TRANSFORMERS:

LOCAL CONGREGATIONS AS AGENTS OF COMMUNITY TRANSFORMATION

KEYS FROM THE LETTERS TO THE SEVEN CHURCHES OF ASIA

Dr. Larry Asplund

ISBN: 978-0-692-00183-7

Many Christians are earnestly searching for help to face the sociological and theological challenges of our day. They wonder how they can positively affect their culture, or whether they will be negatively affected by it. *Transformers* provides an excellent historical and textual study of how the seven churches of Asia faced the challenges of their day. Observing how the Lord guided these churches through their situations provides an abundant source of insight relevant to today.

—Lanny Hubbard

This is a must-read for Christians today who want to make an effective and fruitful difference in this generation. The author offers eye-opening understanding to the book of Revelation and Christ's message to the seven churches, as well as local churches and dedicated followers today. His account is rich in historical understanding, sound in interpretation of the ancient text, and replete in pragmatic application for today's local churches. If you have a genuine appreciation for instruction and impartation, this book will both inspire and challenge you.

—Glenda Malmin

Larry combines his years of research and his passion for authentic revival to give us this wonderful resource. This book is a wealth of information. Examine the challenges the first century church faced and overcame in order to reach their world. Be inspired by the testimonies of what local church and ministries are doing today to transform their cities.

—Mike Servello

It is a privilege for me to recommend the book *Transformers*. I have known Larry Asplund for many years and I find him very faithful in interpreting the Word of God clearly. He brings out the importance of not comparing ourselves among ourselves. Every church, whether large or small, has an assignment from the head of the church, Jesus Christ. We must hear what the Holy Spirit is saying to us and then we will be an influence in affecting the community where we live.

—Dick Iverson

Larry is one of the finest researchers and writers we have. He is a great communicator of truth in a way that makes application obvious and easy. This book is the result of many years of teaching and research. I believe it will be a great resource for all.

—Frank Damazio

TABLE OF CONTENTS

ACKNOWLEDGEMENTS

As is true with every writer, my family shares in my lifestyle, whether they want to or not. Lynda, my wife of thirty-seven years, gets to see me sit at my computer hour after hour, being less than completely available. She also gets to be the first reader and last editor of anything I write. Thanks, Sweetheart. I couldn't do it without you.

Having written books as a "ghost writer" or "co-author," I have often been asked by my parents, "When are we going to see a book with your name on it?" Well, Mom and Dad, here it is.

My colleagues at Portland Bible College and City Bible Church consistently support me, both personally and professionally. Special thanks go to my spiritual father, Dick Iverson. Ken and Glenda Malmin are my oldest friends; I can always count on their support and participation. Lanny Hubbard and Ken Ross are my dearest friends and have supported me with enthusiasm through this project.

I also want to thank my students at Portland Bible College. They kept me young and sharp. They drew out the best from me. They are my brothers and sisters, and my friends. I also need to thank the baristas at the Beaumont Starbucks for allowing me to spend countless hours taking up space, whether I was drinking a mocha or not.

If I could describe the central passion of my life, it would simply be the church. For me, it is the cause worth living and dying for. My prayer is that *Transformers* will make a contribution to an overcoming church in our day.

PREFACE

So many books, so little time! So, why should you read this book? *Transformers* has been written for you if:

You're convinced local churches exist for a purpose, with a mission, namely to be salt and light and leaven in the midst of their communities.

You would like to explore the dynamics involved in local churches bringing transformation to their neighborhoods and cities.

You are a pastor or a member of a pastoral team with a desire to see your congregation fulfill its purpose in your city.

You are a church planter (or potential church planter) and you would like to consider the implications of planting a kingdom congregation in a community.

You are a student of Scripture and you love exploring the meaning and application of Bible passages, including the book of Revelation.

I bring my own story and concerns to bear on this project. I've written this book because:

I participated in planting a local church in 1972, and continue to be vitally interested in the purpose for and process of church planting.

I have taught in a Bible college for the last eighteen years and am passionate about raising up a new generation of pastors and church planters and lay leaders of all kinds.

I'm absolutely convinced that Jesus is building his church in our time and place, and am excited about the possibility of us making a significant contribution in our time and place.

Now that you're reading this, let me set the stage for you.

The Plan of the Book

The first chapter serves as an overall introduction to the whole book. In it I explain the premise of the book, that is, how local congregations can be agents of redemption and transformation in their cities. This is followed by an introduction to the book of Revelation, a description of the first few verses of Revelation chapter one, and the story of the seven churches of Asia. Because all of this must be related to our own situations, I also introduce the context of the twenty-first century church and the need for communities of faith serving as agents of transformation.

The story of the church—of the ancient churches in the province of Asia or of any church—is not possible without understanding the centrality of the Risen Christ. Chapter two explores the foundational vision of Christ in Revelation chapter one, its significance to the letters to the seven churches of Asia, and its significance to the church today.

Chapters three through nine follow the stories of the seven churches of Asia, drawing out certain keys to overcoming in every context. In each chapter I also tell the story of a contemporary local congregation serving their communities and being redemptive change agents as a result. The need for every believer to have "ears to hear" what the Holy Spirit is saying is explored in chapter 10.

I've also included two appendices so that I can explore the background of Revelation 1–3: (1) the principles used in interpreting the book of Revelation, and (2) the phenomenon of Christian "Gnosticism" in the first century—and the twenty-first century.

Much of this book involves biblical studies, a treatment of Revelation 1–3. In these sections I attempt to "rightfully divide" the Scripture passages. However, academic writing was not my goal, so I have attempted to treat those passages and issues in a relevant, applicable way, expounding on keys to being overcomers and transformers.

Important Resources

Being a teacher of both church history and the book of Revelation, my shelves are filled with valuable resources. However, certain ones are referred to often in this book:

The Letters to the Seven Churches by Sir William Ramsay is considered the classic work describing the historical and cultural background of Revelation 2 and 3. Most of his conclusions made in 1904 are still considered valid by contemporary historians.

Colin Hemer updated Ramsay's work with *The Letters to the Seven Churches of Asia In Their Local Setting*. Additional archeological findings enabled Hemer to add valuable insights to Ramsay.

A First Century Message to Twentieth Century Christians by G. Campbell Morgan is one of the best series of sermons based on Revelation 2 & 3. Morgan was not only an excellent Bible expositor, he was also a disciplined Bible scholar.

Henry Barclay Swete's commentary on the Greek text of the book of Revelation, *The Apocalypse of St. John*, is still an excellent source of textual comments and exegesis.

For my money, one of the best contemporary single-volume commentaries on the book of Revelation is *Revelation* by Grant R. Osborne. This work is a readable but scholarly introduction, including both background information and interpretation.

E Quake by Jack Hayford provides a devotional approach to the message of the book of Revelation. Dr. Hayford makes the case for the worship of the Risen Christ being the central theme of Revelation. I also found excellent observations and insights in *The Jesus Letters* by David Ravenhill.

My prayer is that this work will make a positive contribution to a new emerging missional vision for the church, and that those who read it will have a new hope and vision to make a redemptive difference in the world in and through the church of Jesus Christ.

Join the conversation at transformersthebook.blogspot.com.

CHAPTER ONE:

THE CALL FOR TRANSFORMERS

Planting a church was very exciting. We were in a season of harvest with scores of young people coming to Christ. Some called it the "Jesus Movement." Youth centers and youth churches were springing up all over the country. It was clearly time to gather the new brothers and sisters into some kind of community.

My parents had begun reaching out to kids in their Midwestern community and those young people were responding to the gospel with faith and enthusiasm. In fact, so many were responding they had trouble discipling them fast enough. My wife and I were attending Bible college on the West Coast and were hearing reports of the youth revival happening back east. Finally a call for help came. A decision had to be made, and we moved to Missouri to assist in the birthing of a local church.

But church planting raised a lot of important questions. Does this community really need another local church? If God is asking us to plant a congregation, what is our mission? What is our distinctive assignment from the Lord as it pertains to this community? What does it mean to be faithful to that assignment?

Every local church is a unique kingdom of God community. Each one is a representative of God's kingdom in their city. They exist to express the nature of God's kingdom in specific ways. They are planted by the Lord to extend the influence of the kingdom as salt and light. Every congregation must understand what that means for them in their unique context.

Ultimately we must begin our search for answers in Scripture. One of the very best places to begin is the letters to the seven churches of Asia recorded in Revelation 2 and 3.

A Revelation of Jesus Christ

The letters to the seven churches of Asia are found in a very unique context. The book of Revelation is either obsessed over or avoided altogether by most Christians. It is an ancient example of a form of literature unknown in our day. And yet it is God's Word. Therefore, it is our heritage, a gift of God to us. Perhaps we can do our homework and trust the Holy Spirit to give us insight into this wonderful book.

Revelation, the Book

Revelation gives itself the title of an "Apocalypse." This form of ancient and popular writing was highly symbolic, making use of visions and dreams, angels, symbolic numbers, strange composite beasts, and highly figurative language. It was more like poetry than anything else. It was designed to capture the imagination of the reader. It was also intended to empower the reader to take action in the face of danger.

The Greek word *apokalupsis* refers to an uncovering or an unveiling. It is an explanation of or the bringing of a "mystery" into the light. The last book of the Bible is an unveiling of the mystery of Christ and his ultimate rule. But it is also a prophecy. It's almost as though the book of Revelation is the ultimate book of prophecy, a final meditation on all that had been prophesied previously. It's very vocabulary and thought patterns spring from the wells of Old Testament prophetic literature, yet with Jesus Christ clearly at the center. In his well-known commentary, Henry Barclay Swete wrote:

> It is the work of a memory which is so charged with Old Testament words and thoughts that they arrange themselves in his visions like the changing patterns of a kaleidoscope, without conscious effort on his own part. There is not a single instance in which the Christian prophet of

the Apocalypse has contented himself with a mere compilation or combination of Old Testament ideas. His handling of these materials is always original and independent, and he does not allow his Old Testament author to carry him a step beyond the point at which the guidance ceases to lend itself to the purpose of his book.[1]

The book of Revelation is communicated in the form of a letter. There were two kinds of letters in the ancient world: a personal letter and a literary epistle. The first kind was private and the second public. Epistles were intended to be circulated and read aloud. "The letters of this class express general principles of life and conduct, religion and ethics, applicable to a wider range of circumstances than those which have called for the special letter; and they appeal as emphatically and intimately to all Christians in all times as they did to those addressed in the first instance."[2] All New Testament letters were epistles, including the addresses contained in the book of Revelation.

As a result, the book of Revelation is "apocalyptic with a difference." "Revelation is primarily an apocalyptic book of visions described with symbolic language. Through the format of letters to beloved Christians in the churches of Asia, the Book of Revelation speaks the prophetic words of God using visions described in symbolic, apocalyptic language."[3]

This great New Testament apocalypse must be understood in its original context. It was addressed to specific believers facing specific challenges at a specific time. It was intended for the instruction and encouragement of the believers in the Roman province of Asia toward the end of the first century AD. Our ability to understand and apply the message of the book depends in large part upon our understanding of the times. If we were sitting in the congregation at Ephesus, for instance, when the Apocalypse was first read aloud, how would we hear it? And how would we respond to it? Let's try to place ourselves in that audience and listen anew to the Revelation.

The revelation of Jesus Christ, which God gave him to show his servants what must soon take place (Revelation 1:1).

The opening phrase identifies this portion of Scripture as "the revelation (*apokalupsis*)." Although this key word is found only here in the book of Revelation, it is used at other points in the New Testament. The purpose of God in this age is called a "revelation" (Romans 16:25; Ephesians 3:3). The return of Christ is called a "revelation" (1 Corinthians 1:7; 1 Peter 1:7). Paul prays that the saints would be given a "spirit of revelation" (Ephesians 1:17).

Specifically, the mystery being uncovered is "the revelation of Jesus Christ." This statement refers either to a revelation given by Jesus Christ, or a revelation given concerning Jesus Christ.[4] In either case, Christ is the center of the revelation. Christ is the beginning and the end of the message of the revelation.

God gave this revelation to Christ so that he could in turn show it to his servants at a definite point in time. No doubt it was John's visionary experience on the isle of Patmos that was the occasion for this grand unveiling.

Christ is revealed as Lord and God. He is Lord over his church. He is Lord over the nations. And he is Lord over time. An important part of his revelation concerned certain things that "must soon take place." These things "must" take place.[5] They are under God's sovereign superintendence of the affairs of humans. As a result, they will take place with absolute certainty. Nothing will be able to prevent or even delay them.[6] While this certainly refers to the events at the end of the age, they specifically refer to the trials coming upon the churches of Asia at the end of the first century.

He made it known by sending his angel to his servant John (Revelation 1:1).

God gave this revelation to Jesus Christ who sent it on by an angel to John. But he did it in a unique way. The phrase "made it known" indicates that the message was communicated by means of figurative signs and symbols.[7] The message is being revealed by use of apocalyptic imagery. As always, our task is to hear the message, but in this case, we can't do so without also rightly interpreting the symbols.

But why the involvement of an angel? It's easy to observe that all examples of ancient apocalyptic literature were alive with angels. In every case it was important to see that actual angelic beings were in view. It's almost as though the presence of angels symbolized the connection between heaven and earth. Heaven and earth are the two sides of God's one creation. Angels are heaven's representatives, on assignment from God among human beings on the earth. The presence of angels "probably results from the effort to bridge the perceived distance between the transcendent and the human."[8] Jesus Christ is Lord of heaven and earth; Lord of angels and human beings. It shouldn't surprise us to see the message coming to both "his angel" and "his servant John."

> . . . who testifies to everything he saw—that is, the word of God and the testimony of Jesus Christ (Revelation 1:2).

John is functioning as a prophetic witness in this context. The word *martureo* refers to an accurate witness or faithful interpreter of people and events. It was often used to refer to the official witness in a court case who was offering legal evidence. John is accurately and faithfully bearing witness to "everything he saw," namely the apocalyptic vision he is about to lay before us.

The content of the vision was "the word of God and the testimony of Jesus Christ." This is a parallel expression, implying that God's Word, God's self-revelation, is perfectly seen in the testimony about Jesus Christ. Jesus is the perfect revelation of God.

> Blessed is the one who reads the words of this prophecy, and blessed are those who hear it and take to heart what is written in it, because the time is near (Revelation 1:3).

It's amazing that a blessing is pronounced at the beginning of the book of Revelation. Some believers have almost considered Revelation to be a mixed blessing at best. It has been the cause of significant confusion and misunderstanding. And yet, those who read and hear are blessed.[9]

"The one who reads" is a reference to the public reading of the book in the congregation. It was the regular practice of the public reading of Scripture, resulting in the public hearing of the book of Revelation, that will result in a blessing. But reading and hearing will not be enough. The members of the congregations must also "take to heart" the message of the text. This is one of John's key words (Greek *tereo*) in the Revelation. *Tereo* means "to attend to carefully; to take care of; to keep or observe." John uses this verb instead of "obey." It contains a very strong sense that the readers / hearers are to embrace and put into regular practice everything they hear in the Revelation.

I find that most contemporary readers view Revelation as an occasion for end-time speculations. Those who read it at all focus on the mysteries of "the beast" or "666" or "the 1000 years." Those who are seeking the blessing found in Revelation will look for things to observe, to keep, to obey. As with the rest of Scripture, when they read Revelation they will see opportunities to embrace "rebuking, correcting and training in righteousness" (2 Timothy 3:16).

There will be even greater motivation to respond to the Revelation "because the time is near." The word translated "time" is not the idea of linear chronology (*chronos*) but rather the idea of a "set time" or a "prophetic season" (*kairos*). And that time is "near" (Greek *engus*), meaning it is "certain, sure," and under the sovereign control of God.

> *John, to the seven churches in the province of Asia: Grace and peace to you* (Revelation 1:4).

This greeting clearly marks the epistolary nature of the Revelation. There is a specific writer, namely John. And there is a specific destination, namely the seven churches located in the Roman province of Asia.

Transformers

"Grace and peace" was the common Pauline greeting (cf. Romans 1:7; 1 Corinthians 1:3; 2 Corinthians 1:2; etc.). It combined the common Greek greeting (*grace / charis*) and the common Hebrew greeting (*peace / shalom*). Every member of the congregation was included in John's salutation.

> . . . *from him who is, and who was, and who is to come, and from the seven spirits before his throne* (Revelation 1:4).

It's not only the apostle John who is greeting the churches. It is also the very Godhead, Father, Son and Holy Spirit. The first person of the Godhead is here referred as the One "who is, and who was, and who is to come." The phrase translated "who is" is an attempt to communicate the essential being, the self-existence of God.[10] "Who was" communicates his existence in eternity past. "Who is to come" expresses the fact that he is "the coming one," the Lord of history who is actively involved in the affairs of human beings. Once again, to quote Swete:

> As a whole the phrase exhibits the Divine Life under the categories into which it falls when it becomes the subject of human thought, which can conceive of the eternal only in the terms of time. Such a title of the Eternal Father stands fitly among the first words of a book which reveals the present in the light of the past and of the future.[11]

"The seven spirits" could also be translated as "the sevenfold Spirit." They are "before his throne," eternally "proceeding" from the Father. In a similar way, Zechariah 4:10 speaks of the "seven . . . eyes of the Lord." This phrase also appears in the vision in Revelation 4:5 and 5:6. It clearly is a reference to the Holy Spirit, and specifically to the fullness of the Spirit in relationship to the sovereign rule of God in the midst of the church.

> . . . *and from Jesus Christ, who is the faithful witness, the firstborn from the dead, and the ruler of the kings of the earth* (Revelation 1:5).

The oneness of the Son with the Father and the Spirit is a common theme in Revelation. John presents only the very highest view of the full deity of Christ. In his capacity as the Son of God Jesus is here seen as three things:

The faithful witness. Jesus is the perfect witness of the Father. He is also "faithful"; that is, he is trustworthy and reliable; he is consistent. We can put absolute confidence in what Jesus reveals to us about God. In the gospels Jesus himself claimed to be a faithful witness (see John 3:11; 8:14).

The firstborn from the dead. Jesus is the first fruit of the resurrection. As such he is the fount of resurrection life, the head of a new human race for all eternity. This phrase echoes Paul's teaching concerning Christ in Colossians 1:18.

The ruler of the kings of the earth. Jesus has all authority in heaven and on earth (Matthew 28:18). He is not just a ruler; he is the head, the origin, the first place over all kings and all kingdoms. Everything and everyone must bow the knee before his lordship.

> *To him who loves us and has freed us from our sins by his blood, and has made us to be a kingdom and priests to serve his God and Father—to him be glory and power for ever and ever! Amen* (Revelation 1:5, 6).

John now sings a beautiful doxology to the risen, exalted, glorified Christ. In the process he describes three things Jesus has accomplished (and is accomplishing) for us:

He loves us. Jesus is continually loving us with a pure, perfect love.[12] The work of Christ on the cross has made possible an ongoing intimacy with him, if we are willing to receive it and walk in it.

He has freed us from our sins by his blood. At the moment of his death on the cross Jesus boldly announced, "It is finished" (John 19:30). At that moment he "loosed us," he "released us," he "unbound us" and set us free. He set us free "from our sins." He released us from the guilt and the consequences of our tendency to miss his mark. And he did so "by his blood." He paid the penalty for our sins, earning the right to set us free.

He has made us to be a kingdom and priests to serve his God and Father. In the victory Jesus won he established his kingdom, and he established his faithful followers as citizens of his kingdom. Not only citizens, kings and priests, a royal priesthood. God's word to Moses expressed his promise to make the old covenant community "a kingdom of priests and a holy nation" (Exodus 19:5, 6). Now that covenant promise is fulfilled in the new covenant community. In his first epistle, Peter declared, "But you are a chosen people, a royal priesthood, a holy nation, a people belonging to God" (1 Peter 2:9, 10). Those addressed by John were not destined to be a "kingdom and priests" at the end of the age, at the return of Christ. They were then (and are now) a "royal priesthood" because of the work of Christ.

John's revelation of the true King and the true kingdom flies in the face of the claims of the Roman emperor and empire. "The Apocalypse is largely a protest against the Caesar-cult and the attitude of the Empire towards the Church, and at the outset it places the Divine Kingdom in sharp contrast to the imperial power. . . . the Church, redeemed by the Blood of Christ, constituted a holy nation, a new theocracy."[13]

John's introduction uses a beautiful order and symmetry in describing the person and the work of Christ:

The Person of Christ	The Work of Christ
The Faithful Witness	He loves us
The Firstborn from the Dead	He freed us from our sins
The Ruler of the Kings of the Earth	He made us to be a kingdom and priests

The Christ who is "the faithful witness" is the Christ who is encouraging a growing love relationship with him. The one who is "the firstborn from the dead" is the same one who by his death has freed us from our sins. The "ruler of the kings of the earth" has called us to participation in his kingdom as a royal priesthood.

To him be glory and power for ever and ever. John's doxology concludes with a clear expression of worship. Jesus Christ alone is worthy to receive glory and power. This word for "power" is very forceful. It literally means "strength, might, great power and dominion." True dominion belongs to Christ alone, and it will belong to him for ever. He alone is to receive all glory. *"Amen."*

> *Look, he is coming with the clouds,*
>   *and every eye will see him,*
> *even those who pierced him;*
>   *and all the peoples of the earth will mourn because of*
> *him. So shall it be! Amen* (Revelation 1:7).

John then pens a beautiful hymn that combines two passages from the Old Testament prophets. The first line is taken from Daniel's famous vision of the "son of man" and the "ancient of days" (7:13). There Daniel sees "one like a son of man," or simply, a human being. Yet this is a different human. This one is "coming with the clouds of heaven." His point of origin is heaven, not the earth. He is both human and divine. When Stephen was being martyred he saw a vision of the "son of man" (Acts 7:56). This phrase is also used in Revelation 14:14. However, "son of man" was Jesus' favorite way of referring to himself. In fact, he uses it 85 times in the gospels. He is the God-Man referred to by Daniel.

The rest of the hymn is drawn from the prophecy in Zechariah 12:10. The prophet referred to a "spirit of grace" that was going to be given to "the inhabitants of Jerusalem," and that grace would lead them to really see "the one they have pierced," leading to true repentance. However, John takes this idea beyond that of Zechariah. John sees "all the peoples of the earth," representatives from every human tribe, mourning "because of him." Ultimately the gospel will go throughout the earth and every tribe will be represented among the people of God. The reference to "those who pierced him" is "pointing not so much to the original crucifiers as to those who in every age share the indifference or hostility which lay behind the act."[14] (This word from Zechariah is referred to only one other place in the New Testament, John 19:37.)

So shall it be! Amen. As with the greeting "grace and peace," this exclamation combines both the Greek and Hebrew version of the same expression. "Yes" (Greek *nai*) and "Amen." Both expressions acknowledge and confirm the truthfulness of what has been said, and communicates a commitment to seeing it come to pass.

> *"I am the Alpha and the Omega," says the Lord God, "who is, and who was, and who is to come, the Almighty"* (Revelation 1:8).

There are several ways of expressing the all-sufficiency of God in the book of Revelation: the "first and the last," the "beginning and the end," and the "alpha and the omega." This reference to the Greek alphabet is clear: God is the first and last letters, thus encompassing all the letters in between. He alone is God and everything derives its existence from him.[15]

Added to the expression already seen in verse 4 (*who is, and who was, and who is to come*) is the title, *the Almighty*. This is the most exalted title for God in the book of Revelation, and reoccurs at key points (4:8; 11:17; 15:3; 16:7, 14; 19:6, 15; 21:22).[16] "The Almighty" is a translation of the Greek word *pantokrator*, meaning "all-powerful" or "ruler of all." God has all power, all authority, all sovereignty. He rules over all, and therefore we can trust in him in every situation. The churches can put all their confidence in him, even in the midst of very trying times.[17]

Seven Churches and Seven Letters

This risen, glorified Christ is addressing real people participating in real congregations. They lived in real cities at a particular point of time in history. We want to listen to the word of God found in Revelation and receive the blessing of applying it to our own lives. However, to do so we must place ourselves in the original audience. Each of those cities and congregations had an important story to tell, an important contribution to make to the gospel of the kingdom in their time and place. Who were the people Christ addressed in this unusual way? Where did they live? What were their circumstances? Let's try to paint the picture as accurately as we can.

The Province of Asia

The ancient land known as "Asia Minor" is roughly equivalent to present-day Turkey. During the second millennium BC this area was dominated by the Hittite empire and the kingdom of Mitanni whose capitol was Troy. The famous story of the Greek invasions around 1200 BC is told in Homer's account of the Trojan Wars. The oldest cities referred to in the book of Revelation were established by the Greeks in this early period. The kingdom of Lydia, whose capitol was Sardis, emerged as the dominant power during this early time.

The situation changed with the appearance of Cyrus the Persian, known to us from the Old Testament. He defeated the Lydians in 546 BC and established his headquarters at Sardis. From there he conducted a series of wars against the Greeks. Eventually Alexander the Great invaded Asia Minor and conquered the Persians in 334 BC. After his death, his various successors both built and fought over control of the cities of Asia.

One of the Greek kings established a kingdom at Pergamum in 282 BC. This Greek dominion was prominent in the western half of Asia Minor, and was finally bequeathed to the Roman empire in 133 BC. The Romans simply designated it the "Province of Asia."

Asia soon became the wealthiest province in the vast Roman empire. It had a population of 4.6 million inhabitants covering an area of 56,000 square miles. It formed the main connecting bridge between the western and eastern worlds.

To the Romans, a "province" comprised a certain "sphere of duty." This sphere was both administrative and religious. The province had certain administrative duties as it pertained to Rome and the empire. It also had certain religious duties that served to unite the people in the province. Roman officials were responsible for both these duties. This resulted in government and religion being intimately linked. According to the famous archaeologist and historian, Sir William Ramsay, "Loyalty and patriotism were expressed through the provincial religion, i.e., the state cult of the majesty of Rome and the emperor. . . . all who refused to engage in the public worship of the emperors were proscribed by imperial act as traitors and outlaws, possessing no rights."[18] This was especially true in the province of Asia at the specific time John received his Revelation.

Seven Cities and Seven Churches

Revelation 1:4 addresses "the seven churches in the province of Asia." In verse 11 it will list them: Ephesus, Smyrna, Pergamum, Thyatira, Sardis, Philadelphia and Laodicea. But these were not the only churches in Asia. One of the earliest churches was located in Troas (formerly known as Troy; Acts 20:7–12; 2 Corinthians 2:12). There were also churches at Colossae and Hierapolis (Colossians 4:13, 16). And there may have easily been others. So why these seven churches?

The fact that "seven" churches are addressed is significant, especially in apocalyptic literature. Seven churches are representative churches, standing for all the churches in Asia. In fact, in the largest sense these seven churches could possibly be seen standing for all the churches at every place and time in history.

But there also seems to be a first century Asian reason for addressing these specific cities and churches. A look at a map of the Roman province of Asia that includes the trade routes will show that these seven cities were on the main circular route that dominated communication and trade in the province. If a letter was delivered to Ephesus with instructions that it make the circuit throughout the province, it would be sent north to Smyrna next, then on to Pergamum.

It would then be sent southeast to Thyatira, then Sardis, then Philadelphia, and finally, Laodicea.

Sir William Ramsay was perhaps the first to propose an ancient mail delivery route for the seven churches of Asia.

> All the seven cities stand on the great circular road that bound together the most populous, wealthy, and influential part of the province, the west-central region. The gradual selection of seven representative churches in the province was in some way connected with the principal road circuit of the province.[19]

Secondary routes were located in and out of these cities. Ephesus was the chief sea port at the mouth of the Cayster and Maeander rivers. Smyrna was a center of trade for the north Ionian coast at the mouth of the Hermus river. Pergamum served as a center of communication for the northern part of the province. Thyatira was a hub for the inland district. Sardis had long been a center for the central portion of the Hermus river valley. Philadelphia was a cultural center for the area of Lydia. Laodicea was at the crossroads of the trade routes running north-south and east-west. For this reason, the seven churches in these seven cities became focal points for seven groups of churches in the province. "The district of the seven letters contained the entire Asian church as it was organized about the end of the first century."[20]

The seven cities of Asia included ancient non-Greek cultures (Pergamum and Sardis), ancient Greek colonies (Smyrna and Ephesus), and new cities founded by the Greek kings after Alexander (Thyatira, Philadelphia and Laodicea). The cities were established variously as military garrisons, as centers of trade and centers of Greek culture. Settlers were made up of soldiers, Greek colonists, and tradesmen from other cultures, especially those from Israel. The cities often competed with each other for prominence. Several made claims to being the "first of the province." Smyrna claimed to be the "first of Asia in size and beauty." Sardis boldly announced itself as the "first metropolis of Asia, of Lydia, and of Hellenism." Ephesus claimed to be first as the key port on the coast of Asia while Pergamum claimed first place as the imperial capital of the province.

ASIA MINOR
1st Century A.D.

Churches in these cities may have been established from the earliest days of Christianity. On the day of Pentecost visitors from Asia were present to witness the outpouring of the Spirit and respond to the preaching of the gospel (Acts 2:9). We see them participating later in the affairs of the church at Jerusalem (Acts 6:9).

Paul's longest stay was in Ephesus (AD 54–56) from which he spread the gospel and planted churches throughout the province of Asia (Acts 19:10). In AD 61 Colossae, Hierapolis and Laodicea were recipients of letters from Paul (Colossians 4:13, 16). It's probable that the other churches in Asia were planted at this same time. Ephesus functioned as the "mother church" in the province, responsible for the planting and the apostolic oversight of their congregations. However, each local congregation was distinctive and significant in its own right.

Seven Letters

The seven letters communicated in Revelation 2 and 3 identify the destination of the book of Revelation as the seven churches of Asia, and of the province of Asia as a whole. These are to be taken seriously as epistles written to actual congregations at the end of the first century. At the same time, because they appear in an apocalyptic presentation, their contents must be seen in the big, cosmic-historical picture. In that sense they are addressed to local congregations in every time and place. They are indeed addressed to us in our own time. We will be careful to read and interpret them in their context, but we will also be diligent to hear and obey the message ourselves.

Each of the seven letters follows a consistent pattern (a feature we should expect when reading apocalyptic literature):

Address. Each letter begins with a greeting by the risen Christ in terms both borrowed from the opening vision in chapter one and that specifically speaks to the needs of that local congregation. In addition, five of the letters begin by acknowledging, "I know your deeds." The exceptions are Smyrna ("I know your afflictions") and Pergamum ("I know where you live").

Commendation. Jesus then commends the congregation for the ways they are accurately representing him and his kingdom in their community. These are the areas in which the churches are being overcomers. He points out the redemptive fruit they have been bearing, in every case but two: Sardis and Laodicea receive no words of commendation. The chief challenges facing the churches are also addressed. The challenge of the "synagogue of Satan" is referred to in the letters to Smyrna and Philadelphia. The challenge of the Nicolaitans is mentioned in the letters to Ephesus, Thyatira and Pergamum.

Correction. The weaknesses in the churches are also addressed, with a call to repentance. These are ways in which the churches are being overcome by the surrounding culture of the cities. Only the churches at Smyrna and Philadelphia receive no words of correction.

Promise. Finally there are words of promise to the overcomers. Those who "have ears to hear," those who respond to the words of correction with repentance and obedience, will be rewarded in wonderful and eternal ways.

Challenges for the Churches

All the churches of Asia faced certain challenges in common. There was certainly the challenge of living in the Roman empire at the peak of its power. That may have been a blessing in some ways, but it was also a curse. Although the empire was Roman, the culture was Greek. Greek religious and philosophical thought was predominant in the province and was a daily challenge to the teachings of Christ. There was also the ongoing conflict with the synagogues and the transition of the Christian church from a Jewish sect to a universal faith.

Graeco-Roman Culture

The ancient inhabitants of Asia Minor (usually referred to as Anatolians) practiced various forms of nature or fertility religion. Nature religions celebrated the passing of the seasons and the ongoing fertility of crops and herds. Their religious practices usually involved magic and sexual immorality in the pursuit of fertility. This pagan element can be easily seen in the province of Asia at the end of the first century AD, especially in the worship of Artemis or Diana of the Ephesians.

The Greeks added a layer of religious ideas that involved more human gods and goddesses, designed to express Greek cultural ideals. The Greeks also taught a philosophy that proposed a dichotomy between "pure mind / thought" and inferior "matter." The result was a de-emphasis on observable, material things, and an emphasis on intellectual pursuits.

The Romans were all about order, harmony and efficiency. They were prepared to absorb almost any cultural element in a conquered area so long as it did not disrupt the consistency and orderliness of their rule. For the Romans, all religion was "civil religion." All religion was designed to produce good citizens and maintain the unity and stability of the empire.

Ultimately an official Roman religion began to develop: emperor worship. The evidence consistently suggests that emperor worship began in the province of Asia.[21] The first temple dedicated to Roma, the goddess of Rome, was built in Smyrna in 195 BC. The first temple devoted to an emperor was built to Caesar Augustus as the "Savior of the world and the Majesty of Rome" in the city of Pergamum in 29 BC. Not to be outdone, Smyrna built temples to the emperor Tiberius, his wife Livia, and the Roman senate, in AD 26. By the end of the first century AD, every city in the province had one or more temples promoting the imperial cult. One archaeologist noted, "No other province is known to have had more than one provincial cult of the emperors at this time, and several provinces appear to have had none. Clearly, Asia was on the cutting edge of imperial cult activity."[22]

The growing imperial cult took place in the context of the *Pax Romana* (Roman Peace) and the resultant prosperity. Much of it was originally an expression of gratitude for the effective leadership of the emperors. John Yeatts listed three characteristics of emperor worship: (1) It originated with the people, not the emperors themselves. (2) It was not exclusive; other gods could be worshiped as long as the people were willing to confess, "Caesar is lord." (3) Failure to worship the emperor was viewed, not as apostasy, but as political revolt.[23] The emperors recognized a good thing when they saw it, and began to enforce the new imperial cult with more and more energy.

To make matters worse, beginning with Caesar Nero some of the emperors chose to actively persecute the Christian church. They found Christians to be irrational, ignorant and close-minded. Because they refused to worship the emperor or the pagan gods, they were classified as atheists. Worst of all, Christians were considered to be disloyal, subversive and poor citizens, simply because they refused to cooperate with civil religion.

All this greatly intensified under the emperor Domitian (AD 81–96). Domitian was a member of the Flavian family. His father and brother were both emperors before him. His father Vespasian was the general who fought the Jewish war (AD 66–70). When he was named emperor in AD 68 his son Titus finished the job, completely destroying the temple and the city of Jerusalem. This proved to be a key event in the early development of the Christian faith.

Prior to the destruction of the temple, Jews of the Diaspora around the empire were tax exempt. Instead, they sent an annual offering to Jerusalem. After the destruction of Jerusalem Vespasian removed their tax exempt status and required all Jews everywhere to pay the *fiscus Judaicus*, the Jewish tax. The proceeds went toward the support of the temple to "Jupiter Capitolinus" in Rome.

At the death of Vespasian in AD 79 his son Titus ruled briefly until AD 81. He was replaced with his brother, Domitian. By this time many Jewish people either refused to pay the new tax or paid under protest. As a result, Domitian passed a series of laws against Judaism and even against "Jewish practices." These laws were vigorously enforced against Jews, Jewish proselytes, or non-Jews who appeared to be practicing things Jewish—Christians.

In addition, Domitian decided to require those in the

empire to worship him as a god, even though still alive. Domitian insisted that all people confess him to be *Dominus et Deus*, i.e. Lord and God. Those who refused to do so lost all rights to function in the empire. "Every Asian must stamp himself overtly and visibly as loyal, or be forthwith disqualified from participation in ordinary social life and trading."[24] This was especially true in the province of Asia. There is evidence that a large statue to Domitian and temple were set up in Ephesus at this time.

The Christians refused to worship the emperor, resulting in an intense time of persecution. Clement of Rome wrote of "the sudden and successive calamitous events which have happened to ourselves" and "being persecuted" after suffering "terrible and unspeakable torments" (1 Clement 1.7). It was in this context that the letters were delivered to the seven churches of Asia.

Judeo-Christian Culture

The Jewish people had a long history in the province of Asia. Jewish tradesmen may have found their way to Asia during the time of the Persian empire, or even earlier. Alexander the Great favored the Jews, admiring their moral principles and high learning. The Greek kings of Asia also favored Jewish colonists, granting them special rights. In fact, Antiochus III "the Great," one of the most famous of the Greek kings, actively recruited Jewish colonists for his new cities and exempted them from the normal requirements of the inhabitants, including not only taxation but also participation in local religious rites. The Greek kings considered their Jewish colonists their most loyal subjects.

These colonists were great Jewish nationalists, sending generous support to Israel. However, in some cases there was a growing syncretism between their Judaism and local philosophical and pagan religious ideas.

In the first century AD, the relationship between the new believers in "Yeshua HaMeshiach" and the synagogue had been rocky from the beginning. With few exceptions, the gospel was preached to Jews alone during the first decade of the church (Acts 11:19). When entering a new city, the apostles preached the gospel in the local synagogue first (Acts 13:14; 14:1; 17:1; etc.). The policy of Paul was to preach the gospel "to the Jew first" (Romans 1:16). Most of the early Christians were Jewish converts. There is reason to believe that many of them continued to worship in the synagogue as well as within their multi-ethnic Christian community. Conflict between the two seemed inevitable (cf. Acts 13:45f; 14:2f; 17:5f, 13f; etc.). This included Paul's visit to the province of Asia, and especially in Ephesus (Acts 19:33f; 20:3f).

The conflict between the synagogue and the church greatly intensified after the destruction of the city of Jerusalem. That event in AD 70 released a wave of refugees from Palestine that inhabited the synagogues of the Diaspora. This seemed to have the effect of radicalizing those Hebrew communities. During the 80's the Jewish colonies became more exclusive and began excommunicating Jewish converts to Christianity from the synagogue. In about AD 90 the synagogue added a curse to the benediction in the Jewish Prayer Book: "For the renegades let there be no hope, and may the arrogant kingdom soon be rooted out in our days, and the Nazarenes . . . perish as in a moment and be blotted out from the book of life and with the righteous may they not be inscribed."[25]

At the same time, the empire declared that any Jews who chose to faithfully pay the Jewish tax would be exempt from participation in emperor worship. Those who attempted to escape the tax were prosecuted. This seemed a sensible compromise, but it also put additional pressure on the Christian believers. They could escape participation in emperor worship and persecution if they sought refuge in the local synagogue and paid the Jewish tax. However, if the synagogue excommunicated them for heresy and reported them to the Roman authorities, these dis-fellowshipped believers in Jesus came under the full penalty of the law. Colin Hemer put it this way:

> In times of pressure the Jewish Christian had a potential
> refuge from the obligation of emperor-worship by trading

on his radical and religious origin. The situation placed
the Jewish communities in a position of peculiar power.
By disowning a Christian and informing against him, they
might deprive him of his possible recourse to toleration at
a price, and render him liable to the emperor-cult.[26]

At the same time, the Christian church was having its
own internal problems. A new heresy was developing in the
province of Asia. There had been early hints of it in Paul's
epistle to the Colossians, but during the decade of the '80's a
false teacher arose in Ephesus named Cerinthus. He represented the perspective of Greek philosophy, interpreting
Christian doctrine through the grid of Plato. He and his followers wanted the Christian faith to sound more "rational"
and to be more appealing to those in the surrounding Greek
culture.

Thus was birthed Christian "Gnosticism." For these
Greek intellectuals, salvation came through the secret knowledge (Greek *gnosis*) taught by Christ. Those who had been
initiated into this knowledge would learn how to escape the
bonds of matter and be reunited to God as pure thought or
rationality. Since matter was evil, the human body was essentially irrelevant. Since the spirit of the initiated was perfect,
what they did with their body was irrelevant. As a result,
they taught a doctrine of libertinism, absolute freedom from
the law. It was perfectly fine for Christian believers to engage
in pagan rituals, including emperor worship and the accompanying immorality. This early group referred to themselves
as "Nicolaitans."

All of these elements came together toward the end of
the first century AD to form a serious crisis in the churches of
Asia. The believers were facing the prospect of severe persecution at the hands of the Roman authorities. They could
escape persecution in two ways: either by more fully identifying with the local synagogue, or by finding a way to justify
compromise with the surrounding culture.

As a result, there was a strong temptation to defect from
the faith during this time. Some time later the Roman governor Pliny wrote a letter to the emperor Trajan about

Christians who had abandoned their faith twenty years previously,[27] referring to the very time the letters were written to the churches of Asia. "The Churches of Asia knew themselves to be on the brink of an encounter with the greatest power the world had seen. . . . the purpose of these chapters is to strengthen faith and kindle hope in the hearts of the faithful."[28]

The Church and the City

Imagine for a moment that the apostle Paul is sending you out to pioneer a church in the province of Asia during the last half of the first century. You know you are being sent on an apostolic mission, a mission with a purpose and with clear objectives. You are going to establish a beachhead for the kingdom of God in your community. You're going as a representative of Christ in the midst of an anti-Christ culture. Your objective is to express the distinctive nature of the kingdom of God in the city, and to extend the authority and influence of that kingdom everywhere you go.

As you set out, you understand certain things about your kingdom assignment. You know that your assigned city also represents a kingdom. Although it is a counterfeit kingdom with a counterfeit king, a kingdom whose authority does not exist outside of God's sovereign control, you know that the kingdom of darkness will seek to stop your mission at every turn. It will seek to confuse you, to oppose you, to discourage you, and to keep your light hidden.

However, you also understand that it is ultimately only one true King and one eternal kingdom. You understand you are representing the eternal kingdom, on assignment from the King of kings and the Lord of lords. In the end, Jesus Christ is the Lord of your city, the Lord of the province, indeed the Lord of the whole earth.

In speaking of the eternal kingdom of God and its effect on the world, Jesus used several important metaphors:

Salt. He told the disciples that they were to be the "salt of the earth" (Matthew 5:13). Salt is customarily used both to flavor and to preserve. It is important for the followers of

Jesus to be "salty." In fact, Jesus said if we lose our saltiness, we will become essentially irrelevant (Matthew 5:13; 9:50; Luke 14:34). The distinctive flavor must always be present for salt to be salt. As a preservative salt has the effect of "peace" (Mark 9:50) and gracious speech (Colossians 4:6). Salty disciples of Christ would have a redemptive effect on their surroundings.

Light. Jesus also referred to his followers as the "light of the world" (Matthew 5:14). As such they were to be public with their light, allowing it to shine (Matthew 5:14–16; Luke 8:16; 11:33). A light hidden is no light at all. The affect of light is to dispel the darkness and reveal what is true (Matthew 10:27; Mark 4:22; Luke 8:17; 12:3). Although this revelatory affect may result in conflict, it is necessary for light to be truly light. Jesus himself said, "I am the light of the world" (John 8:12; 9:5). Therefore, his disciples reflect his pure light to whoever may be observing.

Leaven. Jesus also compared the kingdom of God to leaven or yeast (Matthew 13:33; Luke 13:21). Leaven has the affect of spreading its influence in hidden ways. A small amount of yeast might be put in a lump of dough, but before it is done, it has spread throughout the entire lump (Galatians 5:9). While light is public, leaven is private; but both have an ongoing redemptive affect.

The churches of Asia were established by Christ to be salt, light and leaven in their cities. To be effective they needed to be aware of the unique challenges facing them. They needed to know the story of their city. Speaking of these churches, William Ramsay remarked, "With unerring insight its leaders saw the deep-seated character of those seven cities, their strength and their weakness, as determined by their actual surroundings, their past history, and their national character."[29]

Representing the kingdom of God would involve exposing the patterns of sin in the city and modeling the righteous alternative. Ultimately the potential existed for the church to be an agent of transformation in the city. In the process, the church would be identified with the city and the city with the church. Colin Hemer observed, "There is at times some

Transformers

measure of identification of church with city. The churches are apt to be judged by their varying response to their surroundings."[30] Ramsay went even further when he concluded, "[Christ] assumes always that the church is, in a sense, the city. The local church does not live apart from the locality and the population amid which it has a mere temporary abode."[31]

If the believers in the local church functioned as "overcomers" in the city, they would eventually overcome the various "strongholds" in the city and begin to see genuine transformation. However, if the church did not overcome, it would eventually be overcome by the city, and would ultimately absorb and become an expression of those very strongholds. That was the challenge of the churches of Asia. And that is still our challenge today.

The Challenge for Today's Church

Every local church today is on assignment. Every congregation exists as salt and light and leaven in a specific, concrete context. We are all called to overcome or be overcome. What is the nature of our challenge today?

Enculturation

In *Dynamics of Spiritual Life*, Richard Lovelace described the ebb and flow of revival in the church. He proposed that the church has a tendency, all things considered, to "enculturate" or absorb elements of the surrounding culture. Where the life of Christ is not the dynamic operating in the church, where the love of God and the life-changing power of the Holy Spirit is not predominant, the church simply learns to co-exist with the values and structures of society. The church I grew up in would have called this "worldliness." In another place the apostle John simply called it a love for the world (1 John 2:15–17). It involves adopting, adapting to, and even spiritualizing, the transient values of a culture.

Lovelace taught that there are two ways to experience "enculturation." One is "destructive enculturation," or "saturation with the godless culture of the surrounding world."

He went on to say, "When men's hearts are not full of God, they become full of the world around like a sponge full of water."[32] This process is so "natural" for us we are hardly aware of it taking place. Yet, if we were completely honest, we would be forced to admit that we place too high a value on some of the things our culture values.

The other way to "be overcome" Lovelace calls "protective enculturation." That involves taking refuge in the safe place of religious forms and traditions. Rather than finding ways "to overcome" and serve as salt and light we tend to build religious walls around ourselves and our friends. We think that if we can keep the world out we won't have to deal with the world. But mere religion is just another form of worldliness. "It appears that when the church begins to draw up codes and taboos which separate it from the world, it is most worldly, most in conformity with the world's understanding of holiness and spirituality."[33] While the churches of Asia had the two optional ways to compromise, either with Graeco-Roman culture or with the synagogue, in a similar way we have the options of destructive or protective enculturation.

We are not here to either absorb the world's cultural values or "protect ourselves from the world" (which is itself an expression of the world's religious values). Rather, we are here to be leaven, to work as agents of transformation in the midst of the world.

Lovelace went on to say that a season of revival results in a process of "disenculturation." A revived church sees clearly the values of the surrounding culture, and clearly discerns what is necessary to see those values transformed into the values of the kingdom of God. That begins by a dynamic witness, a demonstration of God's kingdom values in and through our lives. But is that what we see happening in our day?

A Sanctification Gap

The process of enculturation has resulted in what Richard Lovelace calls a "sanctification gap." After a season of reviving has come and gone, the church tends to become increasingly comfortable with the surrounding culture. It loses the piercing gaze of spiritual discernment it once had. While it may see the more obvious issues with some clarity, others are lost from view.

During the past few years George Barna and George Gallup, Jr. have been bombarding us with statistical information on the American church. It paints a picture of a seriously compromised, enculturated church. In an August 2001 survey it was shown that 33% of all born-again Christians had been divorced at least once. This compared to a divorce rate of 34% among non-Christians. The data further discovered that 90% of the born-again Christians had been divorced since their born-again experience. What's more, the divorce rate in "Bible Belt" states, where 70% of the population is in church on Sunday morning, was 50% higher than the national rate.

Another survey discovered that during the 1990's the number of unmarried couples living together (cohabitation) increased 72% nationwide. However, during that same period the rate of cohabitation increased by a rate of 97-125% in the Bible Belt. Nationally 33% of all adults have lived with a member of the opposite sex without being married. The rate is 25% among born-again Christians. This same survey found out that 26% of born-again Christian do not believe premarital sex is a sin. It also discovered that 13% of born-again Christians in the American church do not believe extra-marital sex is a sin. "What a tragedy for evangelicals to declare proudly that personal conversion and new birth in Christ are at the center of their faith and then to defy biblical moral standards by living almost as sinfully as their pagan neighbors."[34]

The data on the attitudes of American Christians toward "mammon" is also telling. In 2002, Barna discovered that only 6% of born-again Christians tithe. The average American Christian gives $5.00 per year to missions. This in a nation where the average household income is $42,409. Part of the problem is a lack of clear Christian perspective as well as Christian conviction. According to Barna, only 9% of American Christians have a "biblical worldview" (only 2% of born-again American teens). Barna's conclusion: "Every day, the church is becoming more like the world it allegedly seeks to change."[35]

> So are we overcoming, or are we being overcome? What should we conclude?

> Scandalous behavior is rapidly destroying American Christianity. By their daily activity, most "Christians" regularly commit treason. With their mouths they claim Jesus is Lord, but with their actions they demonstrate allegiance to money, sex and self-fulfillment.[36]

The Promise of Overcoming

The letters to the seven churches of Asia were sent at a time of crisis for the church. Some of the churches were, by the grace of God, overcoming in their cities. They were a light shining in the midst of darkness. Other local churches were absorbing the values of their surrounding culture. Some were almost spiritually dead. Yet, to each one Jesus gave keys to overcoming, and precious promises to those who used those keys.

The Message of the Letters

The letters made several very clear points. One was the true nature of the Roman empire. While Jesus was the King of the eternal kingdom of God—he alone was Lord and God—the emperor was the temporary ruler of a temporary kingdom whose real power behind the power was none other than Satan. Rome was the temporal community of the kingdom of Satan. The church was the community of the kingdom of God. "The central question of Revelation is: 'Who is the true Lord of this world?' The answer is that God rather than the emperor Domitian is the Lord and worthy of worship: 'Worship God!'"[37]

The letters understand that with two kingdoms occupying the same territory, conflict is inevitable. However, victory is also inevitable; victory for the kingdom of God and victory for the church. Indeed, because of the victory Jesus already won on Calvary, the victory has already been won for the church.

Although the conflict may involve suffering—sharing in the sufferings of Christ—even those sufferings will only contribute to the ultimate victory. In that sense, Revelation was intended to encourage and empower the saints in Asia to persevere. If they do, if they overcome, they will celebrate their victory for all eternity.

A key to overcoming can be observed in each letter. Whether the saints are commended or corrected, an important insight is revealed about the power to conquer in the midst of any circumstance.

The key of repentance. All five churches corrected by the Lord are commanded to repent. Repentance is not a theme we hear very often these days. What does it mean to repent? How do we know whether or not we have repented? The answer to those questions will provide us with an important key to overcoming.

The key of sharing in the sufferings of Christ. When is the last time your heard a sermon on the subject of suffering? Yet the letters spend a great deal of time on this theme. Indeed, the Bible teaches a theology of suffering, one an overcoming church must understand.

The key of the authority of God's Word. Jesus alone has the authoritative word of God. His word is the final and complete revelation of God and God's will for humanity. His word will be the basis for judgment in the end. The power of the word of Christ is greater than that of the Roman emperors, and the saints will overcome if they put their trust in that word.

The key of perseverance. We all know better than to pray for patience, yet the exhortation to persevere is found at all the key points in Revelation. Why is it such an important virtue? How it is the key to the development of so many other virtues? If we want to keep from being absorbed by the world's system we'll need to cultivate perseverance.

The key of the power of the Holy Spirit. The church is a Holy Spirit community, engaged in a vital partnership with the

Holy Spirit in extending the kingdom of God. And the Holy Spirit is the senior partner. The Body of Christ is a dead body if it is not continuously energized by the vital power of the Spirit. If a local church gets so good at what it does it no longer feels its dependence on the Holy Spirit, it will die.

The key of obedience. Some Christians define faith as a matter of what you believe and how well you say it. The letters define faith as how you live and what the practical consequences of your life-choices are. As soon as we lose sight of the need to be disciples, as soon as we make Christianity a matter of private belief (and the comfort that might bring), we will begin to become like the world.

The key of brokenness. When things are going well for us, when we're healthy and happy and can pay all our bills, we lose sight of our desperate need for Christ. Those who never lose sight of the extent of their spiritual neediness will consistently overcome in a world governed by power and pleasure.

The Message to Today's Church

As we examine the details of these seven letters it will be essential that we apply them to our own lives in whatever context the Lord has us in. There's no question we stand in need of the grace of God and the power of the Holy Spirit. If we're honest, we'll admit that, if left to ourselves too long, we tend to become like the world. It may happen so gradually we're not consciously aware of the process. We may even decide that the temporal values we're absorbing are eternal kingdom values, spiritualizing our backsliding.

At the same time, we acknowledge our desperate desire to see God reign more and more in and through our lives and our communities. We have a genuine desire to be salt and light and leaven in the midst of the world. We have a real commitment to see real transformation happen in our specific contexts.

If there is hope for the churches in Asia, there's definitely hope for us. There's hope for our nation. There's hope for our generation.

The message of the letters to the seven churches of Asia

to today's church is that if we will repent, we can see revival and reformation, restoration and transformation, in our day.

The seven letters of Revelation 2 and 3 lead us to believe that if we heed the call of the Spirit, we can close the "sanctification gap" in our churches. We can see the statistics turn around. We won't seem like hypocrites any more. As a result, we will have the moral authority to call the world to repentance. We will truly be in a position to call the world to Christ.

Taking a careful look at the letters to the seven churches of Asia will give us insight and hope for the future of the church in our day; for the future of your church and mine. And it will stir a fresh faith in people's hearts to believe God for a powerful transforming impact on our cities.

CHAPTER TWO:

THE VICTORIOUS CHRIST IN THE MIDST OF THE CHURCHES

I thought it was just going to be another chapel service. Attendance was required so I was there, sitting toward the back, not really focused on what was being said. Then I noticed a young male student heading toward the front of the chapel, weeping. I saw him speaking to one of the teachers, and the next thing I knew he was standing on the platform with a microphone in his hand, confessing his sins! I have to admit that it made me a bit nervous.

It became worse when students all over the chapel began to weep, and then a line began to form of students going forward to make a public confession. After each one finished and stepped down from the platform, a group of teachers and students surrounded them and prayed for the grace of God to fill their lives. It was obviously a work of the Holy Spirit.

Soon it seemed as though a wave was moving from the front of the auditorium toward the back. I knew I couldn't escape the effect of that wave. I didn't know what I was in for. The spirit of confession and repentance worked throughout that gathering. Then the presence of the Lord fell in an unusual way. That chapel service went on for three days and nights, and our lives were completely undone—and redone.

That was February 3, 1970, the day the Holy Spirit visited college campuses all over the United States. It began what became known as the "Jesus Movement." It overshadowed an entire generation until the cover of the June 21, 1971, issue of *Time* magazine announced, "The Jesus Revolution." A generation became enamored with the person of Jesus Christ. We wanted nothing more than to read, study and proclaim his teachings. We wanted to follow him, to be like him, to serve him. Sure, there were some who spun off into a religious twilight zone (Satan loves nothing more than to corrupt a work of the Holy Spirit), but many of the pastors and leaders of the church today were rescued by Jesus in those early days.

We were (and are) passionate, not about religion, but about a real relationship with a real person—Jesus Christ. We were seekers after truth, but with the new understanding that truth was a Person. It was all about Jesus.

The letters of Jesus to the seven churches of Asia addressed real issues, but most of all, they were all about Jesus.

The Place of Vision

I, John, your brother and companion in the suffering and kingdom and patient endurance that are ours in Jesus (Revelation 1:9).

John continues the Revelation by identifying himself as "your brother." He is not above them as a spiritual champion. He is family. Not only that, he is their "companion." This word (Greek *sunkoinonos*) literally means, "to share or fellowship with someone or something; to participate with others in something; a joint partner." The central idea of the word is *koinonia*, the word for fellowship, a life shared in common. John is sharing in their common experience, communicating an essential solidarity with them.

Specifically, he is sharing three things with the saints in Asia. First, "the suffering," also translated "tribulation" (cf. 2:9, 10, 22). It simply means, "a pressing or pressure; oppression, affliction, or distress." It's certainly not a "happy" word, but it is a real-life description of the experience of the church at the end of the first century. Sharing a *koinonia* in suffering is an idea found elsewhere in the New Testament. Paul commended the Corinthians for sharing in his sufferings (2

Corinthians 1:7; see also Philippians 4:14). He also spoke of the fellowship of sharing in the sufferings of Christ (Philippians 3:10).

Second, John and the churches of Asia are companions in "the kingdom." As in verses 5 and 6, John draws attention to their participation in the royal dominion of King Jesus. Just because they are sharing in tribulation does not mean they are helpless victims. They are citizens of an eternal kingdom. They are royalty. They share in "royal power, dominion and rule." It's just that the spiritual authority of the kingdom of God operates on different principles than the power and authority of the Roman empire.

They are also companions in "patient endurance." This is one of the key terms of the letters, and of the rest of the Revelation. It is a translation of the Greek word *hupomone*, and means "steadfastness, constancy, endurance; a patient, steadfast waiting," and is often translated "perseverance" (see also 2:2, 3, 19; 3:10). This perseverance is not passive but active. Indeed, it is strength and courage in the face of opposition.

These three things John and the believers in Asia share "in Jesus." While they are companions together of these things, most importantly they are companions with Jesus in suffering, dominion and perseverance. Indeed, their motivation to endure hardship, to exercise spiritual authority, and to stay the course no matter what, comes from the realization that they are doing so with Jesus.

I . . . was on the island of Patmos because of the word of God and the testimony of Jesus (Revelation 1:9).

Patmos was a stopping point about seventy-five miles from Ephesus on the journey to Rome. It is a barren, rocky, hilly island, thirty miles in circumference, ten miles north to south, six miles wide, and sixteen square miles in area. This, along with other small islands in the Aegean, were used for the banishment of prisoners. John was on the island of Patmos because of the "word of God and testimony of Jesus." In verse 2 this phrase probably refers to the whole

Revelation. In this instance it no doubt refers to John's activity in preaching the gospel.

According to Sir William Ramsay, the Roman practice of exile "carried with it entire loss of civil rights and almost entire loss of property. Banishment combined with hard labor for life was one of the grave penalties. It was preceded by scourging, and it was marked by perpetual fetters, scanty clothing, insufficient food, sleep on the bare ground in a dark prison, and work under the lash of military overseers."[38] Exile usually occurred at the instigation of a sitting Roman emperor and continued until the death of that emperor.

According to the historical record, Domitian's persecution of the church began in AD 90 and continued until his death in AD 96. John was the only remaining apostle from Jesus' original group. What's more, he was probably in his 80's. He would have made an easy target for Domitian's strategy against the church.

On the Lord's Day I was in the Spirit (Revelation 1:10).

The New Testament church did not have official holy days, as in Judaism. However, it became an early practice to assemble together on the first day of the week, the day Jesus rose from the dead (Acts 20:7; 1 Corinthians 16:2). The early church began to refer to the first day as the Lord's Day. Evidently this practice began in the province of Asia, so it is natural we would see this phrase (used only here in the New Testament) in a passage meant for these very believers.

John testifies that he was "in the Spirit," or literally "in Spirit." Being in the Spirit is to be the common experience of Christian believers (Romans 8:9). The New Testament also refers to "blessing in the Spirit" (1 Corinthians 14:16), "praying in the Spirit" (Ephesians 6:18; Jude 20), "singing with the Spirit" (1 Corinthians 14:15), and "worshiping in the Spirit" (Philippians 3:3). In this passage John was probably referring to a specific, prophetic-visionary experience.[39]

John may have been "on Patmos," but more importantly, he was "in the Spirit." His experience of the Holy Spirit was the higher reality, the more essential truth. John's experience was not limited by his natural circumstances but transcended them to the reality of the Spirit.

> ... and I heard behind me a loud voice like a trumpet, which said: "Write on a scroll what you see and send it to the seven churches: to Ephesus, Smyrna, Pergamum, Thyatira, Sardis, Philadelphia and Laodicea (Revelation 1:10, 11).

John's first experience must have been rather shocking. He heard a loud, unusual sound behind him. It sounded like a trumpet blast. The sound went beyond any description of normal speech. This was a supernatural voice.

The idea of the sound of a trumpet had gained a certain significance by this time. Both Jesus (Matthew 24:31) and Paul (1 Thessalonians 4:16) had made reference to it. This was the sound of the prophetic voice announcing the presence of the King of kings.

The prophet Ezekiel had a similar experience. In his case, the trumpet sound emanated from an angel (Ezekiel 3:12). The same was probably true for John. This great sound was the voice of Christ's angel, preparing John for what he was about to see.

The command is given to "write" and to "send." He is to render an accurate account of what he is seeing. And he is to send that account to the seven churches. A messenger (or messengers) would need to be appointed to deliver the account of the vision. "The messenger would carry the roll to each of the Churches in turn, and by each it would be read and probably copied. His route is indicated by the order in which the Churches are named."[40] These churches are about to become the recipients, and the repositories, of a great revelation.

The Victorious Christ

I turned around to see the voice that was speaking to me. And when I turned I saw seven golden lampstands (Revelation 1:12).

John turned around to "see the voice," confirming that he was having an unusual experience, a visionary experience. The voice had been speaking to him and was continuing to speak to him, and in a way he would never forget.

The first thing John saw was "seven golden lampstands." This image brings us back to the Old Testament tabernacle or temple. Moses received instructions from the Lord concerning a golden lampstand (Exodus 25:31–40). He was to hammer a seven-branched lampstand out of one piece of gold. Each branch contained a candle at the end of it, often in the form of a bowl containing oil and a wick. The lampstand was to provide light for the holy place in the tabernacle. The temple of Solomon actually contained ten golden lampstands, five on the right side of the holy place and five on the left (1 Kings 7:49).

The lampstand was designed to be a bearer of light. Its sole purpose was to bring light into darkness. The lampstand was golden. It was to reflect God's divine character. The lampstand was sevenfold. It was a mature, complete expression of the light that only God could give. The language of the text could be either translated as "seven golden lampstands" or "a sevenfold golden lampstand." In the context of this passage there is not necessarily a contradiction between the two. There may be seven separate lampstands, but in the end, from God's point of view, there is only one.

The prophet Zechariah also had a vision of lampstands (4:1ff). When he asked the angel for an interpretation, he was told that the lampstands were two anointed ones empowered by the Holy Spirit. In this case, the lampstands were human vessels. Such is the case here. As we will see, the lampstands are the churches.

. . . and among the lampstands was someone "like a son of man" (Revelation 1:13).

John then notices a person in his vision, someone "like a son of man." Reference to the "son of man" connects us with verse 7. The one "coming with the clouds" is the "son of man" (Daniel 7:13), the God-Man sent from heaven. Daniel saw the son of man as the King, the one who was given dominion over all the nations of the earth. John sees the son of man "among the lampstands." He was literally in the middle of the lampstands, moving freely from one to the other. Here the emphasis is on Christ as the high priest in the midst of the churches.

The one standing in the midst of these lampstands is not just any high priest. The son of man is the son of God. He is the only true light of the world (John 8:12). He is the source of the light the lampstands provide. The lampstands are not a source of the light in and of themselves. All they can do is reflect a more essential Light.

Jesus is personally present in the midst of the churches. He is walking about among them, actively involved in their life and mission. He is the power and the unifying force in all they are and do.

Jesus' high priestly ministry among the lampstands would be the same for the churches as it was in the tabernacle. The lampstands required tending. They had to be fed oil and the wicks trimmed. In his massive commentary Kevin Conner noted:

> The setting, as John understands it, from his Hebrew background and now his Christian foundations, is that of the Tabernacle of the Lord (or the Temple) and the ministering High Priest. Under the Old Covenant, the priest ministered morning and evening before the golden lampstand in the Tabernacle. There he trimmed the wicks of the lamps, took away the burnt out ashes, and supplied the holy oil for the lamps to burn continually before the Lord.[41]

The wicks had to be trimmed twice every day. The lampstands would soon lose their capacity to shine if they were not regularly "corrected" by the high priest. As David Ravenhill wrote:

If these deposits were not removed, the light gradually weakened, and ultimately, would go out, plunging everything into darkness. And so Jesus comes to lovingly but firmly reprove and direct the Church—to trim away and remove those areas that are contrary to His will. He [also] commends them for those deeds that allow His light to shine in them.[42]

Jesus has an intimate relationship with his church throughout the book of Revelation. The church shares in the victory of Christ. The church is his new covenant community, his kingdom community. The church is the very Body of Christ. For that reason, he is committed to its care.

> . . . *dressed in a robe reaching down to his feet and with*
> *a golden sash around his chest* (Revelation 1:13).

Here Jesus is seen in the high priest's garments. Moses was commanded to make holy garments for the priest that were intended to communicate glory and beauty (Exodus 28:2). This included a robe and a sash (Exodus 28:4).

A long robe with a golden sash also describes the royal garments worn by kings. The golden sash was particularly worn by kings. According to Jack Hayford, "His garment draping the full length of His body is the clothing of a Master, not the shorter garment of a servant. His chestband woven of pure and refined gold is a regal ornamentation, in this case evidencing the purity and perfection that are the hallmarks of this King's rule."[43] Jesus is not only the high priest in God's temple, but he is also King of God's kingdom.

Daniel had a similar vision (chapter 10). In his vision he saw a powerful angel, possibly the archangel Gabriel. The description included a special robe of linen and a belt of pure gold (verse 5). In fact, several features of Daniel's vision seem to be in the background of John's description in Revelation chapter 1.

> *His head and hair were white like wool, as white as snow,*
> *and his eyes were like blazing fire* (Revelation 1:14).

The image of white hair was often used to communicate wisdom or honor or even purity (see Proverbs 16:31; Daniel 7:9). It's also important to realize that any view of the glorified Christ would be filled with splendor and light. John's own experience at the Mount of Transfiguration resulted in a similar revelation of Jesus (Matthew 17:2).

Eyes blazing as with fire is a similar description of the Risen Lord reflecting the essence of the glory of the Lord. His blazing eyes speak of clear discernment and knowledge, making judgment possible. Once again, Daniel's vision describes a similar characteristic (10:6).

> *His feet were like bronze glowing in a furnace, and his voice was like the sound of rushing waters* (Revelation 1:15).

The feet of Christ have the appearance of glowing, red-hot bronze.[44] The image of fire once again reflects the glory of the Lord (as in Ezekiel 1:4–7). Feet of brass also seem to symbolize strength and stability.

His voice is described in supernatural terms. It sounds like the thunder of a thousand waterfalls (compare Daniel 10:6; Ezekiel 43:2). There is a divine strength and authority to his words. He is the perfect expression of the multifaceted word of the Lord. "In the past God spoke to our forefathers through the prophets at many times and in various ways, but in these last days he has spoken to us by his Son, whom he appointed heir of all things, and through whom he made the universe. The Son is the radiance of God's glory and the exact representation of his being, sustaining all things by his powerful word" (Hebrews 1:1–3).

> *In his right hand he held seven stars, and out of his mouth came a sharp double-edged sword. His face was like the sun shining in all its brilliance* (Revelation 1:16).

The right hand of the Lord represents his authority and majesty (see Exodus 15:6). Here he is seen holding the stars in his right hand. To the Jewish mind God held all of creation, ultimately the stars themselves, in his hand (Isaiah 40:12). However, to the Roman mind it was the stars that were in control of the destinies of men. "In ancient astrology, stars were thought to control the universe and to commend emperor worship. That Christ holds them in his hand means that he, not the emperor, controls the powers that govern the universe."[45]

John then notices that out of the mouth of the risen Christ came a "sharp double-edged sword." The word used for "sword" (Greek *romphaia*) is only used in the book of Revelation (except for Luke 2:35). It is literally a large blade or thrusting spear, distinctive to the area of Thrace. The Old Testament spoke of "the rod of God's mouth" as an instrument of authority and judgment (Isaiah 11:4). The double-edged sword (cf. Hebrews 4:12) must have a similar meaning. "Christ's words penetrate and thus are authoritative. In Revelation, Christ's word judges the evil powers, and his only weapons in his final battle against Satan and his followers are the word of God."[46]

The brilliant light coming from his face is another connection to the Mount of Transfiguration. The glory of the Lord is being revealed in the face of Jesus Christ (2 Corinthians 4:6). And it wasn't enough to describe it as a very bright light. It was like the sun shining in its full power. It was the brightest noonday sun. Words fall short of the full beauty of Jesus.

> When I saw him, I fell at his feet as though dead. Then he placed his right hand on me, and said: (Revelation 1:17).

When Daniel had his vision of God's glory he had a similar response (10:8, 15; see also Ezekiel 1:28). John was overwhelmed with his experience of the Lord. His body and mind could only cope with so much glory. It's even more amazing when we consider that this is John the beloved disciple who leaned his head on Jesus during the last supper (John 21:20). He knew Jesus intimately. Yet when he saw him in his glory, all he could do was fall down in amazement and worship.

Transformers

When John was overwhelmed in the presence of Jesus the Lord responded by placing his right hand on him. The same hand that holds the stars is now placed personally and affectionately on his brother John, to strengthen and uphold him.

> *Do not be afraid. I am the First and the Last. I am the Living One; I was dead, and behold I am alive for ever and ever! And I hold the keys of death and Hades* (Revelation 1:17, 18).

The followers of Jesus had heard encouragement to not fear before (Mark 6:50; Matthew 28:5). Jesus came to encourage faith, not fear. While respectful worship and awe was appropriate, anxiety was not. Jesus wants John to be in a state of mind that will enable to him fully receive the revelation.

Jesus then makes certain "I AM" statements as claims concerning his person. The gospel of John contains a series of these statements (see for example 6:35; 10:7; 14:6; etc.). Several very important ones are added here.

I am the First and the Last. This was a title for God in the book of Isaiah (44:6; 48:12), and the Apocalypse, ascribed to the exalted Christ. Jesus is the *protos* and the *eschatos*. He has first place in all things. He has the highest degree of rank and dignity. He is supreme. He is also the culmination of all things. He is the ultimate expression of God's self-revelation.[47] Christ is the initiator and the finisher of everything pertaining to the purposes of God. He is the source and the goal for all God's people.

I am the Living One. God is often referred to as "the Living God" (Deuteronomy 5:26; Psalm 42:2; Jeremiah 10:10; Acts 14:15). Jesus is here seen as the essence of God's life.[48] Jesus has the life of God in himself (John 5:26). He is the very life of God (John 11:25; 14:6), and as such, is the only true source of divine, eternal life, to all who believe on him.

I was dead, and behold I am alive for ever and ever! As the incarnate son of man, Jesus died once and for all on the cross. He tasted death for all people (Hebrews 2:14). But his ongoing state is life! "I am living!" Jesus cannot die again—he can only live. And he will live for ever, literally "from age to age."

I hold the keys of death and Hades. Jesus is holding in his hand certain keys. "Keys" always imply authority—authority to open and shut, to bind and loose. Jesus has authority over death and hell. He had spoken of those keys during his ministry among his disciples: "I will build my church, and the gates of Hades will not overcome it. I will give you the keys of the kingdom of heaven; whatever you bind on earth will be bound in heaven, and whatever you loose on earth will be loosed in heaven" (Matthew 16:18, 19). Jesus had spoken of a time when his church would exercise the authority of heaven over hell. He would give them the keys necessary in order to effectively use that authority. Here we see that it is the risen Christ who has the keys in his hand. Jesus will give keys to the church, but they must understand that the keys belong to him alone. All authority in heaven and earth belongs to him (Matthew 28:18). Authority over death and Hades will not be given to him at his second coming; they belong to him right now. The risen Christ is "engaged in superintending the churches, in ordering the events of the cosmos, appearing in judgment, and finally establishing the promised kingdom and bringing the affairs of earth to a victorious conclusion."[49]

These words would be especially meaningful to those facing persecution, suffering, and even death. Even if they die for their faith, the resurrection of Christ has given them authority over death. The saints at the end of the first century, and those who follow Jesus today, can put their trust in him. Even when it looks like sin and death are winning the fight, we are confident that Jesus has already won the victory; he is reigning as King now; he is in control.

> The vision of Jesus is one of a kingly being, clothed in magnificent regalia of divinity. The impact of this vision is that Jesus should not be seen as a defeated Messiah, but as a powerful reigning Lord. Jesus holds the seven stars in his right hand, indicating that it is He who controls the eternal destiny of the universe, not Caesar. Jesus is the reigning Lord of the universe. He is also the one

Transformers

who is very present in the life of the church, walking constantly among the seven churches. No matter what circumstances are to be faced by the church, the church is guaranteed Jesus' abiding presence.[50]

Write, therefore, what you have seen, what is now and what will take place later (Revelation 1:19).

John now receives his commission and commandment to write, to faithfully record what he is being shown. He is to record what he has seen. The background of his revelation is what he has already observed of Christ and of the churches. Specifically, he has just seen an exalted vision of Christ in his glory. That vision is to be the foundation of everything else he will see and write.

He is also to record what "is now." The present state of the church and its context in the Roman province of Asia is the context of the Revelation. John's original audience had a special need to receive the report of what he has seen and is seeing. They also need the hope that comes from hearing about "what will take place later." Coming events involve much more than tribulation. History is moving toward a culmination. Jesus is the beginning of the story; he is also the culmination. Testing times are about to take place, but they are not the end of the story. In the end there will be only one King and one kingdom on the earth.

The mystery of the seven stars that you saw in my right hand and of the seven golden lampstands is this: The seven stars are the angels of the seven churches, and the seven lampstands are the seven churches (Revelation 1:20).

John is now going to receive the revelation of the mystery. He is going to receive Jesus' own interpretation of two of the symbols used in the vision thus far.[51] The first symbol interpreted is "the seven stars." Jesus tells John that these stand for "the angels of the seven churches." And that settles the matter. Or does it? Unfortunately, although we can easily agree that the seven stars are the angels of the seven churches, there is little agreement as to who (or what) the seven angels are.[52]

Once again, the vision in Daniel 10 might be helpful. In that context we read of the angel Michael who represented Israel, and even Daniel himself (vv. 13, 21). Michael not only represented heaven in the case of Israel, he also protected them by actively opposing fallen "princes" who represented Persia and Greece (10:13, 20; 12:1). Representative angels are also referred to in the New Testament (Matthew 18:10; Acts 12:15). "Hence, 'the angels of the seven churches' are best understood as the heavenly, spiritual identities of the earthly, physical churches in the province of Asia."[53] They are heaven's representatives in the church, and the church's representatives before the throne of God.

While the "stars" are angels, the "lampstands" are churches. The stars represent the kingdom community in heaven while the lampstands represent God's community on earth. At the center of it all is the risen Christ. He is the one who holds the stars in his hand, and he is the one who is walking in the midst of the lampstands. He is in control of the destiny of his people, and he is involved personally in their lives.

A New Jesus Movement

There would be no church without Jesus. There would be no kingdom without the King. There would be no Christian faith apart from Christ. The whole Christian movement depends on people who are dedicated followers of Jesus.

Sociologist Christian Smith recently conducted a survey of American Christian teens ages 13-17. He discovered that the concern for religious faith in our day has to do mostly with what he calls "the instrumental good," or the practical outcomes that faith might bring. American teens (and their parents) are primarily concerned about whether or not faith will help them do better in life. They're committed to Christian faith because it's good for them. It improves their lives in empirical ways.

Smith calls this "Moralistic Therapeutic Deism." Its creed

Transformers

would read something like this: "God exists. God created the world. God set up some kind of moral structure. God wants us to be nice. He wants me to be pleasant, wants me to get along with people. The purpose of life is to be happy and feel good, and good people go to heaven. And nearly everyone's good."[54] He said this has become the *de facto* religious faith of the majority of American Christian teens, a faith encouraged by their parents and churches.

His study shows that these teens do not grasp the most elementary concepts of the gospel. Understanding the Bible is not really necessary. Understanding God is probably impossible, nor is it really required. "You don't have to get too personally involved with this God. But when there is a problem—when you need him—he will solve it as soon as you snap your fingers or ring the bell."[55] What's wrong with this picture? Smith concludes that "Moralistic Therapeutic Deism is not just an inadequate version of Christianity. It's a different religion."[56]

This approach to faith seems to work in many cases. Teens who follow it behave better than those who don't. But is that the bottom line of Christianity? Why did we choose to become Christians in the first place? And what is the church doing to further that motivation? "The question is, what is the interest of the Christian church? Is it to make kids wear their seat belts more often? Is that their goal? Or is there some higher commitment—to understanding the world, to practicing a way of life, Jesus' way, whether or not it makes you happier and healthier and gives you a longer life."[57]

When I read about the condition of Christian faith in the American church, among teens and their parents and leaders, my conclusion is simply this: It is a picture of a Christless Christianity. The person of Jesus Christ is almost irrelevant. There is not a passion for Jesus at the center of this Christian religion.

We are once again at a time when we see a desperate need for a new revelation of Jesus Christ. A new generation needs to rediscover Jesus and fall in love with him all over again. In fact, all of us could benefit from a refreshing of our love for Jesus. Our hearts need to be captured by him again.

Our highest desire in life must be to see Jesus, to really hear his words, to follow him and become more like him. If we do, the Christian church will have the power and purity it needs to more accurately represent the lordship of Jesus in our own time and place.

The Central Revelation

Jesus Christ is the central revelation of the Christian faith. The revelation of Jesus is the central vision of the book of Revelation. The vision of the risen Christ in Revelation chapter one is only the first of seven visions. Each one adds something new to the glory and majesty of our understanding of Jesus.

The Lamb in the center of the throne. We catch a fresh glimpse of Jesus in Revelation 5. There he is seen as the "Lamb of God," standing on the throne with the scars of slaughter. He is the Redeemer of people from every tribe. But he is also the Lion of the tribe of Judah, the sovereign Lord. How is it possible to be a lamb intended for the slaughter and a king at the same time? This is the mystery of Christ. He rules over all, but not by human power or manipulation. He rules by love and self-sacrifice. As a result, he alone is "worthy . . . to receive power and wealth and wisdom and strength and honor and glory and praise."

The Son who rules all the nations. In Revelation 12 we see a vision of a woman giving birth to a male child. But this is no ordinary child. This is one who will rule all the nations "with an iron scepter." He is a child, born in the ordinary way. But he is a king—the King over all the nations of the earth. He not only rules, he rules with an iron, immovable authority. A child who rules. A baby with a rod of iron. Satan saw the need to eliminate this child, but instead he ascended "to God and to his throne" where he will reign for ever.

The Lamb on Mount Zion. In chapter 14 we once again see the Lamb, this time standing in the midst of his community of 144,000.[57] These followers of the Lamb are fully identified with him. They are dedicated worshipers, singing the song of redemption. They have become like Christ, pure and blameless. They have a simple childlike lifestyle of following the Lamb wherever he goes. They are the ones the Lamb has purchased with his own blood. It's a picture of the community of the Lamb.

King of kings and Lord of lords. Revelation 19 is the great vision of the triumphant Christ returning to receive his kingdom. He is "Faithful and True." He has won the right to be the Judge of the whole earth, bringing in a reign of justice. He is the "Word of God." He is the full and perfect expression of the nature and the will of God. He is the ruler of all creation with his armies following him. He alone is worthy to reign.

The bright Morning Star. The last vision of Christ is in Revelation 22. Jesus is the bright hope of the church. He is coming back, and his reward is with him. He is the source and the goal of all his followers. He comes to feed his people from the tree of life, and they will live and reign with him for ever. He is the son of David. He is the Son of God. He alone has living water. Anyone who is thirsty can come to him freely, and drink of that water.

Christ and the Seven Churches

There is nothing more central to our understanding of the message of the book of Revelation than a clear and compelling view of the risen Christ. There is also no more important key to our understanding of the message of the letters to the seven churches of Asia than the sovereign superintendence over and the intimate solidarity of Christ with those churches. They were his own dear followers, his family. He stood in their midst, holding their lives and their destinies in his hand. Grasping the implications of that will be the key to their ability to overcome in their circumstances.

Every letter opens with an address from the risen Christ that has special meaning to that church. It presents Christ in a way that is the answer to that church's challenge. If the church would focus on the image of Christ in the address, it would successfully overcome.

The Churches	The Christ
Ephesus—*Him who holds the seven stars in his right hand and walks among the seven gold lampstands* (2:1).	"One among the lampstands" (1:12, 13). "Seven stars in his right hand" (1:16).
Smyrna–*Him who is the First and the Last, who died and came to life again* (2:8).	"I am the first and the last" (1:17). "I was dead and am alive for ever" (1:18).
Pergamum—*Him who has the sharp, double-edged sword* (2:12).	"Out of his mouth came a sharp double-edged sword" (1:16).
Thyatira—*The Son of God, whose eyes are like blazing fire and whose feet are like burnished bronze* (2:18).	"His eyes were like blazing fire" (1:14). "His feet were like bronze glowing in a furnace" (1:15).
Sardis—*Him who holds the seven spirits of God and the seven stars* (3:1).	"From the seven spirits before the throne" (1:4). "Seven stars in his right hand" (1:16).
Philadelphia—*Him who is holy and true, who holds the key of David* (3:7).	"I hold the keys" (1:18).
Laodicea—*The Amen, the faithful and true witness, the ruler of God's creation* (3:14).	"The faithful witness" (1:5). "The ruler of the kings of the earth" (1:5).

Christ is not only in the midst of the churches, directing and caring for the churches; he is reason the churches exist. He is the meaning and the objective of the churches.

The churches of Asia have entered into a period of increasing persecution. The commitment to Christ is being sorely tried. Now more than ever they need to see Jesus, the one who has already overcome the world and who will be with them, empowering them to overcome. "The central message of Revelation is suggested here: those who endure persecution with Christ will rule with Christ."[59]

Each of the seven letters begins with a crucial revelation to that church. Each letter ends with a promise to those who overcome—who conquer in the midst of their circumstances.

Transformers

This promise focuses back on the fact that their destiny is with Christ. All they will ever need is ultimately to be found only in eternal life with Christ.

Overcomer Promise	Eternal Life With Christ
Ephesus—*I will give the right to eat from the tree of life, which is in the paradise of God* (2:7).	They will know true life and fulfillment with Christ in Paradise.
Smyrna—*Will not be hurt at all by the second death* (2:11).	Instead of judgment they will live for ever with Christ.
Pergamum—*I will give some of the hidden manna. I will also give him a white stone with a new name written on it, known only to him who receives it* (2:17).	They will be nourished by the true bread of heaven, Jesus Christ. They will receive an eternal inheritance in God's house.
Thyatira—*I will give authority over the nations . . . just as I have received authority from my Father* (2:27). *I will also give him the morning star* (2:28).	They will share in Christ's authority. The will walk in the true light, Jesus Christ.
Sardis—*Will . . . be dressed in white. I will never blot out his name from the book of life, but will acknowledge his name before my Father and his angels* (3:5).	As overcomers they will be acknowledged as citizens of God's kingdom.
Philadelphia—*I will make a pillar in the temple of my God. Never again will he leave it. I will write on him the name of my God and the name of the city of my God, the new Jerusalem, which is coming down out of heaven from my God; and I will also write on him my new name* (3:12).	They will know true stability and security. They will have a new, permanent identity in Christ.
Laodicea—*I will give the right to sit with me on my throne, just as I overcame and sat down with my Father on his throne* (3:21).	They will share in Christ's rule and they live in fellowship with him.

Christ and the Church Today

When we consider this vision of the risen Christ, what can we do but worship? Indeed, worship is the ultimate response called for by the Revelation. Worship is the central activity of heaven. Worship is the key to overcoming. Worship is the primary vocation of the overcomers. Worship is the most powerful weapon against the strategies of the enemy. Worship is the key to victory. "If Jesus is worthy of worship for these qualities that are present in Him, then the Church's worship is the pathway to remedy the Church's problems. Jesus, not methods, is the answer to any weakness present among His people."[60]

The church today is not really that different from the church at the end of the first century. We face our share of challenges and have our share of weaknesses as well. The key is the same for us as it was for them. Our answer is a clear vision of Jesus. Our strength comes from a passionate love for Christ and a commitment to him and to his rule.

Our examination of the seven churches of Asia and the letters of Christ written to them will give us guidance along the way. We will be able to see ourselves in their stories and will learn wisdom and be encouraged. With Christ at the center, we too will overcome.

CHAPTER THREE:

THE PROMISE OF BEING A MOTHER CHURCH IN A GATE CITY

THE LETTER TO EPHESUS

Sixty-five years before John sent his letter to the church at Ephesus there were Jews from the province of Asia in Jerusalem (Acts 2:9). They were in Jerusalem for the Feast of Pentecost, the anniversary of the founding of the Jewish nation. While there they witnessed the birth of another nation. They heard multiple languages being spoken from an upper room, and they heard Simon Peter announce the coming of the Holy Spirit in fulfillment of the promise of God. They heard about the coming of the kingdom of God, and its King was proclaimed—Jesus of Nazareth. Some of those visitors accepted Jesus as their Messiah and stayed for a time in Jerusalem, participating in the life of the new congregation (Acts 6:9). Some of them eventually returned home to spread the word.

Some years later the apostle Paul wanted to preach the gospel in Asia, but the time wasn't quite right (Acts 16:6). A few years later Paul paid a brief visit to Ephesus, the chief city of Asia, and left Aquila and Priscilla to begin a work without him (Acts 18:18–21). Finally, almost twenty-five years after the first Jews from the province of Asia had heard the gospel on the Day of Pentecost, Paul settled in for his most extended stay in the city of Ephesus. He actually encountered a group of Hebrew Christian followers of John the Baptist (Acts 19:1–7). After baptizing them in the name of Jesus Christ he began to preach the gospel in the local synagogue (Acts 19:8, 9). From Ephesus the gospel was preached and local churches established throughout the entire province (Acts 19:10).

For the Romans, Ephesus represented the whole province. It was a "gate city" into the entire region. It also represented the greatest obstacles to the preaching of the gospel and the founding of a congregation. Surely Paul understood the strategic benefit of establishing a viable local church in Ephesus first, and from there, planting congregations throughout the province.

More than forty years later the apostle John delivered a very important message from the risen Christ to this "mother church." He was addressing the second and third generation of believers in that great city. A lot of history had already gone by. To understand the significance of John's message we need to understand the challenges faced by the believers in Ephesus.

The Story of Ephesus

The city of Ephesus had a long history going back over a thousand years before the New Testament. During that time the city faced many changes, and was actually moved from location to location. The first founding of the city occurred around 1100 BC by the early Ionian Greek colonists from Athens. It was built on the north slope of Mt. Pion. A temple to the Greek goddess Artemis was built around the same time one mile outside of the city walls.

King Croesus of Lydia conquered Ephesus in 560 BC. He destroyed the city in the process and rebuilt it adjacent to the temple, adding to both the city and the temple precinct. However, in 356 BC the temple was destroyed by fire. During this period Ephesus tended to take the side of the Persians in their wars against the Greeks.

In 335 BC Alexander the Great captured the city of Ephesus. Shortly thereafter the temple began to be rebuilt.

The city came under the rule of King Lysimachus in 287 BC.[61] Under the Greek kings the city was moved again, this time two miles away next to the harbor, at the mouth of the Cayster River. Both the new city and the new temple reflected classical Greek culture and architecture. This development resulted in Ephesus becoming the center of commerce and trade in western Asia Minor.

In 196 BC the city was captured by the Seleucid King Antiochus III, who made the city the capital of the region. In 189 BC Ephesus came under the control of Pergamum. They in turn gave the city to the Romans in 133 BC, and the new province of Asia was formed. At first Ephesus resisted Roman rule, siding with a rebellion led by Mithridates IV, king of Pontus, that was eventually crushed by general Pompey in 69 BC. Caesar Augustus brought in the *Pax Romana*, the Roman peace, and the stability and prosperity that came with it. After that, Ephesus became one of the four most powerful and prosperous cities in the Roman Empire.

From the time the city was located at the harbor it suffered the instability caused by the silting of the harbor. In fact, the harbor had to be periodically closed down in order to dredge it. This problem eventually caused the decline of the city's place of prominence. (So much silting has taken place that the current location is four miles from the sea.)

The three major trade routes in Asia Minor culminated at Ephesus. It was the first city encountered by travelers from Rome heading east. It was also the sea port encountered by those traveling from the east to Rome. Ephesus was the most cosmopolitan city in the province of Asia, housing representatives of many cultures.

Among other people groups there was a large Jewish population in Ephesus. This Jewish colony had gained prominence under the Greek kings. Josephus remarked that "the Jews of Ephesus and throughout the rest of Ionia 'bear the same name as the indigenous citizens.'"[62] They were Roman citizens with special privileges in the city. Since most of the early Christians were converted in the synagogue, there was growing hostility between the Jews and Christians (Acts 19:9).

By the time of the first century AD Ephesus had a population in excess of 250,000. The main street was lined with marble columns, sidewalks, shops, fountains and temples. The sidewalks were adorned with beautiful mosaics. Ephesus was considered a center of rhetoric. It included the library of Celsus, the third largest library in the world. The library contained a famous lecture hall, possibly where the school of Tyrannus met (Acts 19:9). The *agora* or marketplace was the largest and most beautiful in the world. The great theater of Ephesus had a seating capacity of 24,000 (Acts 19:29).

By far the most auspicious structure in Ephesus was the temple to Artemis. The rebuilt Greek structure was the largest marble structure in the world: 425 feet long, 220 feet wide, with 127 columns 60 feet high. Thirty-six of the columns had finely sculptured gold-covered bases. The Great Altar that stood in front of the temple was 130 feet long and 68 feet wide. The statue of Artemis was a squat, basalt figure covered with fertility motifs and astrological symbols. The temple was considered one of the seven wonders of the ancient world.

The Greek goddess Artemis (sometimes known by the Latin "Diana") was the Hellenized version of a more ancient fertility earth-mother goddess. In ancient times she was symbolized as a queen bee. Her priestesses were called "worker bees" and her priests "drones." As a fertility figure she was the "birth-goddess." Artemis was said to be the daughter of Zeus and the twin sister of Apollo. She was the "Virgin-Huntress," the "Lady of Wild Things" and the "Huntsman-in-Chief" to the gods. She was considered to be a savior goddess and a protectoress of youth. However, according to Homer, Artemis required the Greek fleet to sacrifice a maiden to her before she allowed them to sail to Troy.

Ephesus was the *Neokoros* or warden of the worship of Artemis. Not only was the chief temple located in Ephesus, but the priests at the temple were also responsible for the worship of Artemis worldwide. Artemis was considered the patron deity for the whole province of Asia, with temples in several other cities. As a result, the temple precinct, or "Artemision," became the focal point of life in Ephesus. The

Artemision was built around a sacred date-palm surrounded by a royal park. The temple precinct was considered a sacred asylum for criminals. The area was eventually enlarged to the extent that it overlapped the city limits of Ephesus, resulting in a high crime district. In fact, that part of Ephesus became a center of organized crime.

Worshipers deposited large sums of money in the temple for safe-keeping. For that reason, the temple eventually became a prominent banking center, bringing great wealth to Ephesus. Support industries surrounding the worship of Artemis also brought prosperity to the city (Acts 19:24–28).

The temple became a center of the occult and the magic arts. The "Ephesian Letters" were famous throughout the empire as magic charms (Acts 19:18–20). "The city was a hotbed of cults and superstitions, a meeting-place of East and West, where Greeks, Romans and Asiatics jostled one another in the streets."[63] Thus, the growth of Christianity represented a threat to the well-being and status of the city (Acts 19:26, 27).

Ephesus became increasingly prominent in the empire. It became a seat of proconsular government, or an "Assize town." The Asian Assembly was governed by the Asiarchs ("officials," Acts 19:31) who served not only as civil administrators for the province but also priests of the provincial religion. And that religion was the worship of the glory of Rome and of her emperors.

Caesar Augustus himself had commissioned a temple to Julius Caesar in 29 BC. There were also temples honoring both Claudius and Nero in the city. There was an area in the Artemision dedicated to emperor worship. Eventually citizens were required to burn incense to the emperor before they could enter the agora to conduct business.

During the reign of Domitian Ephesus was named the Neokoros of the imperial cult. A large temple to Domitian was built, the central feature being a statue to the emperor fully twenty-seven feet high. No one could enter or leave the city without acknowledging the lordship of Domitian.

When Paul first entered the city around AD 52, he must

have realized he was entering the "gate city" for the province. But that gate not only represented the authority of Rome, it also represented the authority of hell. If he could successfully establish a beachhead for the kingdom of God there, the entire province would be opened up to the gospel. And he succeeded in doing so, as it was later recorded, "All the Jews and Greeks who lived in the province Asia heard the word of the Lord" (Acts 19:10). Because of the power of Paul's witness in Ephesus, "The word of the Lord spread widely and grew in power" (Acts 19:20).

After Paul, Timothy became the senior leader of the congregation in Ephesus. Some time during the 80's the apostle John also moved to Ephesus. During this time the congregation grew to forty thousand to sixty thousand members.

During the same period a heretical faction developed in the church under the leadership of a man named Cerinthus. It was a libertine Greek movement known as the "Nicolaitans." They eventually became known as Gnostics. "Their purpose . . . was to effect a reasonable compromise with the established usages of Graeco-Roman society; they taught that Christians ought to remain members of the pagan clubs, and that they might do so without disloyalty to their faith."[64] Before long they separated themselves from the main congregation to form their own alternative congregations. The church father Irenaus relates that John, who ordinarily never made use of a bath, went to bathe on some extraordinary occasion, but understanding that Cerinthus was within, started back, and said to some friends that were with him, "Let us, my brethren, make haste and be gone, lest the bath, wherein is Cerinthus the enemy of the Truth, should fall upon our heads" (*Against Heresies* 3.3.4).

At the same time the worship of the emperor Domitian was being established in Ephesus. Resistance on the part of Christians and Jews resulted in an outbreak of persecution in AD 90. As a result John was sent to Patmos as an exile. Toward the end of that time Timothy was martyred for his opposition to the ongoing paganism and Artemis worship in the city. Timothy may have still been the senior leader in the church when John wrote his letter.

Ephesus was a church waging a valiant struggle against heresy within and persecution without. Their zeal for the struggle never waned. However, something else very precious was beginning to fade.

The Letter to Ephesus

To the angel of the church in Ephesus write: These are the words of him who holds the seven stars in his right hand and walks among the seven golden lampstands (Revelation 2:1).

Jesus begins his message to Ephesus by emphasizing special aspects of his character and his relationship with the church. Because Ephesus is the mother church in the province Jesus makes general reference to the "stars" and the "lampstands" of the churches. He is the one who is in control of the churches, from the perspective of both heaven and earth. He is standing in solidarity with the church, intimately aware of their circumstances and overseeing their struggles.

There are some interesting differences between the description of Jesus in chapter one and the address of Christ in this letter. In 1:16 we read that Jesus "had" the stars in his right hand. In 2:1 it changes to Jesus "grasping" the stars in his right hand. Jesus does not simply have control of the situation in Ephesus; he has a firm grip on the church and on their circumstances. They don't need to fear or try to control the situation; they can trust him. And while 1:13 describes Jesus as being "among" or "in the middle" of the seven golden candlesticks, 2:1 says that Jesus was "walking about" or "living" among the seven gold candlesticks. Jesus was not just standing in the middle of the churches, he was walking around among them, sharing their lives in very personal ways, having direct authority over them. The Ephesian church had a need for a firm grip and the watchful safeguarding of Jesus. If they would focus their eyes and hearts on him, they would be able to rest in him and in his good purpose for their lives—and for the city.

I know your deeds, your hard work and your perseverance (Revelation 2:2).

Jesus began five out of seven letters with the acknowledgement that he was perfectly and personally aware of their deeds—their work, their labor, their walk with him. In the case of Ephesus, there were certain characteristics that qualified their labor further. "Your hard work" literally refers to "labor to the point of exhaustion." Paul used this same word to describe his own hard work (1 Corinthians 15:10). Their deeds were also marked by "perseverance," or patience endurance. Paul used this word to describe his own patience in the midst of afflictions (2 Corinthians 6:4). The Ephesian believers were marked by self-denying labor and the strength and courage to stay the course no matter what the obstacles.

Paul commended the Thessalonian believers in similar terms (1 Thessalonians 1:3). He also noted their work (*erga*), their labor (*kopos*) and their endurance (*hupomone*). However, Paul connected their work to their faith, their labor to love, and their endurance to hope.

I know that you cannot tolerate wicked men, that you have tested those who claim to be apostles but are not, and have found them false (Revelation 2:2).

In addition, the Ephesians have succeeded in identifying and rooting out false apostles. They are not able to "put up with" false teachers. In the case of Cerinthus and his followers, the Ephesians had taken a clear stand against their teaching. Jesus is commending them for their discernment and their lack of tolerance for them. He identifies the false teachers as "wicked men," base, troublesome, injurious, destructive men. Their false teaching had the potential to destroy the church and the faith of the believers. But the Ephesians had "tested them," had examined them to prove their character and their true motivation, and they had found them to be false.

Paul had warned the Ephesian elders to be on guard against "savage wolves" that he predicted would come among the flock and not spare them (Acts 20:29). That prophecy had eventually come true in the case of the Nicolaitans, but the Ephesians had indeed been on guard. Evidently Cerinthus and his followers claimed to be more than teachers; they claimed apostolic authority. They claimed to be "itinerant teachers with a mission which placed them on a higher level than the local elders."[65] But their authority did not come from Christ. They were "deceivers." They were consciously attempting to lead the believers astray. They had to be stopped, and they were being stopped by the tireless Ephesian church.

You have persevered and have endured hardships for my name, and have not grown weary (Revelation 2:3).

Jesus now repeats his commendation for emphasis. They are a hard-working, self-sacrificing community. They have stood their ground in the face of fierce opposition, from within and without. They have refused to compromise with their detractors "because of my name." They were zealous to guard the honor of the name of Jesus. They have toiled to the point of exhaustion and have not given up. They are a large, influential, fruitful congregation. They are a faithful, apostolic church, guarding the gate into the province and the churches of Asia.

Yet I hold this against you: You have forsaken your first love (Revelation 2:4).

The Ephesian church had not allowed weariness and constant hardship to deter their struggle in the cause of Christ. But in the heat of the battle something vital had begun to fade. Because he loves them, Jesus now comes to correct the thing that is against them.

The church has released and let go of their "first love." John's phrase literally means "the love you had at first." In the days of their founding they had a passion that motivated everything they did. Although they were still very effective, that passion had grown cold.

There is one other place where John uses both the word "first" and "love" in the same place: "We love, because He first loved us" (1 John 4:19). Jesus had summarized the law by saying that the first and greatest commandment was, "You shall love the Lord your God with all your heart, and with all your soul, and with all your mind" (Matthew 22:37, 38). The first love is the personal, passionate love believers have for Jesus himself. It is that love that motivates all their deeds. It is possible to continue to work hard and be effective, but to be motivated by something other than love. Paul had previously taught, "If I give all I possess to the poor and surrender my body to the flames, but have not love, I gain nothing" (1 Corinthians 13:3). Their "pure devotion to Christ" had become complicated by long and hard dissensions (2 Corinthians 11:3).

Love for Christ is soon translated into love for one another. If we love God, we will also love our brothers and sisters (1 John 4:20, 21). That same divine quality of love will spill out to all people, for "God so loved the world" (John 3:16). Love is the entire fulfillment of the Law (Romans 13:10).

A great apostolic church, faithful, effective, a tireless warrior against the dangers within and without, had lost love as its chief motivation. Their apostolic task had taken the place of a simple, pure love for Jesus, for one another, and for the people of Ephesus.

> *Remember the height from which you have fallen! Repent and do the things you did at first* (Revelation 2:5).

Jesus commands them to do three things to see their love restored:

Remember. They were to begin by engaging in a process of recalling to mind their passionate love relationship they had in the beginning. They were not only to bring it to mind, they were to act on it. They were to reenter into their past experience of "first love" and bring it back into the present. They were to remember their early love for Jesus as a high point in their experience, a height from which they have tragically fallen.

This process was designed to prepare the way for the next two steps.

Repent. They were to turn back, to return to their simple, pure devotion to Christ, and to allow that love to reenergize their deeds. They were to change their thinking in a decisive moment, and to allow that to change their actions and their motivations. [66]

Do the first works. There were "first works" involved in the peoples' "first love." Surely those works involved acts of love toward God and people. The ancient Greek commentators suggested that the members of the Ephesian church had become increasingly indifferent toward the needs of their poorer brethren. [67] It could be that a large, powerful, perhaps even wealthy church, had lost their heart of compassion toward those who seemed weaker or poorer (see 1 Timothy 6:10). If so, they needed to turn back to the first love that had motivated their first works.

> *If you do not repent, I will come to you and remove your lampstand from its place* (Revelation 2:5).

If they refuse to remember, repent and return to their first love and first works, Jesus said, "I am coming to you." This seems to indicate a special coming or visitation from the Lord in judgment. It could refer to their immediate time but also has in view the judgment at the end of the age.

When he comes, he will "remove" their lampstand. He will set them in motion and move them to another place. Specifically, they will be moved out of their rightful place. They were in a place of influence as an apostolic church. They were the mother church in the gate city of the province of Asia. But that place of responsibility was going to change if they did not repent. They had been salt and light in their community, but that community influence would cease without love guiding them. Their "role should not be defined simply by [their] hard work and defense of doctrinal purity, but by love—love for Jesus and love for people." [68] The bright light of their apostolic witness would go out if they did not rediscover love as their driving force.[69]

> *But you have this in your favor: You hate the practices of the Nicolaitans, which I also hate* (Revelation 2:6).

Unless the Ephesians misunderstand the intent of these words of correction, Jesus repeats his commendation, not only of their lack of tolerance of wicked men, but their actual hatred of their deeds. While they were to love God and love people, they were to hate wicked deeds. The practices of the Nicolaitans involved idolatry and immorality, practices which Jesus also hated.

Their love for Jesus will result in a love for everything Jesus loves and a hatred for everything Jesus hates. Their love for people will result in a passionate hatred for the things that are injurious to those people.

> *He who has an ear, let him hear what the Spirit says to the churches* (Revelation 2:7).

Jesus gives a general invitation to all those who read and hear the words of this prophecy in all the churches. Every individual is required to apply the message of every letter. Having "ears to hear" calls to mind the saying of Jesus in the Gospels (Matthew 11:15; Mark 4:9, 23; Luke 8:8; 14:35). In every case Jesus is implying that something more than passive listening is required. The hearers are to open their hearts and minds to the truth being revealed. They must take to heart and obey what they are hearing. Some refused to really hear what Jesus was saying (Mark 8:18). As a result, the word spoken had no effect on their lives.

Specifically, the Ephesians are to practice listening to what the Holy Spirit is saying. The Holy Spirit often spoke to the servants of God, guiding them on the way (see Acts 8:29; 13:2). The Spirit was speaking certain things to the churches, acting as their teacher and counselor. Indeed, the church was engaged in a partnership with the Holy Spirit, one that worked only if there was an ongoing sensitivity to the speaking of the Spirit to and through them.

To him who overcomes, I will give the right to eat from the tree of life, which is in the paradise of God (Revelation 2:7).

Jesus concludes his letter with a promise to the overcomers. It is possible for members of the church in Ephesus to conquer, to triumph, to win the victory.[70] The idea of overcoming is a very important theme in the book of Revelation, not only in the seven letters but in the rest of the vision as well (cf. 5:5; 12:11; 15:2; 17:14; 21:7). In the Gospel of John Jesus is quoted as saying, "In this world you will have trouble [tribulation]. But take heart! I have overcome the world" (16:33). When the believers faced difficulties on their kingdom journey, they were to fix their hearts on the fact that Jesus had already won the victory over the world. In his first epistle, John told the believers, "You, dear children, are from God and have overcome them, because the one who is in you is greater than the one who is in the world" (4:4). The indwelling Spirit of God was the victorious one, and was the key to the overcoming potential of the saints.

The opposite of victory is defeat. If the believers did not carry off the victory, they would end in defeat. So the question is, what did the Ephesians need to conquer? And what is the potential victory laying before them? This congregation had been providing an apostolic witness in the city of Ephesus for more than a generation. They had brought significant levels of transformation to the city. The beginning of their witness was fired by love. Now that love had grown cold and they were in danger of losing their witness.

This church was the "mother church" of the other churches established in the province of Asia. That very phrase indicates they were not only to lead those churches, they were to nurture them, to care for them, to look out for them with a sensitive, soft heart of compassion. Without first love, they would not be able to do so.

Their victory would activate their full potential as a mother church in a gate city. What threatened that victory was the waning of love as the motivation for all they said and did. Their tireless labor and endurance in the face of continual hardships makes it easy to see how that could happen. Nevertheless, they must triumph over that enemy or be defeated themselves. And if they overcome, they will continue to fulfill their destiny in Christ.

Above and beyond that, if they triumph, they will be given the ultimate reward, "the right to eat from the tree of life, which is in the paradise of God." The tree of life first appears in the garden of Eden (Genesis 2:9), placed next to the tree of the knowledge of good and evil. Adam and Eve sinned by disobeying God and eating from the latter tree. And human beings have mastered the fruit of that tree ever since. The Ephesians had mastered the knowledge of good and evil. Their doctrine was pure and their dedication to rooting out evil was firm. But the flow of God's life was being threatened.

Because of their disobedience, humans were denied access to the tree of life (Genesis 3:22). In Proverbs the tree of life is a symbol of a lifestyle of wisdom and righteousness (3:18; 11:30; 13:12; 15:4). Ultimately, the tree of life is heaven's source of healing for the nations (Ezekiel 47:12; Revelation 22:2).

The word "paradise" comes from a Persian term for an enclosed garden or park. It referred to a temple complex made up of a sacred tree surrounded by a royal park. When the thief called upon the name of Jesus while dying on the cross, Jesus promise him that he would be with him in Paradise (Luke 23:43). At one point Paul testified to being caught up to Paradise in a vision (2 Corinthians 12:4). In Ephesus, the vast Artemision represented a "paradise." Domitian participated in the destruction of the temple in Jerusalem and then built a temple to himself in Ephesus. All these were false paradises. There was no future in any of them.

The faithful labor of the Ephesians must have made them wonder whether or not there would be a reward. They must have been exhausted and even discouraged at times. Eating from the tree of life in the paradise of God refers to a restoration of an eternal life of intimacy with God promised in the beginning, before sin entered into the world. There is no greater reward. "To eat of the Tree is to enjoy all that the life of the world to come has in store for redeemed humanity."[71] Ephesus had persevered, but they were sick at heart. "But the fruit of the tree of life is the infallible cure, the tree whose very leaves were for the healing of the nations."[72]

The Key of Repentance

The letter to the church at Ephesus presents a clear key to consistently overcoming: "Repent." This is such an important key it was commanded of five of the seven churches (see also 2:16, 21; 3:3, 19). In these letters it is the main word telling the churches how to respond to their spiritual problem.

The Old Testament word translated "repent" is *shuv*, simply meaning to turn or return. It was a relational word describing a return to a former love relationship that had grown cold. "In the covenantal sense, it refers to turning affections from one partner or turning to a stronger relationship with another."[73] The prophet Jeremiah, speaking for the Lord, declared, "They turned their backs to me and not their faces" (32:33). The people had started with an intimate relationship with the Lord that faded from generation to generation. "Therefore this is what the Lord says: If you repent, I will restore you that you may serve me" (Jeremiah 15:19).

We have already seen that the New Testament word is *metanoeo*. It is a compound verb literally meaning "another mind set." It refers to an essential change of thinking, including ones ideas and decisions. The idea is to return to the Lord from the heart so thoroughly that the inner perspectives and values change to increasingly conform to the Lord's own mind and heart.

"Repent" was the first word in the preaching of John the Baptist, of Christ, and of the apostles (Matthew 3:2; 4:17; Acts 2:38). Jesus told his listeners, "Unless you repent, you will all likewise perish" (Luke 13:3). The apostle Paul testified, "I preached that they should repent and turn to God and prove their repentance by their deeds" (Acts 26:20). God commands everyone everywhere to repent (Acts 17:30).

Repentance happens when we respond to God's love. "God's kindness leads you toward repentance" (Romans 2:4). When we consider the faithfulness and the mercy of the Lord, when we see the price he has paid to have a relationship with him, we are moved to turn to him with all our hearts.

Godly sorrow produces repentance. "Godly sorrow brings repentance that leads to salvation and leaves no regret, but worldly sorrow brings death" (2 Corinthians 7:10). There is more than one kind of sorrow. All of us know what it's like to simply be sorry we were caught. By definition, self-centered sorrow does not contribute to repentance. Godly sorrow is a God-centered, God-directed sorrow. Esau gives us an example of a sorrow that does not lead to repentance. He mourned the loss of his birthright but he did not mourn his separation from God (Hebrews 12:17). Godly sorrow involves being sorry our relationship with God has been harmed by our sin, with a passionate desire to return to intimacy with him.

God gives us the power to repent. ". . . the hope that God will grant them repentance leading to a knowledge of the truth" (2 Timothy 2:25). It's one thing to repent in our minds. It's another thing to repent in our wills, from the heart. True, deep repentance leads to genuine change. Our wills are often too self-centered to fully turn, and we need the Lord's help. Fortunately, as we set our hearts to return to him, he is with us to empower us to turn all the way back.

Repentance is foundational to our faith in God. "Not laying again the foundation of repentance from acts that lead to death" (Hebrews 6:1). A personal, dynamic, increasingly intimate relationship with God is not possible without repentance. We are determined to move toward the Lord, not away from him. We desire to turn our faces to him, not our backs. Relationship develops from that desire.

God wants everyone to come to true repentance. "He is patient with you, not wanting anyone to perish, but everyone to come to repentance" (2 Peter 3:9). God is continually calling us to return to him, drawing us along with cords of love. He seeks a real relationship with us and patiently works toward that end.

The Parable of the Lost Son (Luke 15:11–32) provides us with one of the best pictures of repentance. At a certain time the younger son left his father's household and "set off for a distant country." There he squandered his entire inheritance. There was every reason to expect that the pig pen was his just reward. Then, Jesus said, "he came to his senses." This was the beginning of repentance for him. He began to think differently. He realized that he was not worthy to be a son in his father's house, so he would offer himself as a servant. His new humble heart attitude led him to leave the pig pen and set out for home.

"But while he was still a long way off, his father saw him." Evidently the father had been looking for the son every day. Because of his heart of love he ran to greet his son, who responded with words of repentance: "Father, I have sinned against heaven and against you." He knew the relational consequences of his sin and sought reconciliation. The father responded by fully restoring his son. The father was willing to do whatever was necessary to see his son restored to the family. In the same way, God always responds to genuine heart repentance. He meets us "half way" with arms open wide.

Repentance bears observable fruit. "Produce fruit in keeping with repentance" (Luke 3:8). The power of repentance transforms our lives. When we are reconnected with the heart of God, his love and life changes us. John the Baptist mentioned such things as sharing with the poor (Luke 3:11), being honest in business (3:13), and being content with our wages (3:14). These kinds of things would be evidence that the penitent one had adopted God's perspectives, God's values, God's attitudes, and the evidence would be apparent to all. In that sense, repentance is a lifestyle. Ron Sider said it this way:

> Biblical repentance . . . is a deep, heartfelt sorrow for offending the Holy Sovereign of the universe and a strong inner resolve to embrace the conversion—the complete reversal of direction—that our forgiving Savior longs to bestow. We cannot manufacture this radical change using our own strength. But we can beg our Holy God not only to forgive but also to change us. Daily, we can pray to the Lord to transform us more and more into the very likeness of Jesus.[74]

Repentance has the power to prepare for revival. Daniel's

prayer is one of the greatest examples of revival praying in the Bible. When Daniel prayed for his people he confessed, "We have sinned and done wrong. We have been wicked and rebelled; we have turned away from your commands and laws" (Daniel 9:5). Daniel had not personally committed any of these sins. But as a prophet, he was standing in the gap for his people. He understood the power of forgiveness to clear the spiritual atmosphere and prepare for a fresh visitation of God. In fact, revival goes deep only to the extent that repentance has gone deep. If it worked for Daniel, it will work for us.

> Anguished, persistent prayer for revival must become more central in evangelical life. We need to pray mightily for a sweeping movement of revival. God has responded with powerful movements of revival in the church when God's people united in intense, sustained periods of prayer.[75]

Repentance has the power to heal the land. It's possible to be so busy with apostolic efforts to reform the land that we forget the need for the land to be healed. That healing will take place only if the people of God begin with genuine, heart-felt repentance. "If my people, who are called by my name, will humble themselves and pray and seek my face and turn from their wicked ways, then will I hear from heaven and will forgive their sin and will heal their land" (2 Chronicles 7:14).

The Message of the Letter to Ephesus

The fact that a large, successful apostolic church could, at the peak of its influence and effectiveness, be said to have lost its first love, and that the consequence of that would be the loss of its influence, forces us to examine the issues more carefully. How could such a dilemma happen, and how could it be avoided?

The Challenge of the Second and Third Generation

The first generation, the pioneering generation, of any movement is energized by a clear vision and a pure passion.

They are the recipients of the first mandate that burned brightly in their hearts. They are the ones who gladly dedicated their lives to the cause of Christ, and they give themselves sacrificially to the work.

The second generation grows up hearing about the vision. They see the zeal of the first generation and admire it. They share in the work with fervor. But they don't necessarily share the same heart motivation and passion. It is then possible for activities to replace priorities, for the work to become the focus of their labors, not their love for Christ and for people.

Jack Hayford observes how this can work in the business place:

> People who study corporations that rise to a great place of success observe that they often plateau and lose their momentum or they absolutely lose their place and disintegrate. The dynamics that occasioned the rise to a place of effectiveness are forgotten and lost because the machinery, the bureaucracy, takes over and loses the vital life of the corporation.[76]

Institutionalism sets in when subsequent generations focus their creative efforts on maintaining the institution. When that happens in the church, its vital force begins to wane.

A multi-generational church will have more than an initial pioneering generation carrying the banner of the kingdom of God. Every generation must catch its own vision and have its own passion. Every generation must experience its own revival.

The Challenge of Dissension

The church at Ephesus not only struggled with opposition from the synagogue and the state, they struggled with heresy and the resultant immorality on the inside. This struggle with the Nicolaitans eventually led to division, to a "church split." Times of conflict always make us vulnerable. There is always the possibility that the "spirit" of the conflict can enter into the community.

Because the church is a living organism, the Body of Christ, division affects it like a virus. Paul encouraged the church to have "no divisions" among them (1 Corinthians 1:10) and taught them how to avoid divisions (1 Corinthians 12:24, 25). Jude spoke of those who cause division as the ones who "follow their own ungodly desires" (vv. 18, 19). There is always a great deal of carnality involved in an atmosphere of dissension. Even those fighting on the right side can go away with a "spirit of division" from the fight. There was the danger of that for an apostolic church like Ephesus, fighting heresy, testing false teachers, guarding the church and the truth.

What's more, the Nicolaitans were known for their lovelessness. Many of the statements in John's first epistle were aimed at their arrogant attitudes. Fighting lovelessness can result in absorbing some of that very same spirit, especially if one's identity becomes attached to the fight. All situations of dissension, even when we are convinced we're on the side of right, must be carefully guarded. It is essential we maintain a soft heart and a loving spirit, not allowing the "fight" to get into us.

The challenge of dissension is the challenge of speaking the truth in love (see Ephesians 4:15). Truth without love is not truth, and love without truth is not love. There must be an equal amount of both if both love and truth are to prevail. "If men have lost their first love, they will do more harm than good by their defense of the faith. Behind the denunciation of sin there must always be the tenderness of first love if that denunciation is not to become evil in its bitterness."[77] If the love side of the formula begins to wane, truth becomes a blunt instrument that injures more than it heals.

The Challenge of Intimacy and Busyness

"First love" is to love the Lord first—with all your heart, mind, soul and strength. "God is love," implying that everything God does is motivated by love. To the extent that we represent God in all we do, we too will be motivated by love.

We have been created for relationship, with God first—

and as an overflow of that relationship, with others. Everything depends on our growing intimacy with the Lord. Cultivating that intimacy is our highest priority. G. Campbell Morgan defined "first love" as "marital love, the response of love to love, the subjection of a great love to a greater love, the submission of a self-denying love to a love that denies itself. First love is the abandonment of all for a love that has abandoned all."[78]

The story of the relationship between Jesus and the family of Lazarus, Martha and Mary illustrates the point well (see Luke 10:38–42). Martha had a wonderful ministry of hospitality. When Jesus came to town it was Martha who "opened her home to him." It was Martha who received Jesus and immediately began to work hard to meet his needs. There was nothing wrong with Martha's behavior. She would be a pillar in any local church today. Her hard work and attention to detail were admirable.

However, Jesus noticed that she "was distracted by all the preparations." The tasks before her soon became more important than they really were. She forgot that the work involved in serving Jesus was a means to the end, not the end itself. Jesus himself was the end. He was the goal.

Mary's response was to sit "at the Lord's feet listening to what he said." If she had been off in another part of the house, refusing to assist Martha, her negligence would have been a problem. Instead, she is focused on Jesus as her first priority. More than anything else she wanted to spend time in his presence. Just listening to his voice gave her immense pleasure. And her response to Jesus gave him pleasure as well. Martha had become "worried and upset." Her preparations had become a burden instead of a joy. Mary had "chosen what is better." She had chosen to waste time with Jesus. And her desire to do so was not going to "be taken away from her."

Martha's first love had been overshadowed by her work. As a result, even her work ceased to be a blessing. "All zeal for the Master that is not the outcome of love to Him is worthless. Activity in the King's business will not make up for neglect of the King. He who has lost his first love cannot satisfy with work and labor and patience, and hatred of sin and orthodoxy. The Master waits for love."[79]

The Ephesian church had perfected "Martha ministries." They had worked to the point of exhaustion, and then kept on working. But something was now missing. "In Ephesus, something has changed from the early days when everything about their faith was fresh and new. Now their passion has been replaced with other priorities. There is work to be done—a world to win."[80] We would have considered the church at Ephesus to be a model church in every way. But that was not the perspective of the Lord of the church. "The intensity of 'first love' . . . cannot be measured by numbers or programs. Not can it be valued by budgets or buildings. We deceive ourselves if we look at a marriage as being based solely on the size of the house, the spouse's income, or the size of the family. None of these visible assets reveal the love the couple shares together."[81] The church is the Bride of Christ. We are engaged to be married. No matter how many preparations might be called for, nothing is more important than pouring out our love to our Bridegroom.

Jack Hayford has left us an important challenge: "This passage then explains that the fountain of your power is your relationship with Jesus, not the dominion or authority you seem to be able to manifest in ministry. Is Jesus the center of it all? Not just His name being used, but are you drawn to Jesus, to love Jesus?"[82] If Jesus is the center, all we do will be driven by love.

The Story of City Bible Church

Portland is the largest city in Oregon and one of the major urban centers in the Pacific Northwest. Incorporated in 1851, its early history is fairly shady, known for drugs and alcohol and the practice of "shanghaiing" young men. When the railroad arrived in 1883 the city began to grow into a major economic force on the west coast. Portland is known for the beauty of its rivers and mountains and the friendliness of its citizens.

Bible Temple was established in 1951 as a nondenominational Pentecostal church. It was founded by members of the same family, namely Ivy and Sylvia Iverson, and their son and daughter-in-law, Dick and Edie Iverson. The background of the church was the healing revival of the late '40's, the Iversons having been a part of the ministry of T. L. Osborne. Father and son pastored the church together for almost ten years until poor health forced Ivy to turn the church over to his son. Altogether Dick Iverson pastored the church for forty-four years, until 1995, when he appointed Frank Damazio to be the new senior pastor.

Pastor Frank came to Portland from Eugene, Oregon with a passion for impacting the city. Bible Temple had been known for its apostolic outreach, including church planting and missionary sending. The church had begun Portland Bible College to train pastors and missionaries, including Frank Damazio, who had been sent out to plant a church in Eugene in 1981. The new pastor brought with him a deep desire to reach the city in new ways.

The first symbolic step in that process was to change the name of the church, no small feat for an older, well-established congregation. In 1998 Bible Temple changed its "brand" to City Bible Church, a church in the city for the city.

Frank began to reach out to the other pastors in the city, from both denominational and nondenominational churches. His desire was not to form a quasi-city denomination but simply to be a source of encouragement and resources to all the churches of the city and to promote unity and effective ministry among them. As a congregation of over 4,000 members C.B.C. is a "regional" congregation, impacting the metropolitan area and beyond. Part of the opportunity afforded such regional churches is the honor of actively serving other congregations in the region. Pastor Frank began to host pastors' prayer meetings for mutual intercession, encouragement and fellowship. Before long there were so many local pastors attending they had to have two groups meeting together at different times in the month.

As the pastors joined together in prayer they began to see the needs of the city from a broader perspective. And they saw clearly that all of them together could effectively address some of those needs. On one Sunday evening members of all the congregations represented by the pastors met together for a citywide prayer meeting. At the meeting they took an offering for the homeless. The next week several pastors met with members of the local government and presented the funds to them. It goes without saying that such an event had never happened before.

At another time the Portland school district ran into budget problems and no longer had the funds to adequately maintain school properties. The first to hear about it was City Bible Church's Generation Ministries, who organized young people to mow the lawn of the elementary school closest to the C.B.C. campus. It soon became obvious that much more was needed, so members of the C.B.C. congregation worked together to maintain an area middle school, including mowing and painting and whatever else was needed. Now many congregations are working together to serve the Portland school district.

And then it happened. A member of the congregation presented the elders of City Bible Church with a year-end gift of $100,000 with a clear proviso—the money could only be used to feed the poor. The decision to accept the gift would require a long-term commitment to an intentional ministry to the poor. It seemed to be another opportunity to serve the community, so "City Reach" was formed. A food distribution facility was rented and a couple hired to coordinate ministry to the poor. The strategy was to make such a ministry as personal and pastoral as possible. Food would be delivered personally to the homes of needy families by a pastor or small group leader, with an offer of prayer and other forms of support. In addition, arrangements were made with a local second-hand store to give vouchers for clothing and household goods to needy families. That ministry continues to grow.

Every year a variety of city outreach projects are aimed at being salt and light in the city of Portland. The "City Summer Celebration" began as a July 4 picnic and soon became a community-wide event. One year 5,500 people attended the celebration. Along with food, games and attractions for children there were community services offered such as free oil changes for single mothers, free food for needy families, and a blood drive organized by the Red Cross. There were also a variety of "prayer booths" where prayer was offered for visitors with a variety of personal needs.

The movie phenomenon, "The Passion of the Christ," affected cities across the U.S. and around the world. It was obvious not everyone in Portland who wanted to see the movie would be able to. Portland has one of the highest rates of homelessness in the nation. So the congregation of City Bible Church rented space in two local theaters and went downtown to invite homeless people to a "Passion" party. Over 600 people accepted the invitation, loaded into buses and saw the movie for free. They were then taken to the C.B.C. campus for a pizza party. An opportunity to pray with someone was offered and 169 accepted the offer. All the homeless were given gift bags containing soap, toothpaste and toothbrushes, socks and Bibles.

Then a weekly "recovery ministry" was launched. A variety of groups, led by trained leaders, were offered free of charge. From "Chemical Dependency" to "Codependency," "Eating Disorders" to "Marriage Builders," Celebrate Recovery ministers to over one hundred people in small groups. Testimonies from the community indicate that the power of God is at working liberating and healing many.

Thanksgiving is traditionally a time to celebrate the faithfulness of the Lord in our lives. For C.B.C. it has also become a time to recognize that not everyone is equally blessed. Some in fact are in desperate straits. As a result, money and food for the poor are collected every year. During a recent year over six hundred food boxes that included a Thanksgiving turkey were assembled and distributed to families in the community. That opportunity to give and serve was such a blessing to the congregation a Christmas follow-up was planned. In 2004 Portland was experiencing a high rate of unemployment and many families were not going to have extra money for the holidays. So the City Bible Church congregation raised money and bought toys for over seven hundred families. In addition, a special Christmas dinner was planned and invitations sent to needy families. Around six hundred fifty people were served a sumptuous dinner they would not have enjoyed otherwise.

Easter seemed another good opportunity to reach out to the community. Needy families were invited to an Easter Day brunch and egg hunt on the C.B.C. campus. Those who needed transportation were accommodated. Three hundred fifty people, including children, attended the brunch.

Then came March 3, 2004. The Multnomah County Commissioners decided to begin issuing same-sex marriage licenses and before long over 3,000 gay weddings had been performed. This was a difficult moment for the churches of Oregon, and especially of those in Portland, one of its counties being Multnomah Country. City Bible Church had reached a fair number from the gay community in Portland and was committed to communicating the gospel and the love of Christ to them. Yet the need to make a biblical moral statement about marriage seemed to be called for. So the "Defense of Marriage Coalition" was formed by a group of C.B.C. pastors, including Pastor Frank. The relationships that had been formed with pastors in Portland led to a very rapid unity on the issue of marriage in the state of Oregon and a strategy for defending its traditional definition.

Churches from around the state gathered for prayer and decided to offer a constitutional amendment on the November ballot. Oregon's friendly, tolerant (if not libertarian) culture seemed to doom such a ballot measure, but when the votes were counted, 59% of Oregonians chose to defend the traditional definition of marriage. For City Bible Church, being salt and light involved serving the community in a variety of creative ways, but it also involved a prophetic witness to righteousness in the midst of declining morals. For some, being a redemptive, transformational presence in the city is either compassionate deeds or moral advocacy. For C.B.C. it is clearly both.

CHAPTER FOUR:

THE PROMISE OF BEING A CHURCH OF CONQUERING FAITHFULNESS IN A CITY OF CONVENIENT FAITHFULNESS

THE LETTER TO SMYRNA

One of the most ancient cities in the province of Asia was the coastal city of Smyrna. The early church fathers reported that Paul, on the way from Corinth to Ephesus, passed through Smyrna and found a small group of disciples already there (cf. Acts 19:1). However, he went on to establish the work in Ephesus first, and then eventually sent a team to Smyrna to build the Christian community in that city.

Evidently they were very successful. There are only two churches that are not corrected by Jesus in the Revelation, and Smyrna is one of them. What if you had been a member of that team sent out by Paul in Ephesus? What challenges would you have encountered? What would your vision for the city have been, and how would that determine your plans and priorities? You would certainly want to study the story of Smyrna first, and then prayerfully allow the Holy Spirit to set your course.

The Story of Smyrna

The original city of Smyrna was founded by Greek settlers sometime between 1200 and 1000 BC. It was located on the Aegean Sea 35 miles north of Ephesus. According to tradition Homer was born in Smyrna around 800 BC. Between 800 and 600 BC the city was afflicted by a series of attacks from the Lydians until Alyattes, king of Lydia, destroyed the city around 600 BC. For the next several hundred years there was only a simple village where a former city had been located.

When Alexander the Great passed through the area in 334 BC he authorized the rebuilding of the city and personally oversaw the laying of the new foundation, closer to the sea than the ancient city. He intended it to become a prominent Greek maritime and trading center and a starting place for a trade route heading east. The Greek king Lysimachus finished the rebuilding project in 290 BC, situated at the head of a well protected gulf with an ample harbor. This was a literal rebirth of Smyrna. A Greek writer, Aelius Aristides, likened the city to Phoenix, the mythical bird that burned to death and was reborn out of the ashes.

The rebuilt city soon became known as the most beautiful city in Asia. An acropolis was built 500 feet high on the top of Mt. Pagos. It had a series of buildings that spread many miles around the head of the land-locked gulf. The acropolis included a beautiful roadway called the "Street of Gold." These buildings were so strikingly beautiful they became known as the "Crown of Smyrna." The agora had a large courtyard nearly 400 feet long, surrounded by columns. The city contained large temples to the Greek god Zeus and the goddess Cybele, connected by a mall that was the envy of the ancient world. It also had a large stadium that seated 20,000. The Roman geographer Strabo referred to Smyrna as the "First of Asia in beauty and size." Aelius Aristides considered Smyrna the ideal city on earth, the very flower of beauty.

The earth-mother goddess Cybele was the patron deity of Smyrna. That meant there was an ancient underlying layer of nature religion in Smyrna. The Meles River was worshiped for its healing powers. Smyrna was the first city to build a temple dedicated to the glory of Rome and the goddess Roma in 195 BC. This was over 60 years before the establishing of the Roman province of Asia. In fact, Smyrna was so pro-Rome, when in AD 26 they competed with ten other cities to build a temple to the Roman emperor Tiberius, Livia (the mother of Tiberius) and the Roman Senate, they were granted the honor and named the *Neokoros* of the imperial cult. In Smyrna "each person was required to worship the emperor regularly, and certificates were at times issued for such worship."[83] The Roman Cicero referred to Smyrna as "the most faithful of our allies." As a result of their ability to conform to the standards and expectations of Rome, Smyrna had a history of unbroken peace and prosperity under the empire.

By the end of the first century AD Smyrna was second in wealth only to Ephesus (and would eventually surpass Ephesus). It was at the end of a great trade route that penetrated the interior through Sardis. It was also at the end of the very fertile Hermus River valley. It had a population of over 100,000 and had a reputation for being the "Ornament of Asia."

The history of Smyrna resulted in certain traditions. The Phoenix-like death and rebirth of the city reflected the Egyptian myth of the Phoenix that emphasized the use of myrrh (a spice used by the Egyptians in the embalming process). In fact, the word "smurna" is the Greek word for myrrh. The local goddess Myrrha became their universal type for mourning. "Life from death" was a unifying theme in the city's history.

The so-called "Crown of Smyrna" on the acropolis, combined with the fame of their local athletic games, gave rise to a strong tradition of "crowns" or laurel wreaths.[84] This crown was used in several different contexts, including as a sign of festivity, a public honor, or the visit of a king, as well as the crowning of an athletic champion. If the city of Smyrna wanted to bestow an honor on a deceased citizen, they did so by awarding a crown.

There was a large, prosperous Jewish colony in Smyrna from the days of Alexander. They were granted citizenship and tax exemption from the beginning. Most of the early Christian converts were members of the synagogue. When the conflict between the church and synagogue intensified under

Domitian, hostilities were particularly sharp in Smyrna.

History indicates that there were some in the synagogue in Smyrna who took it upon themselves to use the Roman authorities to persecute the Christians. They did so by instigating legal action against the Hebrew Christians in the synagogue, making the charge that they were not true Jews. This strategy exposed those Christians to the full wrath of the empire. Just as with the city of Smyrna itself, some in the synagogue had learned to accommodate themselves to Rome in order to gain the desired benefits.

It appears as though this situation continued 60 years after John's letter. The early church father Polycarp was the famous bishop of Smyrna in AD 155. Polycarp was brought before the Roman officials and commanded to "revile Christ." Polycarp replied, "Eighty and six years have I served him, and in nothing has he wronged me; and how, then, can I blaspheme my King, who saved me?" (*The Martyrdom of St. Polycarp* 9.3). When threatened with death by beasts or by fire, Polycarp refused to deny his Lord. At that point, "The whole multitude, both of Gentiles and Jews, that inhabit Smyrna, with irrestrainable anger and a loud voice called out . . . with one voice that Polycarp should be burnt alive" (12.2, 3). When the authorities gave in to the mob, "The multitude quickly collected logs and brushwood from the workshops and baths, the Jews especially lending their services zealously for this purpose, as was their custom" (13.1). Before the fire was lit, Polycarp prayed:

> O Lord God Almighty, Father of thy beloved and blessed Son Jesus Christ, through whom we have received our knowledge concerning thee, the God of angels and powers, and of the whole creation, and of all the race of the just who lived before thee, I thank thee that thou hast deemed me worthy of this day and hour, that I should have my portion in the number of the martyrs, in the cup of thy Christ, unto the resurrection of eternal life, both of the soul and body, in the incorruptibility of the Holy Spirit. Among these may I be received before thee this day as a rich and acceptable sacrifice, even as thou hast prepared and made manifest beforehand, and hast ful-

filled, thou who art the unerring and true God. On this account, and concerning all things, I praise thee, I bless thee, I glorify thee, together with the eternal and heavenly Jesus Christ thy beloved Son, with whom to thee and the Holy Spirit be glory both now and for ever. Amen (14.1–3).

The character of the church of Smyrna described in the letter of the risen Christ lived on. In fact, a viable church continues in Smyrna (present-day Izmir) to the present day.

The Letter to Smyrna

In many ways the letter to Smyrna is unique. It is the shortest of the seven letters—only four verses long. Only two letters do not begin with "I know your deeds," one of them being this letter. Only two letters contain no words of correction, including the letter to Smyrna. This letter also has the fewest references to the Old Testament.

To the angel of the church in Smyrna write: These are the words of him who is the First and the Last, who died and came to life again (Revelation 2:8).

When John saw the vision of the risen Christ in 1:17, Jesus said, "I am the First and the Last." Jesus identified himself as the origin and the culmination of all things. This greeting would be especially appropriate in the city that claimed to be "the first" city in Asia. Smyrna does not have the highest place, the place only the Son of God could claim. In addition, Jesus is the sum and the conclusion of all things. He is eternal. No matter how great Smyrna is, it is temporary.

In 1:18 Jesus revealed himself as "the living one." Although he died, he is alive for ever. In his letter to Smyrna Jesus identified himself as the one who had died but then lived. The language of the address in the letter to Smyrna is a more specific reference to the resurrection of Christ on the third day. Jesus had actually died, but he had risen from the dead. It was not a symbolic truth, it was a historic fact. Christ went before the saints in Smyrna by suffering death, but a death that led to resurrection.

The city of Smyrna prided itself on its history of having died in 600 BC, only to live again after Alexander. "Life out of death" was the chief cultural theme of the city. Jesus fulfilled that theme in the highest sense. And he offered the same level of life from death to his faithful followers.

> *I know your afflictions and your poverty—yet you are rich!* (Revelation 2:9).

Instead of telling the Smyrnean Christians, "I know your deeds," he acknowledged three things: "I know your afflictions . . . poverty . . . slander." Jesus began by expressing his understanding of their difficulties. "Afflictions" (Greek *thlipsis*) means "a pressing, pressing together, or pressure." It refers to the pressure of the stones that grind the wheat, or that force the juice out of the grape. It means "trouble, oppression or distress," and is also translated "tribulation," "suffering" or "persecution." When Jesus taught the parable of the seed and the sower, he said that the seed sown along the path springs up quickly until it encounters "trouble" (Matthew 13:21). Jesus also taught his disciples they would eventually be handed over to be "persecuted" (Matthew 24:9). Although they would experience "trouble in the world," they should find hope in the understanding that he had already overcome the world (John 16:33). Paul testified that he rejoiced in his "sufferings" (Romans 5:3). John had also testified that he was a partner with them in their "suffering" (Revelation 1:9). The clash between the kingdom of God and the kingdom of the world will always result in these kinds of difficulties. However, the church in Smyrna found affliction to be their daily bread. They need to understand Jesus' personal view of their troubles.

Jesus also acknowledged that he was personally aware of their "poverty." This is the strongest word for poverty, referring to destitution that leads to a life of begging, to be conspicuously poor. Jesus uses this word when he says, "Blessed are the poor in spirit" (Matthew 5:3). Jesus came to preach "the good news to the poor" (Luke 4:18). Paul testified to being "poor, yet making many rich" (2 Corinthians 6:10). James pointed out that God has "chosen those who are poor in the eyes of the world to be rich in faith" (James 2:5). The extreme poverty of the believers in Smyrna could have been caused either by the Roman mobs destroying their property, or by the loss of jobs due to their Christian stand. In either case, they had become destitute as a result of their afflictions.

Their outward circumstances could be described as extreme poverty. However, from God's point of view, "You are rich." Being "rich" (Greek *plousios*) means "abounding in material resources, abundantly supplied." Jesus commented on those who lay up treasure for themselves but are "not rich toward God" (Luke 12:21). It is the Lord who is ultimately "rich" toward all (Romans 10:12). Paul taught that the poverty of Christ has resulted in believers being truly "rich" (2 Corinthians 8:9). On the other hand, those who "want to be rich fall into many harmful desires" (1 Timothy 6:9). Real poverty marked the lives of the persecuted saints in Smyrna, but they were truly rich. As Sir William Ramsay observed:

> The Smyrnean church had had a more trying and diffi-
> cult career than any other of the Asian churches. It had
> been exposed to constant persecution. It was poor in all
> that is ordinarily reckoned as wealth, but it was rich in
> the estimation of those who can judge of the realities of
> life. There is here the same contrast between appearance
> and reality as in the opening address: apparent poverty
> and real wealth, apparent death and real life.[85]

I know the slander of those who say they are Jews and are not, but are a synagogue of Satan (Revelation 2:9).

The third thing Jesus noticed about believers in Smyrna was the "slander," a word referring to "railing, reviling, speech injurious to another; reproachful speech." Blasphemy was considered a sin against God. Jesus warned against "blasphemy against the Spirit" (Matthew 12:31). "Slander" comes out of an evil heart (Mark 7:22). Paul exhorted the Ephesians to get rid of all "slander" (Ephesians 4:31).

In this case, the reproach was coming from the synagogue.

Certain members, if not the leaders, of the local synagogue were conspiring with the Roman authorities to persecute the Christians. Their accusation against the Christians was, "They say they are Jews, but are not." Now Jesus communicates his perspective. Jesus cannot be accused of being anti-Semitic, since he was Jewish. He is simply pointing out that the slander against his people was a sin against God—it was blasphemy.

Paul had taught a doctrine of "spiritual Israel." A "Jew" is "one inwardly . . . by the Spirit" (Romans 2:28, 29). It's not circumcision that creates a child of God, but "a new creation" (Galatians 6:15). The true circumcision "worship God by the Spirit" (Philippians 2:2, 3). John insisted that the true people of God is a spiritual nation, not an ethnic group (see John 8:44). John also viewed the Roman empire, and especially emperor worship, to be satanic. Rome was "the beast." For anyone in the synagogue to cooperate with Rome meant they were cooperating with Satan, and were to that extent, "a synagogue of Satan." According to G. Campbell Morgan, "It is a terrible indictment, called forth by the fact that they had vilified His people, and so had proved themselves under the leadership of the slanderer whose perpetual aim it is to degrade our God and His Christ."[86]

> *Do not be afraid of what you are about to suffer. I tell you, the devil will put some of you in prison to test you, and you will suffer persecution for ten days* (Revelation 2:10).

Although Jesus does not correct the saints in Smyrna, he does give them a very clear word of encouragement. "Do not be afraid" is a command literally meaning, "Stop being afraid," or "don't be afraid of anyone." Jesus had taught his disciples, "Do not be afraid of those who kill the body but cannot kill the soul. Rather, be afraid of the One who can destroy both soul and body in hell" (Matthew 10:28). They had every reason to be afraid, but the fear of God would empower them to overcome every other kind of fear.

After telling them to not be afraid, Jesus gives them even more reason to be afraid. They are about to "suffer" even more

Transformers

intense trials. This word for "suffer" refers to the feelings one has in any experience, either good or bad. In a negative context it means "to undergo evils; to be afflicted." Specifically, their imminent experience will involve imprisonment and possible death. The author of their suffering will be "the devil." *Diabolos* is the Greek equivalent of the Hebrew *Satan*, and means "accuser, slanderer, adversary." The same devil who was using some in the synagogue to slander them would soon use the Roman authorities to imprison them. In either case, their true enemy was neither Jew nor Roman but Satan.

The devil would be putting some of the believers "in prison." Imprisonment was not used by the Romans to get criminals off of the street and out of society. Prison was only used as detention pending trial, or detention pending execution. Prison clearly implies the possibility of execution, of martyrdom. This will be an opportunity to "test" the Christians. Satan is attempting to trap them into compromising their loyalty to Christ. However, from God's point of view, this is an opportunity for the believers to demonstrate the authenticity of their faith and to bear a powerful witness to Christ. Jesus had been lead by the Holy Spirit into the wilderness to be "tempted by the devil" (Matthew 4:1). God will not allow us to be "tempted" beyond what we can bear (1 Corinthians 10:13). Indeed, we are to "examine" ourselves (2 Corinthians 13:5). Although their trial will be severe, it will give them an opportunity to prove that Jesus Christ is in fact who he claims to be.

They will experience tribulation or persecution "for ten days." This phrase brings to mind the experience of Daniel in the Old Testament. Daniel submitted to a ten-day trial (1:12–14), during which time he established God's favor upon him. "Ten days" is a limited but full time of testing. It is a test under God's specific control. Like Daniel, they will have an opportunity to bring glory to God and preach the gospel with their own lives. As Paul had written, "For our light and momentary troubles are achieving for us an eternal glory that far outweighs them all" (2 Corinthians 4:17).

Be faithful, even to the point of death, and I will give you the crown of life (Revelation 2:10).

In the face of intensified persecution, the command of Christ to the church at Smyrna is to "be faithful." Jesus does not offer to alleviate the suffering. He simply instructs them to stand strong, to be consistent and reliable in the heat of the battle. The city of Smyrna lauded their reputation for faithfulness in the empire. But the faithfulness of the city was motivated by a desire for peace and prosperity. Jesus is calling for a different kind of faithfulness from his people. They faced suffering and death, not peace and prosperity, as the reward for their faithfulness.

Instead of "faith" John emphasizes the importance of "faithfulness" in the face of suffering.[87] "'Faith' in the Book of Revelation is the way we persevere, by putting all our trust in the God who is sovereign over history and will indeed vindicate his people for their suffering. It does not mean that suffering is not our lot but rather that God will bring victory out of seeming temporary defeat."[88] Their confidence in the faithfulness of Jesus will embolden them to be faithful in afflictions, even if that leads to their "death."

"To the point of death," or "until death," literally means "up to and including death." This phrase is found one other place in the book of Revelation. "They overcame him by the blood of the Lamb and the word of their testimony; they did not love their lives so much as to shrink from death" (Revelation 12:11). The key to the power of the overcomers was the fact that they did not love themselves "until death." They knew something about life and death that made them fearless and faithful.

"I will give you the crown of life."[89] True life is not limited by mortality. True life is found only in Christ. To die for him does not end true life; it only releases it to a new dimension. Those who remained faithful until death would be given the victor's crown, the laurel wreath of triumph and festivity. How fitting in the context of the "Crown of Smyrna" and the famous athletic contests. How ironic in the context of Smyrna's custom of awarding "crowns" as a way of honoring the dead. The fearless and faithful followers of

Christ in Smyrna will receive God's own victor's crown. "God had been faithful to Jesus and had raised Him from death to victory and a crown. So too would God, through Jesus and His Holy Spirit, raise the disciples to victory and a crown."[90]

> *He who has an ear to hear, let him hear what the Spirit says to the churches. He who overcomes will not be hurt at all by the second death* (Revelation 2:11).

Here is the message of the Holy Spirit. The life, death and resurrection of Jesus Christ have changed everything. It has redefined life and death for every human being. Just being alive physically does not necessarily constitute true life. In the same way, dying physically does not necessarily imply true death.

The "second death" is also referred to in Revelation 20:6, 14; 21:8, where it is also called "the lake of fire." The second death is true death. It is God's final judgment (see also Daniel 12:2; John 5:29). The overcomers will be given immunity from the second death. They cannot truly die.

Jesus had said, "I am the resurrection and the life. He who believes in me will live, even though he dies; and whoever lives and believes in me will never die" (John 11:25, 26). "Jesus does not guarantee Christians immunity from suffering and death, but He does promise them eternal life and victory for their martyrdom."[91] The overcomers will be guaranteed true life.

What do they need to overcome? What are the enemies that need to be conquered? What will be the distinctive characteristic of overcomers in Smyrna? These followers of Jesus lived in a city famous for its faithfulness, but it was a convenient faithfulness. It was a faithfulness of a people who had learned what to do and what to say in order to maintain the favor of the Romans. The Christian church was being given the opportunity to serve as salt and light in the city by modeling true loyalty. But they had an enemy, and its name was "fear": fear of affliction, fear of poverty, fear of slander, fear of death. If they could consistently triumph over fear, if they could continue to put their confidence and trust in Jesus who had proven his faithfulness to them, they would be faithful—until death.

The Key of Sharing in the Sufferings of Christ

Meditating on the letter of the risen Christ to the church at Smyrna can be a bit uncomfortable for an American Christian. It is filled with suffering and trials, affliction and poverty. It is all about having a radically new value system based on a new understanding, God's understanding, of life and death. For the most part, the American church does not have a theology of suffering. Yet, it is a common theme in the Bible. It could even be said that a right understanding of "suffering" is central to our understanding of the cross and God's plan of redemption.

God is aware of human suffering. Suffering has been the common experience of human beings since the entrance of sin into the world. But God is not unconcerned. In fact, his heart of compassion goes out toward those who are suffering. "I am concerned about their suffering" (Exodus 3:7). In his ministry, Jesus met human beings at the point of their suffering. All those who were suffering were brought to him, "and he healed them" (Matthew 4:24).

Jesus came into the world to share in our suffering. Isaiah had prophesied that the Messiah would be "pierced for our transgressions" and "crushed for our iniquities" (Isaiah 53:4, 5). Although they didn't understand why, Jesus told his disciples that it was necessary for him "to suffer many things" (Matthew 16:21; 17:12). After his resurrection Jesus explained that it had been necessary for him "to suffer these things" (Luke 24:26). The preaching of the apostles clearly declared that it was God's will that "Christ would suffer" (Acts 3:18; 17:3; 26:23).

God's plan of redemption, his method for removing human sin from creation, was not to wave a magic wand, speak the word and abolish it. His plan was to enter into humanity, to enter into human suffering that had come as a result of sin, and to release love and life and healing from the inside out. God's plan of redemption arises out of the fundamental fact that he is love. And that is "the power of the cross" (1 Corinthians 1:18). Jesus was crowned with glory and honor "because he suffered" (Hebrews 2:9) and became the author of our salvation "through suffering" (Hebrews 2:10). The power of suffering is the power of the cross—the power to bring life out of death, to replace beauty for ashes.

The followers of Christ have the privilege of sharing in his sufferings. Redemption didn't end at the cross. The redeemed ones are now a redemptive presence, agents of redemption, in the world. In fact, we are co-heirs with him if "we share in his sufferings" (Romans 8:17). Those sufferings are not to be compared to the glory that will follow (Romans 8:18). The sufferings of Christ "flow over into our lives" so that the comfort of Christ will overflow our lives to others (2 Corinthians 1:5–7). We are granted the ability not only to believe in Jesus but also to suffer with and for him (Philippians 1:29).

Paul declared that his deepest desire was to share in the sufferings of Jesus, even "becoming like him in his death" (Philippians 3:10). As a result, he rejoiced in his suffering (Colossians 1:24), and he invited other believers to "join me in suffering for the gospel" (2 Timothy 1:8). Paul was not ashamed to suffer for Christ (2 Timothy 1:12). Although Paul's suffering may have resulted in him being put in chains, it had unchained the gospel (2 Timothy 2:9).

We are commended by God if we suffer for the sake of Christ (1 Peter 2:19). If we suffer for what is right, we are blessed (1 Peter 3:14). Indeed, we are to rejoice if we receive the privilege of participating in the sufferings of Christ (1 Peter 4:13). When we find ourselves in a situation of suffering, we are to respond by committing ourselves to God as our faithful Creator (1 Peter 4:19). "The gospel of Jesus Christ, when it is declared in its entirety, tells us plainly that the only way to enter the Kingdom of God is through the doorway of suffering and letting go of self and its agencies."[92]

Meditating on the sufferings of Christ was a constant source of comfort to the Christians in Smyrna. Their experience paralleled the experience of Christ. Participating in that experience was their joy. "The parallel with the sufferings of Christ had a message of encouragement for the suffering

Smyrnean Christian. Christ is the First and the Last, and the reality of his victory over death is the guarantee of the same victory for his followers."[93]

Suffering is our preparation for glory. The meaning of this life in the end is that it is preparation for the life to come. Suffering liberates us from our addiction to temporary things, including our addiction to our temporary life. As a result, we draw closer to the Lord, lean more heavily on him, and find new enlargement of spirit. "Trusting in outward things will always weaken spiritual character. Only under the pressure of hardship and persecution, are we reminded of the world's shallowness and the deception of its promises."[94]

Our tribulation will lead to triumph. We are companions with Christ on the journey, sharing in his life and his work. As G. Campbell Morgan wrote:

> That is the whole philosophy of suffering. When presently all the tribulation is passed, and the painful processes of the little while are over, and the last grim pressure ceases, then we shall be crowned with life, then we shall know the meaning of life. This is the heart and centre of the great truth delivered to the suffering saints at Smyrna. "I am your companion in distress. I am your comrade in the darkness. I know, and I am with you, and just beyond I will be with you still, leading you to the fountains of living waters."[95]

The Message of the Letter to Smyrna

It's easy to see how the letter to Smyrna might apply to the church in China or Pakistan. But is there a message to churches in the West? How are affliction and poverty and slander relevant to churches that are comfortable, rich and influential?

The Challenge of Faithfulness

The church at Smyrna had the continual challenge of trusting in the Lord in the midst of very trying circumstances.

They needed to be able to see Jesus in every situation and put the focus of their hearts on him. What if they had thought that faith was the power that enabled them to escape all suffering? If they had enough faith, they shouldn't have to endure poverty; faith would make them wealthy. If they had enough faith, they would have been rescued from imprisonment and death; faith would have kept them "safe."

These believers had to go deeper in their understanding of faith and then live it out in a radical faithfulness. They would have eventually come to understand that great faith is simply great trust in God's great faithfulness. Both Old and New Testaments reveal God as completely faithful (cf. Deuteronomy 7:9; 32:4; Psalm 33:4; 36:5; 1 Corinthians 1:9; 2 Thessalonians 3:3; etc.). The Lord is absolutely trustworthy. He is consistent, dependent, reliable. Our faith holds that understanding at the center.

As a result, people of faith are principally faithful people (cf. Number 12:7; Psalm 101:6; Ephesians 1:1). Faithfulness is a fruit of the Spirit (Galatians 5:22). In the end, we will be judged according to our faithfulness (Matthew 25:21). Faith is our heart response to the faithfulness of God. Faith is our response to God's voice speaking in our lives (Romans 10:17). Faith is not a magical way out of suffering; faith keeps us focused on Christ in the midst of suffering. We may need to understand that some day.

The Challenge of Values

The difference between the kingdom of God and the "world" is significantly an issue of values. The world, or the "worldview" of our culture, is based on transitory values, while the kingdom of God is based on transcendent values. Our culture is focused on temporary things. The church of Jesus Christ is to be focused on permanent things. And the difference is profound.

When Moses had to choose between living in the midst of power and wealth in Pharaoh's household, "He chose to be mistreated along with the people of God rather than to enjoy the pleasures of sin for a short time" (Hebrews 11:25). That was a rather counterintuitive choice. Why did he make it? "He regarded disgrace for the sake of Christ as of greater value than the treasures of Egypt" (Hebrews 11:26). His treasure was the more abiding reward of eternity.

When Jesus fed the crowd of 5,000 men (not counting women and children), they all of a sudden became huge fans of his. They followed him around and even thought about drafting him to be their king. They boarded a group of boats "in search of Jesus" (John 6:24). They were looking for Jesus. They were passionate about finding him, but what was their motivation? When they found him, Jesus confronted them with the truth. "You are looking for me . . . because you ate the loaves and had your fill" (John 6:26). They were looking for a free meal. They were not pursuing Jesus so they could commit their lives to him and be faithful followers no matter what it might cost them. They wanted relief from their hunger.

So Jesus attempted to adjust their values. "Do not work for food that spoils, but for food that endures to eternal life" (John 6:27). They needed to lives their lives based on eternal, transcendent values. A life in pursuit of temporary things is no life at all.

In his first epistle, the apostle John exhorted the brethren in the province of Asia to not "love the world or anything in the world" (2:15). In fact, if anyone loves the world, if he places his affections on the world, "the love of the Father is not in him." He then described what he meant by "the world." It is "the cravings of sinful man, the lust of his eyes and the boasting of what he has and does" (2:16). The world is a culture whose values are fixed on temporary things. Adopting that value system is diametrically opposed to the culture of the kingdom of God. "The world and its desires pass away, but the man who does the will of God lives forever" (2:17).

The poverty of the saints in Smyrna forced them to keep their values clear and pure. In the end, it made them even more effective citizens of God's kingdom. While it may be more difficult to keep our values aligned with God's in a prosperous culture, if we want to be effective representatives of Jesus in our generation, we will dedicate ourselves to doing so.

The Challenge of Persecution

We have great compassion for Christians undergoing persecution. When we hear of the genocide launched against Christians in Sudan we pray and send money. But that persecution rarely touches us. For us in the West, persecution is someone being rude or greeting us with an unfriendly hand-gesture. So how is persecution relevant to us?

When Jesus described their kingdom inheritance to his disciples, he told them about houses and brothers and sisters and lands. So far so good! But then he added, "with persecutions" (Mark 10:30). The New Testament church seemed to consistently experience persecution wherever they went (cf. Acts 8:1; 11:19; 13:50). Paul had warned them they would enter the kingdom of God "through many tribulations" (Acts 14:22). Persecution was the regular experience of the apostle Paul (cf. 2 Corinthians 12:10; Galatians 5:11; 2 Timothy 3:11). In fact, he stated that false teachings tended to develop in order to avoid persecution (Galatians 6:12). Paul commended the church for their faith in the face of persecution (2 Thessalonians 1:4). He even went so far as to say that all who strive to live godly lives in the midst of the world "will suffer persecution" (2 Timothy 3:12).

So why don't we experience more persecution? Is it because we have so absorbed the values of the surrounding culture people don't even notice us? And when we are persecuted, is it for the right things?

On the other hand, some today believe that persecution always purifies the church, and may even be heard praying for persecution in the American church. An examination of severe persecution in the history of the church and in our own time shows that persecution does not so much purify the church as it graphically reveals what is already true about the church. To the extent that believers are faithful to Jesus, persecution will bring that to light and intensify it. If believers are "serving" Jesus for what they can get from him, persecution will expose their selfish agenda and intensify it. So in that sense, persecution purifies the church, but only those who are already deeply committed to him experience purification. Perhaps we should repent and intensify our commit to Christ now, and not wait for persecution to come. Then we'll be ready for anything.

The Challenge of Martyrdom

Under the Roman empire the persecuted church eventually had to develop a theology of martyrdom. Some Christians were doing whatever they had to do to avoid martyrdom, while others were turning themselves in and voluntarily seeking martyrdom. So the church fathers and mothers had to define the truth about martyrdom.

The only time I've ever heard a teaching on the theology of martyrdom was by an eastern European theologian prior to the fall of the communist regimes in that area. And yet, martyrdom is a daily issue for Christians in many nations of the world. The "Great Persecution" under the emperor Diocletian (AD 303) resulted in 500,000 martyrs, the most of any period of persecution in those days. However, there have been more Christians martyred in Sudan alone during the last decade. Martyrdom is a living issue.

The apostle Paul faced many dangers during his ministry, including the danger of death. In fact, in his heart he took upon himself "the sentence of death" and was fully prepared to give his life if necessary (2 Corinthians 1:9). In another place Paul described the fact that he was always being given over to death for the sake of Christ. As a result, "death is at work in us, but life is at work in you" (2 Corinthians 4:11, 12).

Hebrews chapter 11 lists the champions of faith, starting with Abel, Enoch and Noah, and including Abraham, Isaac, Jacob and Joseph. It speaks of Moses, Joshua and the judges. In some cases, "women received their dead raised to life again" (Hebrews 11:35). In other cases, champions of faith "were tortured, not accepting deliverance." They were mocked and scourged and imprisoned. They were martyred by stoning, sawing and the sword, "of whom the world was not worthy" (11:38). They were not victims; they were heroes.

The book of Revelation contains the clearest statements

regarding the meaning of martyrdom. At the fifth "seal" in chapter 6 we see the martyrs under the altar in heaven (verses 9–11) asking the Lord when the final judgment was going to come. The answer was, not "until the number of their fellow servants and brothers who were to be killed as they had been was completed." From God's perspective, there were no accidental martyrs. Each one who witnessed to their faith in Christ by giving their lives did so in the center of God's will. When the "two witnesses" successfully completed their assignment, they were overpowered and killed (Revelation 11:2–7). Prior to that moment, any attempt to kill them was completely foiled by God. They were essentially indestructible until the moment came when they were called upon to bear witness with their lives. At the end of the Revelation, we see the martyrs living and reigning with Christ from his throne in heaven (20:4). There is a heavenly reward for the martyrs, while remembering that, "If I . . . surrender my body to the flames, but have not love, I gain nothing" (1 Corinthians 13:3).

Martyrdom is an important theme of the letter to Smyrna. "The major single theme of this letter is that Christ will bring 'life' out of 'death.' Nothing they could suffer would fail to lead to God's vindication and their reward. In the book as a whole, as well as in the church of Smyrna, this was a promise especially for those who would pay with their lives."[96]

There is a valid biblical role for martyrdom in God's plan of redemption. When Satan appeared before God in the book of Job, he accused Job of serving God because God blessed him. In essence, he was accusing God. He was claiming that God's purpose for human beings, to have a people who would serve him because they loved him, was a failure. Even his most choice servant was in reality a mercenary. "But stretch out your hand and strike everything he has, and he will surely curse you to your face" (1:11). And so the test was on. Was Job serving God because God blessed him? Was it impossible to find a human being who served God because he loved him?

Every time a believer gives his life for the cause of Christ, he is demonstrating before principalities and powers that there is someone willing to serve God without being "blessed," and the accusation of hell is thwarted.

The Challenge of Fear

According to the letter to Smyrna, their biggest challenge was fear. Fear is not something we always have control over. Fear can be a bio-chemical response in the body and in the brain. We don't have to stop and think, "I'm going to be afraid now," in order to experience fear.

Yet fear is an enemy. The biggest danger of fear is that it tends to paralyze faith. Sometimes before we can effectively engage faith, we need to spend time overcoming fear.

After Jesus fed the 5,000 he sent his disciples ahead of him across the Sea of Galilee to Capernaum (John 6:16f). During the crossing a fierce storm came up suddenly, threatening to swamp the boat and drown the passengers. Any of us would have experienced panic in that situation. Jesus saw their predicament and came to them, walking on the water. "And they were terrified." Jesus, knowing their state of mind, simply said, "It is I; don't be afraid." The answer to their fear was a tight focus on Jesus. If they could allow their vision and their thoughts to be filled with him, coming to them in the midst of their terror, they would be empowered to overcome the enemy of fear.

In a similar situation, Jesus and the disciples were crossing the Sea of Galilee when a storm arose and threatened their lives again (Luke 8:22–25). In the midst of the storm, Jesus "fell asleep." He was not intimidated by an apparent threat to his life. His trust was so fully in his Father he was able to sleep through it all. Not so the disciples. They were convinced they were going to drown. After Jesus rebuked the wind he asked the men, "Where is your faith?" Their fear had paralyzed their faith and they were not able to see Jesus, sleeping in the boat, resting in the Father's will.

There have been times when I have been stricken with fear. During those times I've found it helpful to see Jesus in the boat with me, asleep, resting in the Father's loving arms.

If Jesus isn't afraid, maybe he knows something I don't know. If I can keep my focus on him, I too will be able to overcome fear and "only believe." And "this is the victory that has overcome the world, even our faith" (1 John 5:4).

The fear of death is one of the most basic human fears. At the very least, the fear of the unknown is involved. We've never died before so it is the great "undiscovered country." However, in Christ this fear too can be overcome. Jesus has fully shared in our humanity, including his very human experience of death. In the process, he destroyed the power of death, and has freed "those who all their lives were held in slavery by their fear of death" (Hebrews 2:14, 15). To the extent that we are controlled by the fear of death, we are limited in our ability to do God's will. There are some things we would simply be unwilling to do because of the threat to our lives. On the other hand, if we are liberated from the fear of death, there will be no stopping us. We will be prepared to face anything that might be in front of us without flinching. Conquering faithfulness in every situation will be the result.

The Story of New Covenant Community

On the outskirts of Kuala Lumpur, Malaysia, is a "squatter camp" made up of illegal immigrant families. This community called Sentul is tightly packed with substandard housing units occupied by the very poor who came looking for work. They are from Indonesia, India, Pakistan, Bangladesh, and beyond. They are Hindus, Muslims and Buddhists. Not able to find work many of the men have resorted to crime, drugs and alcohol. Many of the children are being raised by their mothers without access to basic human services.

Into this quagmire Elisha and Petrina Satvinder planted a Christian community. Elisha grew up in a Sikh Punjabi family and Petrina in a Buddhist Chinese family, both in Malaysia. They met as young Christian believers, married and attended Portland Bible College in the U.S. After graduation they returned home to plant the New Covenant Community.

If you were going to plant a new congregation in the beautiful city of Kuala Lumpur, where would you locate it? There are many upscale neighborhoods in the city. Although Malaysia is a Muslim country, there is a large Christian population in K.L. A church could have easily been planted in a friendly environment that would have guaranteed rapid "success." Instead, the Satvinders chose to start in a very needy part of town.

Part of the reason for their decision was their vision for the church. As Elisha said, "For too long the church has remained a community within its community . . . as a segregated entity. For us, to be involved in caring for the poor as a Christian congregation is not just a matter of choice but a mandate from the Bible." Elisha and Petrina viewed the local church as a redemptive representative of Jesus in the community, and that meant serving the least and the lost.

For them, "The church must present the gospel as good-news. Good news to those who hear it. Good news because the oppressed are being liberated. Good news because issues of injustice are being effectively addressed. Good news because God's standards of righteousness are being restored in the land." The gospel of Jesus Christ is not just relevant to personal faith and spirituality. It has clear and concrete implications for the lives of human beings. Elisha comments, "Sad to say the gospel therefore continues to be a strange message to many."

The needs they faced seemed overwhelming. Poverty and the injustices that cause poverty seemed insurmountable. And beyond that, there was the question of how to break the generational cycle of poverty? And where to begin? Their conclusion was to focus on the children of Sentul. Their mission: "breaking the cycle of poverty by educating the children."

Why children? Elisha and Petrina say it this way: "We focus on children because they are at their formative years, and regardless of their difficult situation, they are highly resilient, making our interventive efforts highly successful." The Satvinders sought to address social problems before they took root. It was also simply true that a great majority of the people in developing nations are children, and that means the majority of the poor are children. It seemed natural to focus their ministry efforts on the poor children of Sentul.

The Satvinders also chose to focus on the education of children. Elisha said, "Education is one of the most powerful tools in helping the poor to come out of the rut of poverty, changing the face and characteristics of any community." While a whole range of services are offered by N.C.C., the core of their vision is education.

In the process, the Satvinders have had a thorough education about poverty and the effects of poverty on children. They have discovered that poor children have higher rates of illness and disabilities. They inevitably have lower IQ scores due to slower cognitive development, lack of family support, malnutrition and disease. They come to school less ready to learn and therefore do less well in school than more privileged children. They are twice as likely as non-poor children to repeat a grade and are less likely to go on to college. As adults, they are more likely to be poor, thus continuing the cycle of poverty to another generation.

As a result, Elisha and Petrina and their team have focused on preschool education. Their goal is to not just address cognitive problems but also issues such as the formation of healthy habits, the prevention of malnutrition, the cultivation of healthy social relationships, and the formation of godly attitudes. Their method is compassionate and simple, but also a great deal of work. They began with house-to-house visitation. They brought parcels of food with them as well as items of clothing. They also offered community medical services. Eventually, they made known their long-term plan of establishing an education center for the children. In the process they established personal relationships with the people in the community leading to an attitude of trust.

When I visited New Covenant Community I walked the by-ways of Sentul with Elisha. Everywhere we went the people called out, "Pastor, Pastor." All of them—Muslims, Hindus, Buddhist and Christians—consider Elisha their pastor. To them, he is not only the pastor of New Covenant Community, he is the pastor of the community of Sentul. I went with Pastor Satvinder as he was invited into neighbors' homes to counsel young people getting caught up in drug use or children who simply needed a father figure. Over time he had become a prominent, unofficial leader of the community.

The Satvinders are passionate about offering quality educational opportunities to the poor. They report, "For the first time in the history of Sentul, the poor are not discriminated against or kept from a high quality of education. The children especially are given an equal opportunity to receive an excellent education." And the results are becoming obvious. The community of Sentul is benefiting. In addition, the Christian believers in New Covenant Community are being benefited.

Not all of the believers at N.C.C. are from poor neighborhoods. In fact, many are young professionals who share the vision of the local church as redemptive salt in the community. They don't view their ministry in Sentul as a "department" of the church, but rather as the biblical mandate for the congregation in their city. Their involvement in Sentul has provided all of them with an education. There are now a variety of ethnic groups in the congregation. The Sunday School has been transformed. There are both Christian and non-Christian children regularly involved. The children from Christian homes have begun to catch a vision for the world outside of their four walls. Elisha reports, "They have been awakened to the issues of justice and righteousness. They have become strong prayer warriors and active advocates for the issues that impact their friends living in poverty."

The children from the Sentul community are now hearing the gospel and receiving teaching from the Word of God on a regular basis, and their lives are changing. In fact, as Elisha says, "They have become carriers of the principles of God's Word into their families and their community." These children are themselves being transformed into change-agents. The community as a whole is beginning to see a clearer vision of God, of the Bible, and of Christian faith.

As a result, a great door of opportunity has opened up to N.C.C. Everyone in the community is more open to dialogue about the gospel. The Satvinders have been included in various government projects aimed at serving "at risk" children. Even foreign embassies have begun to take note of the exceptional work of N.C.C. and are providing financial support.

The long-term vision of the Satvinders is to see a full-service community center established by N.C.C. in Sentul. This would include a youth center and expanded educational facilities. They have a vision to see a full range of educational opportunities for the poor, as well as other services that will enable them to permanently break the cycle of poverty. They are also working to increase the awareness of the other Christian congregations in Kuala Lumpur and the surrounding areas. They also serve as trusted advocates for the poor in the nation of Malaysia.

Elisha and Petrina Satvinder state their mission this way: "Community transformation by raising a whole new generation that knows the purpose of God and lives by His principles." In every way they seek to penetrate the community with "redemptive acts of kindness." They've earned the trust of the whole community. Now they are in the process of serving the community as salt and light and seeing it transformed by the power of the gospel.

CHAPTER FIVE:

THE PROMISE OF BEING A CHURCH OF CONVICTION IN A CITY OF COMPROMISE

THE LETTER TO PERGAMUM

I magine that the apostle Paul has just come to you and said, "We're going to send you with a team to establish a new congregation."

You reply, "Wonderful! Where is it going to be?"

"I'm sending you to one of the most beautiful cities in the world," Paul might respond.

"That sounds great. Is it a large city?"

"Yes," Paul says, "and very prosperous."

"Where is it? Which city? What's its name," you might say, growing excited.

"Well, it's the city where Satan lives!"

The Story of Pergamum

The old city of Pergamum was founded in the region of Mysia in the fifth century BC. It was built about 40 miles north of Smyrna and 15 miles inland on the plain of the Caicus River. It was not ideally suited for commerce but had the potential of becoming a great military fortress. The city took the side of the Greeks in their wars with the Persians.

After Alexander's defeat of the Persians Pergamum was

controlled by his successors who began to build it into a great city. The son of Alexander, Heracles, ruled the city for about twenty years. Lysimachus, king of Thrace, assumed control of the city in 301 BC and began to build the acropolis at the top of a huge granite hill rising over 1,000 feet above the plain. Other structures were built at the base of the hill.

The commander and treasurer of Lysimachus, Philaeterus, became the new ruler of Pergamum in 281 BC. Philaeterus expanded the territory of the city that eventually became the kingdom of Pergamum. His successor was his brother, Eumenes I (263–241 BC). Eumenes I defeated Antiochus I in battle and became independent of the Seleucid kings from Antioch in Syria. His son Attalus I (241–197 BC) defeated the Gauls in battle and built an altar to Zeus to commemorate his victory. He also adopted the goddess Athena as the patron of the city. The royal "Attalid" dynasty was named after him. Attalus I assumed the title "King and Savior" and began a cult of the divine ruler in his dynasty. He was the first Attalid king to seek an alliance with Rome. Pergamum became the major power in Asia Minor as a vassal of Rome.

He was succeeded by Eumenes II (197–159 BC) who continued the policy of his father against the Seleucid rulers, eventually prompting the direct intervention of the Romans. This culminated in the defeat of Antiochus III at the battle of Magnesia in 190 BC. Eumenes II further developed the acropolis by adding a circular wall around it. He also built a library that eventually housed 200,000 volumes, the second largest in the world, second only to the library in Alexandria, Egypt. The story is told that king Eumenes sought to buy papyrus from the Egyptian ruler Ptolemy V, but because Ptolemy wanted to block the planned library, he refused to sell the papyrus. As a result, the Pergamenes treated sheep and goatskins to produce "parchment" (Greek *pergamene*). This new material made possible the development of the "codex" or what we call books. A large theater was also built containing 80 rows seating a crowd of 10,000. It was the steepest theater in the ancient world. During this time Pergamum became one of the intellectual centers of the world. Eumenes II was so proud he called himself "Savior and God."

Eumenes II was succeeded by Attalus II (159–138 BC) and Attalus III (138–133 BC). The last act of Attalus III was to bequeath his kingdom to Rome. As a result, the Roman province of Asia was established in 133 BC with Pergamum as its capital. That meant that the Senatorial representative, the Proconsul, resided in Pergamum.

The city of Pergamum joined in the rebellion of Mithridates IV in 88 BC, killing all the Romans in the city. When they were defeated by the general Pompey, the city went into a period of decline until the reign of Caesar Augustus. At the end of the first century AD the city had a population of around 120,000 and was the most famous city in Asia.

From early times Pergamum was the religious center of Asia, a major center of pagan religion in the ancient world. Athena was the patron goddess of the city. In Greek mythology Pallas Athena was the daughter of Zeus, a warrior goddess, ferocious and undefeatable. Athena was committed to defending the state and the native land against outside invaders. She was also viewed as the goddess of urban civilization. She was thought to be a virgin goddess, the incarnation of wisdom, reason and purity. Her temple was built at the top of the acropolis in Pergamum.

The great altar to Zeus "Soter" ("savior") was located eighty feet below the Athena temple. It contained three levels, the base measuring 110 feet long, 105 wide and 40 feet high, and was covered with images of snakes. In Greek mythology Zeus was the supreme ruler of Mount Olympus and the gods and goddesses who resided there. In ancient times Zeus was a weather god and was symbolized by a lightning bolt. He was committed to upholding law, justice and morals, and was the spiritual leader of both the gods and of human beings. Zeus was honored by Pergamum as the savior of the city, specifically in the war with the Gauls.

These two deities represented the later Hellenistic development of the city. Of even greater importance were the gods Asklepios and Dionysus. The famous sanctuary and temple to Asklepios was built at the end of a road called "the Sacred Way," one mile from the base of the acropolis. The early sanctuary was built around 350 BC. Asklepios "Soter" was the ancient god of medicine and was represented by the serpent. The god Asklepios was used to symbolize the city of Pergamum. The temple complex eventually spread out over a space occupying five acres. It included a tunnel about 100 yards long with streams of water running along the sides. This tunnel ended in a large, circular treatment room 300 feet in diameter. There were several small chambers located on the perimeter of the room with fountains in the center.

Sick people would come from all over the world to be treated. This began with the "rite of incubation," when they would be given a drug and allowed to sleep in one of the small chambers. While they slept they hoped to be visited by the god and either miraculously cured or given the proper treatment. When they awoke they met with a priest physician who prescribed a treatment for them. They were then treated in a series of pools and baths. After their treatment patients recorded their name and cure on white stone pillars. The medical center in Pergamum became the second most important in the ancient world (the first being Epidaurus in Greece). Galen, the most famous physician in the ancient world, was born and trained in Pergamum.

Dionysus was the patron god of the Attalid dynasty. Dionysus (known as Bacchus in Rome) was the bull-god and a slightly Hellenized version of a more ancient Phrygian fertility god. Dionysus was said to be the son of Zeus and a human princess, Semele, making Dionysus the only Greek god with a human parent. The myth surrounding the birth of Dionysus proposed that Semele was killed by Zeus when she was forced to look upon his glory. Zeus then rescued the unborn Dionysus and protected him until he could be safely born, making him the "twice-born." Dionysus was then torn apart by the Titans, only to be brought back to life. Thus the fertility theme of "life from death," especially as seen in the pruning of grape vines in preparation for the new growing season, was represented by the story of Dionysus. The god was also said to have brought his mother back from the dead; worshiping him guaranteed life after death.

Dionysus was the god of fertility and wine, and was said to have turned water into wine. He supposedly invented wine and spread the art of tending grapes. Those who worshiped Dionysus believed that becoming intoxicated from wine resulted in a direct encounter with the god. The effect of the wine meant that the god actually entered into the worshiper, making him greater than himself and enabling him to do works he could otherwise not do. This brought on a divine ecstasy and even a brutal, unthinking rage.

The festival of Dionysus occurred in mid-February as the first leaves began to reappear on the vine. His followers would worship him in the woods. Here they might go into mad states where they would rip apart and eat raw any animal they came upon. In Greek literature there were many complaints about the detrimental influence of Dionysus' orgies on public morality. In the second century BC the "Bacchanals" in Rome took such enormous proportions the Senate had to declare a prohibition on these rites. However, they continued to be very popular in Pergamum. A temple to Dionysus was built in Pergamum where these festivals occurred.

The city also contained a temple to Demeter, a fertility earth-goddess. Demeter was the goddess of the earth and of agriculture. She was credited with making the crops grow each year. The myth of Demeter and her daughter Persephone was used to symbolize the life-death-life cycle of the seasons. According to the myth, Persephone was abducted by Hades to be his wife. While Demeter searched for her daughter no crops would grow. Eventually a deal was made with Hades allowing Persephone to stay with him in Hades for four months each year, resulting in winter. The worship of Demeter centered around the Eleusinian Mysteries and became a popular mystery religion that included the worship of Dionysus. Part of these mysteries involved bathing in the blood of a bull.

Pergamum also contained temples to Hera, Heracles, Hermes, and others. Hera was considered the wife of Zeus and the goddess of marriage and birth. Heracles was a famous hero in Greek mythology, a human being who was the son of Zeus and a mortal woman. Heracles was famous for his strength and his exploits of valor. Hermes was another god born of Zeus. He was the god of shepherds, merchants, oratory and literature. He was known for his cunning and shrewdness, and functioned as the messenger of the gods. Visiting Pergamum would have been a veritable tour of ancient paganism.

After the rebellion of Mithridates, Pergamum worked hard at getting back in the good graces of Rome. In 63 BC the city dedicated a statue of Julius Caesar. Pergamum was the first city to declare the Roman emperor to be divine, building a temple to Caesar Augustus and the glory of Rome in 29 BC. From that point on Pergamum had primacy in the imperial cult. Two other imperial temples were built in later years.

Great pressure was put on the church to compromise their convictions concerning Christ and perform their civic duty to the emperor. Because they refused to do so, the Christian faith was classified by Rome as a "superstition," not a legitimate religion. Christians were also accused of "hatred of the human race" because they refused to show loyalty to the Roman emperor and the Roman people. They were hated for their exclusivism and intolerance of the traditional gods. "Christians were persecuted in Pergamum due primarily to the prevailing imperial cult rather than popular cults like Asklepios. Emperor worship was linked to civic loyalty and patriotism. Thus refusal to participate was not only godless but subversive."[96]

The Roman proconsul exercised the "right of the sword" (Latin *ius gladii*) from Pergamum. This was the symbol of his total sovereignty over every area of life in the province, including the right to execute the enemies of Rome. The Roman proconsul had the power of life and death—or at least he thought he did.

The Letter to Pergamum

To the angel of the church in Pergamum write: These are the words of him who has the sharp, double-edged sword (Revelation 2:12).

In addressing the church in Pergamum Jesus draws from the image in 1:16. There John saw that "out of his mouth came a sharp, double-edged sword." In the address to Pergamum Jesus is seen more simply as "the one having the sharp, double-edged sword." Just as the sword is the symbol of authority, the sword coming out of the mouth of Christ is a symbol of his authoritative word, even his word of judgment. This is another reminder of the Old Testament theme of God ruling the nations with "the rod of his mouth" (see Isaiah 11:4). We also see the Messiah declaring, "He made my mouth like a sharpened sword" (Isaiah 49:2).

The apostle Paul refers to "the sword of the Spirit, which is the word of God" (Ephesians 6:17). The writer to the Hebrews teaches that the word of God is "sharper than any double-edged sword" (4:12). Later in the book of Revelation we see a sharp sword coming out of the mouth of Christ "with which to strike down the nations" (19:15). Roman authority and Roman law, the Roman sword, was considered to be supreme in Pergamum. However, Jesus is not convinced of that fact. He insists that he alone has the sharp, double-edged. Jesus alone has the final authoritative word. This fact should guide the believers in their worship of God and their refusal to worship Caesar. The ultimate power belonged to God, not to Rome. This was a source of strength and courage to the persecuted believers.

I know where you live—where Satan has his throne (Revelation 2:13).

Instead of saying, "I know your deeds," Jesus begins his letter to Pergamum by confirming that he is personally aware of their habitation. He knows that their dwelling is located in the city where Satan has his headquarters. "Throne" always refers to the center of power and authority. The word "throne" is used more in the book of Revelation than in the rest of the New Testament combined. It usually refers to the place of God's authority, God's headquarters. Only in this verse is there a reference to the throne of Satan. (There are also references to the throne of the "beast" in Revelation 13:2; 16:10.)

Was John referring literally to the earthly headquarters of Satan? If so, what were the signs that Satan was ruling from Pergamum? It's clear that John thought of the Roman empire, and especially emperor worship, as Satanic. "It was emperor worship that most directly occasioned the persecutions under Domitian . . . and Pergamum was the center of the imperial cult for all the province of Asia."[98] In Pergamum the loyalty of the Christians was tested by their willingness to participate in the imperial cult. Indeed, the whole history of the church at Pergamum was determined by the fact that it was located closest to the seat of Roman power—to the throne of Satan. The presence of so much paganism and the immorality that went with it also evidences the intense presence of the influence of Satan in Pergamum.[99] The believers in Pergamum were facing an unusually intense spiritual battle in the process of becoming overcomers in that city.

Yet you remain true to my name. You did not renounce your faith in me, even in the days of Antipas, my faithful witness, who was put to death in your city—where Satan lives (Revelation 2:13).

Even in the face of fierce persecution, the Christians in Pergamum had refused to budge in their loyalty to Christ. They were holding fast to his name, refusing to deny Christ. The "name" of Jesus represented his person, his character, and his authority. These believers were putting all their confidence in the name of Jesus. "To remain true to Jesus' name means to live up to the responsibility of this new identity, to resist the lure of this pagan world."[100]

Specifically, they had not been disloyal to him, they had not denied their faith in Christ, in a time of persecution that had included the martyrdom of Antipas. Not renouncing faith in Christ implies perseverance in the face of persecution.

The "days of Antipas" refers to a break-out of imperial persecution that had already happened some time in the past. No doubt Antipas, and possibly others with him, were brought before the Roman authorities and tried for their crimes against the state. They had remained true to their confession of faith in Christ, and as a result, Antipas had been called upon to give his life. Jesus had told his disciples, "Whoever acknowledges me before men, I will also acknowledge him before my Father in heaven. But whoever disowns me before men, I will disown him before my Father in heaven" (Matthew 10:32; see also Luke 12:8; 1 John 2:23; 4:2, 15).

Jesus referred to Antipas as "my faithful witness." This is the way Jesus described himself in 1:5. Just as Jesus had faithfully borne witness to the Father by giving his life, so Antipas had proven to be a faithful witness of Christ.[101] Antipas had proven his faithfulness in the city "where Satan lives." This is the same verb used when Jesus told the Pergamenes, "I know where you live." Pergamum was the place of Satan's throne, his habitation on earth. Antipas had proven that it was possible to be loyal to Christ and to his Kingdom, even in the face of such opposition. "Antipas is an example of others tempted to deny the faith in the face of persecution. Those who, like Antipas, overcome this temptation will be given the titles faithful and witness."[102]

> *Nevertheless, I have a few things against you. You have people there who hold to the teaching of Balaam, who taught Balak to entice the Israelites to sin by eating food sacrificed to idols and by committing sexual immorality. Likewise you also have those who hold to the teaching of the Nicolaitans (Revelation 2:14, 15).*

The believers in Pergamum had been triumphant in the face of the most intense imperial persecution seen anywhere in the province of Asia. But they were being conquered internally. They have overcome in most areas, but Jesus has a few things against them. Specifically, they have some among them who have grabbed a hold of false teaching. The majority of the members had a firm grip on their loyalty to Christ. A few had a similar grip on "the teaching of Balaam." The

Old Testament figure of Balaam (see Numbers 22-24) was a false teacher and a false prophet. Balak, the king of Moab, had paid him to get God to curse Israel. When the Lord refused to cooperate, Balaam "taught Balak to entice the Israelites." The word used for "entice" is the Greek *skandalon*, from which we get the English word "scandal." It literally means, "a trap or snare; the name of the part of the trap to which the bait is attached; a stumbling block." Balaam taught Balak how to trap the Israelites in a way that would result in the breaking of their covenant with the Lord.

Balak learned how to trap Israel "to sin by eating food sacrificed to idols and by committing sexual immorality." He got certain Moabite women to seduce the men of Israel. "The men began to indulge in sexual immorality with Moabite women, who invited them to the sacrifices to their gods" (Numbers 25:1, 2). Involvement in pagan ritual always involved these two things. One led to the other. "The people ate and bowed down before these gods" (Numbers 25:2). The gods of the Moabites were ancient fertility gods and goddesses, similar to those worshiped at Pergamum. False worship of these gods included sexual immorality. It's possible that in some cases the lure of sexual immorality led to specific idolatry (spiritual immorality). "So Israel joined in worshiping the Baal of Peor" (Numbers 25:3). Idolatry, spiritual adultery, led to a covenant with Baal, which automatically included breaking covenant with the Lord. "And the Lord's anger burned against them" (Numbers 25:3). As a result, a plague broke out among the Israelites, stopped only by the zeal of Phinehas. Balaam was eventually killed "with the sword" (Numbers 31:8, 16; Joshua 13:22).

The infamy of Balaam continued into the New Testament and the early church. Peter referred to false teachers in the church who "left the strait way and wandered off to follow the way of Balaam" (2 Peter 2:15). The epistle of Jude refers to certain "dreamers" who "pollute their own bodies" and who "reject authority." Their error is that "they have rushed for profit into Balaam's error" (Jude 11). These were libertine teachers who abused the doctrine of grace, flaunted their liberty, and led whoever was willing to follow into a life of idolatry and immorality. And they did it "for profit," for the personal gain they were seeking.

The followers of Balaam's error were also known as Nicolaitans. The early church father Irenaeus said that the Nicolaitans were early followers of the false teacher Cerinthus who had begun teaching "gnostic" ideas in Ephesus. Their early attempts to "Hellenize" Christian doctrine resulted in increasingly erroneous doctrines. Theirs was "an attempt to effect a reasonable compromise with the established usages of Greco-Roman society. It affected most of all the cultured and well-to-do classes in the church."[103] These false teachers were members of the Greek intelligentsia and upper class who sought a more culturally acceptable expression of the Christian faith.

Among other things, they taught that because the spirit of "enlightened" believers was perfect, what they did with their body was irrelevant. Therefore, outward compromise, even if it involved idolatry and resultant immorality, did not compromise their loyalty to Christ. In this way they were able to justify participation in pagan worship and in the imperial cult. Obviously this insidious doctrine would eventually undermine the believers' faithfulness as Christian witnesses.

Teaching a justification for idolatry and immorality was contrary to the decision of the Council of Jerusalem (Acts 15:20). The early apostles had agreed that Gentile converts would not have to be circumcised and follow Jewish tradition. However, they were required to "abstain from food polluted by idols, [and] from sexual immorality." Even during the time of Paul some believers disagreed with these stipulations, using his doctrine of grace as an excuse for license (see Romans 6:1, 2). Paul specifically addressed the issue of "food sacrificed to idols" (1 Corinthians 8), and pointed out that the exercise of their freedom might result in a stumbling block. Later Paul said that "the sacrifices of pagans are offered to demons" and exhorted the believers to not "be participants with demons" (1 Corinthians 10:20, 21). Peter was aware that some were distorting the teaching of Paul, resulting in lawlessness (2 Peter 3:14–17).

The Nicolaitans were a libertine party in the church who

sought a way to avoid persecution through philosophical sleight of hand. "Nicolaitanism was an antinomian movement whose antecedents can be traced in the misrepresentation of Pauline liberty, and whose incidence may be connected with the special pressures of emperor worship and pagan society."[104] The Nicolaitans minimized the effects of fulfilling the civic duty to the emperor. After all, just a pinch of incense at the altar, just a few meaningless words—how bad could it be? Nevertheless the Nicolaitans slipped deeper and deeper into false doctrine and immorality. Later Clement of Alexandria testified concerning the Nicolaitans that "they abandoned themselves to pleasure like goats."

It's interesting that both the name "Balaam" and the name "Nicolaus" have the same meaning—"to conquer the people." The teaching of Balaam and the teaching of the Nicolaitans was designed to bring spiritual defeat to the people of God, a people who were destined to be overcomers, not overcome.

Although idolatry and immorality were in view, the basic issue was "the teaching" of the Nicolaitans. There was a series of doctrines, gnostic doctrines, that not only undermined the faith and the faithfulness of the believers in Pergamum, but which also led to drastic changes in the way they lived. In fact, it completely reversed their sense of a faithful life before Christ. Concepts always have consequences.

Repent therefore! Otherwise, I will soon come to you and will fight against them with the sword of my mouth (Revelation 2:16).

The situation in Pergamum was the reverse of that in Ephesus. While Ephesus was commended for hating the deeds of the Nicolaitans, Pergamum was corrected for not forbidding the teaching of the Nicolaitans in their midst, resulting in compromise with the values of the surrounding culture. Ephesus was corrected for having lost their first love while the quality of relationships in Pergamum was healthy and strong. Nevertheless, the solution for both churches was the same. They were both called to repent.

For Pergamum, repentance, changing their heart and mind, meant exposing and disallowing the teaching of the Nicolaitans, as well as the lifestyle choices resulting from it. "The Church was already compromised by undue tolerance of the Nicolaitans; she had not purged herself of complicity with them as the Church at Ephesus had done."[105]

The whole church is exhorted to repent. And if they don't, Jesus said, "I am coming to you quickly." Jesus will come to them without delay in order to bring discipline. When he does, he will not judge the entire church but only the false teachers. Jesus is giving the church a short amount of time to bring correction and remove the evil influence of the Nicolaitans from their midst. That's the best solution. If he comes to judge them, he will literally "make war against them with the sword of his mouth." In essence Jesus was saying, "Unless you exercise your discipline as a church, and exclude these people, I will come and fight against them. Unless you repent and deal in discipline with these men, I must fight against them with the sword of My mouth, and that sword will not be found in the method of argument, or a new enunciation of truth. It will be a judgment swift and sure upon the evil workers, in order that the church itself may be free and may be pure."[106]

The idea of warfare (fighting, conflict) is found mostly in the book of Revelation in the New Testament. In 12:7 Michael is seen making war against the dragon and his angels. We also see human rulers making war against the Lamb, but the Lamb overcomes them (17:14). In 19:11 Jesus is called Faithful and True, the one who judges and makes war.

Specifically, Jesus is seen making war with the sword coming out of his mouth, referring to the fuller expression in 1:16. It is his word of authority, his word of judgment, that will deal with the teaching of the Nicolaitans once and for all. The Roman governor had "the right of the sword" in Pergamum. In reality it was Christ, the Ruler of all the rulers of the earth, who had the final word, the final right of the sword. It was the word of Christ that alone would prevail in the end. Just as Balaam had been judged with the sword, so would the Nicolaitans in Pergamum.

> *He who has an ear, let him hear what the Spirit says to the churches. To him who overcomes, I will give some of the hidden manna. I will also give him a white stone with a new name written on it, known only to him who receives it* (Revelation 2:17).

The faithful followers of Christ in Pergamum are invited to listen to what the Holy Spirit is saying to the churches. The Spirit is saying something specific to Pergamum, but it has implications important to the other churches as well, and to us. "Hearing" implies obeying. To overcome, the believers will have to listen intentionally and obey diligently.

The promise of overcoming is given to the church. What is it they must conquer? What would being overcomers in Pergamum look like? They have already proven to be overcomers in the face of persecution. However, they are being overcome in the face of false doctrine. They are confident enough in their faith in and commitment to Christ to resist pressure from Rome to conform to paganism. They clearly see the enemy in the face of Roman authorities and pagan priests. But they do not clearly discern the danger coming from false teachers in their own congregation. And if they don't see the danger, they will end up compromising with paganism and imperial worship anyway.

The overcomers in Pergamum must be clearer in their appreciation for doctrinal correctness. They must have more confidence in the authority of God's Word in every area of life. They live in a city and a culture governed entirely by compromise. For the Romans, it was silly and narrow-minded to refuse to burn incense to the emperor. You didn't have to really believe he was a god; you just had to perform your civic duty. The faithful in Pergamum had refused to compromise with Rome, but they were allowing the same spirit of compromise into the church in the form of gnostic teaching. Not having overcome that spirit of compromise in Pergamum, they had absorbed it. To consistently overcome, they must stop compromising with false doctrine in their midst.

Transformers

In the case of Pergamum Jesus offers two gifts to the overcomers. The first gift is "some of the hidden manna." This is obviously a reference to the supernatural food God provided Israel in the wilderness (Exodus 16:31–35; Numbers 11:7–9). As a memorial of God's provision the Israelites were instructed to put a pot of manna beside the Ark in the Holy of Holies (Exodus 16:32; Hebrews 9:4). Later Rabbinic tradition taught that when the temple was destroyed, Jeremiah hid the manna in a cave on Mount Sinai, and that when the Messiah would come, that manna would be restored to Messiah's temple. Another Rabbinic tradition taught that God would restore his provision of manna at the coming of the Messiah.[107]

The truth is God did send manna from heaven when the Messiah came. In fact, the Messiah himself was God's heavenly food. Jesus identified himself as that manna (John 6:31–34, 49–51). Jesus is the "hidden manna" of tradition, hidden no more but revealed in the person of the Messiah. Jesus will give himself, and the nourishment and fulfillment only he can provide, to the overcomers.

Pagan worship centered around banquets that included food offered to idols. The Nicolaitans sought to justify participation in those banquets. Jesus promised those who overcome the teaching that allowed such compromise a better food, an eternal food, eternal life in him.

The second gift promised by Jesus to the overcomers was "a white stone with a new name written on it, known only to him who receives it." This is literally a reference to a smooth stone or pebble. It can also refer to a "vote," since such stones were used to cast votes in ancient times. This "stone" was sometimes a small cube of ivory with words or symbols engraved on one or more faces, functioning as a sort of ticket. There were in fact several usages of such stones in Pergamum.[108] The most relevant to this letter seems to be the means of admission to pagan banquets. People gained entrance to such events by invitation only. They had to be a secret member of the cult in order to participate in its immoral rites, their names communicated in a secret code. Jesus was inviting the overcomers to his banquet, one that would include eternal pleasures in the presence of the Lord.

The use of white stones in the Asklepios cult also has interesting parallels. When patients were treated in the sanctuary, they hoped to be visited by the god who would initiate the sick one into the cult. As a token of that initiation the patient was given a white stone with a secret name on it known only to the god and the new cult member. That code name gave the worshiper influence with Asklepios. In addition, when this treatment led to a cure, the recovered patient engraved his or her name on a white stone pillar on the temple precinct testifying to his cure. On the other hand, those who had a relationship with Jesus testified faithfully to the peace and wholeness only he could bring.

When people in Pergamum came to Christ, they received a new name, a new identity in Christ. That new identity included a new character, a new life, new potential, and a new destiny. In fact, it was common for believers in the early church to take a new name when they were baptized in water, a name that included the name of God. The benefits of participation in pagan religion were no substitute for the reality, the eternal reality, of abundant life in Christ. Those who put their trust in God and his Word would overcome and be richly rewarded.

The Key of the Authority of God's Word

The root of the weakness in the church at Pergamum was a certain teaching, namely, the teaching of Balaam, known in their time as the teaching of the Nicolaitans. The believers in the church obviously had a very strong personal sense of loyalty to Jesus and to one another. Relationships were more important to them than anything else, including doctrine. The solution was not necessarily to become trained theologians. The solution was to put more confidence in the Word of the Lord. An important key to being an overcoming church is to fully appreciate the authority of God's Word.

Only the Word of God had the power to create something out of nothing. In the beginning there was nothing but emptiness, until "God said." The Word of God brought light out of

Transformers

darkness (Genesis 1:3). It brought order to the "waters" of creation (1:6, 9) and to the lights in the heavens (1:14). God's Word brought life into creation (1:20, 24), and ultimately brought forth humankind (1:26). We believe that the universe "was formed at God's command" (Hebrews 11:3). The heavens came into existence by the Word of God (2 Peter 3:5). There is nothing more powerful than God's Word.

God has given his authority to his Word. God has exalted his Word and his name above all other things (Psalm 138:2). No word spoken by the Lord will fail (Joshua 23:14). Jesus stated that "the Scripture cannot be broken" (John 10:35). The Word of God is the power of God (1 Corinthians 1:18). But for that power to be effective, we must receive it for what it really is, "the word of God" (1 Thessalonians 2:13). To embrace the authority of God's Word is to release its power in our lives.

God's Word is true truth. It may be difficult to say some things are "truth," but the sum of God's Word is in fact the very truth (Psalm 119:160). Concerning God's Word Jesus testified, "Your word is truth" (John 17:17). In fact, "all Scripture" is inspired by God—it is the product of God's breath—and is profitable to completely equip the servant of God (2 Timothy 3:16, 17). Nothing in Scripture is without a purpose (James 4:5). Every Word of the Lord is a result of the personal activity of the Holy Spirit (2 Peter 1:20, 21). If there is any "truth" I can build my life on, it is the truth of God's Word.

God's Word is a proven source of protection to those who obey it. Because the Word of the Lord is tried, it is a shield to those who trust in him (Psalm 18:30; Proverbs 30:5). Treasuring God's Word is the key to a life of holiness (Psalm 119:11). Mary's fruitfulness came from her willingness for the will of God to be done in her life, "according to your word" (Luke 1:38). Jesus proved his faithfulness to the Father by obeying his word (John 17:6). Sin has the effect of shutting up Scripture, keeping us from seeing the truth of it (Galatians 3:22). On the other hand, anyone who chooses to obey God's Word will see it for what it is, the very teaching of God (John 7:17).

The seed of the Kingdom of God is the Word of God. In the parable of the sower and the seed Jesus explained that the "seed" was really God's Word (Luke 8:11). That seed contained the "DNA" of God's Kingdom, but it had to be embraced from the heart in order to bear fruit. When the early believers spoke God's Word with boldness, the influence of the Kingdom was extended (Acts 4:31). Church growth was essentially the spreading of God's Word (Acts 6:7; 19:20). It is the seed of God's Word that brings about the new birth (1 Peter 1:23). Therefore, we should seek any and every door of opportunity to preach God's Word (Philippians 1:14; Colossians 1:25; 4:3), even if it involves imprisonment (2 Timothy 2:9).

The Word of God is the key to winning the battle against hell. The "sword of the Spirit," the only offensive weapon in the battle against the kingdom of Satan, is the Word of God (Ephesians 6:17). The Word of God is more powerful than any natural sword (Hebrews 4:12). The authority of God's Word in our hearts and our mouths is the only authority that will be effective in the areas where we need to conquer.

We have a responsibility to handle the Word of God accurately. As God's workmen we will labor diligently and conscientiously at accurately hearing and proclaiming God's Word (2 Timothy 2:15). Even our lifestyle choices must reflect an accurate understanding and appropriation of the truth of the Word (Titus 2:5). We are to be like the Bereans who examined the Scriptures daily to see if the preaching of Paul was accurate (Acts 17:11). Before accepting any teaching, it is important to ask, "What does the Scripture say?" (Romans 4:3). We are to give ourselves to the reading of Scripture and to its teaching (1 Timothy 4:13). Those who distort the Scriptures do so to their own harm (2 Peter 3:16). It's not just who we believe in but what we believe that is essential to our faithfulness to Christ.

God's Word is a sufficient revelation of God and must not be tampered with. Moses commanded the people to not add to or take away from God's Word (Deuteronomy 4:2). The Word of God is flawless (2 Samuel 22:31). God's Word is settled in heaven (Psalm 119:89). Everything else may fail, but God's Word will stand for ever (Isaiah 40:8). The book of Revelation ends with a warning to those who might be tempted to add anything to God's Word (22:18, 19). The Nicolaitan teachers were both adding to and taking away from the Word of God, and the faithful believers in the church were not stopping them. The cost to both would be enormous, and eternal.

The Message of the Letter to Pergamum

No matter how ungodly the city we may live in, chances are it does not compare to the level of paganism found in Pergamum. The daily pressures on the believers in that city must have been overwhelming. In most areas their response was exemplary. Yet some of the challenges they faced proved their potential undoing. We may face some of those same challenges and therefore can learn wisdom from the experience of those ancient believers.

The Challenge of Elitism

The prestige of the city of Pergamum gave rise to a prominent upper class in the city. Pergamum was an intellectual center as well as the political and religious capital of the province. Conversions to the Christian faith were not limited to the poor and uneducated. Prominent citizens began to see the value of following the teachings of Christ.

But coming to faith in Christ does not necessarily guarantee humility and spiritual maturity. Wealthy, intellectual leaders of the community who joined the church would notice that many of its members were poor and uneducated, at least by comparison. It's a short step from that observation to the conclusion that the traditional expression of faith seemed a bit too simple. Surely more sophisticated believers needed a more sophisticated communication of the teachings of Jesus.

It's simply true that the Nicolaitans were upper class men and women who began to proclaim themselves as the "enlightened ones" and that true enlightenment, true salvation, could come only by being initiated by one of them. Frankly, the Nicolaitans thought they were better than the average Christian. Their elitism set them up for a fall for, as Jesus taught, greatness comes by being "the servant of all" (Mark 9:35).

Concerning the Nicolaitans Jack Hayford commented:

It is the belief that these are the truly important ones, and the rest are peons. It is the notion that the Church is an institution and the people who head the institution and hold the power are really the ones who are important to God. They are the ones who have the real contact. They are the "movers and shakers."[109]

They sought to dominate the local church and the people in it. Eventually, they sought to dominate the Christian faith itself and fell into greater and greater error.

I also see the danger of intellectual arrogance at work. It's one thing to be a diligent student of God Word and be passionate about communicating accurately and helpfully. It's another thing to attach one's ego to the process; to teach doctrine in a way that is significantly motivated by a desire to sound intelligent. It's not about IQ. It's not even about education. It's about taking God's Word and God's thoughts seriously, submitting our lives to them, and encouraging others to do the same.

The Challenge of Cheap Grace

Bible commentators and church historians have all noted the connection between the early Gnostics and the earlier misuse of Paul's doctrine of grace. Paul sought to give all the glory to God for our salvation and the new life in Christ. He was very clear about it: "By the grace of God I am what I am" (1 Corinthians 15:10). But some among the Gentile converts concluded that if the Christian life is all due to God's grace, it shouldn't make any difference what lifestyle choices we make. From the beginning Paul clearly exposed that view as an erroneous misunderstanding and abuse of his teaching. "What shall we say, then? Shall we go on sinning so that grace may increase? By no means!" (Romans 6:1, 2). The treasures of God's grace were opened to us, not so we could live a guilt-free life of sin, but "in order that the righteous requirements of the law might be fully met in us" (Romans 8:4).

The doctrine of salvation by grace is a beautiful distinctive of Christianity. But what would motivate some believers to misapply it? The story of Balaam would lead us to the conclusion that the temptation of sensuality, the lure of great parties, is simply too much for some people. It's one thing to repent, it's another to truly leave the past and burn our bridges behind us. It's one thing to be delivered out of Egypt by the grace and power of God. It's another thing to have Egypt delivered out of us. The lusts of the flesh and the lusts of the eyes continue to find an answering attraction in our souls. Grace is for more than salvation. Grace is needed for the ongoing process of the formation of the image if Christ in our souls.

G. Campbell Morgan saw this as the primary error of the Nicolaitans:

> You have people, who in order that they may eat of the things sacrificed to idols, and in order that they may indulge in the sin of fornication, are holding a doctrine which excuses the actual wrong. Thus, there was heresy in that church at Pergamum, their heresy which has come to be known in later days as the Antinomian heresy, the heresy which says, "You are so safe in the name and in the faith, that it matters little about your conduct. You may mix with the sinners at Pergamum, and follow their habits, and yet share the benefits of the covenant."[110]

There is a need in some parts of the Body of Christ to rediscover the doctrine of grace. Some are still trying to achieve their salvation and are finding that it cannot be done. Others, having a new appreciation for God's grace and our dependence on it, are celebrating that fact by flaunting their new-found liberty. Instead of growing in grace they are moving away from grace into license. Instead of reflecting the image of Christ in a dark world, they are reflecting the darkened values of the surrounding culture, and will eventually move back into bondage. The letter to the church at Pergamum can perhaps restore a true knowledge and appreciation of God's grace and begin to appropriate the power of the grace that cost Christ so much to live as his faithful followers in the world today.

The Challenge of Syncretism

The teaching of the Nicolaitans was a classic example of syncretism. Syncretism involves a thorough blending together of disparate ideas, making one new idea that is neither one nor the other. The Nicolaitans so thoroughly mixed ideas from Greek philosophy with Christian doctrine that the result was not Christianity at all.

It's not uncommon for missionaries to face the challenge of syncretism in other cultures. Some people find it easy to accept Jesus and the validity of his teaching but end up simply adding that new commitment to other religious ideas. To accept that Jesus is truly God and that he is the only true source of salvation seems very narrow and closed-minded. That would have certainly been the attitude of those in a Greco-Roman culture. Why couldn't Christ-followers just be a little more culturally flexible, burn a little incense before a statute of the emperor, and go their merry way? Why did they have to be so stubborn?

Obviously some of the believers decided that flexibility, open-mindedness and cultural relevance were more important than faithfulness to the gospel of Christ, especially when that faithfulness would result in persecution and death. The result was eventually another gospel and another Christ.

We in the West have the temptation to add ideas and values from the surrounding culture to our Christian faith, especially when those ideas will make us more "successful." Although it's possible to be narrower than Jesus, it's also important to question whether or not our teaching, and the motivations for that teaching, is faithful to the teaching of Christ and the apostles. Or is it an accommodation to the surrounding culture? At what point do we begin to preach "another gospel"?

Because our beliefs directly affect our behavior, syncretism can be seen in the real lives of people. Adding foreign ideas to Christian faith can serve as a justification to almost any kind of behavior. Eventually we will just blend into the world. No one will know we are Christ-followers, and they will simply leave us alone. If you were brought into court

Transformers

and tried as a Christian, would there be enough evidence to convict you?

The Challenge of Compromise

Ultimately, the challenge in Pergamum was compromising the distinctive message of Christ. Those in the surrounding culture could not understand why the Christians refused to participate in the normal functions of the culture. What could be so wrong with an occasional Bacchanal? Didn't they realize that failure to demonstrate civic loyalty to the emperor was tantamount to treason?

Peter had warned of this challenge. Christian believers who had been converted out of a pagan context would stand out in a crowd. Their family and friends would question whether or not these new Christians hadn't gotten out of balance somewhere. Maybe they were being influenced by some unscrupulous leader. Maybe they now thought they were better than everyone else, just because they refused to live like everyone else. "They think it strange that you do not plunge with them into the same flood of dissipation, and they heap abuse on you" (1 Peter 4:4). Some would not be able to resist that kind of pressure.

The Nicolaitans only made it worse. Now there were members in the church who were applying the same kind of pressure, and coming up with very intelligent reasons for compromising with pagan values and lifestyle choices. The more faithful saints, who were no doubt poorer and less educated, may have been insecure in the face of this bombardment. Who were they to say that the Nicolaitan teachers didn't have a point?

It was certainly easier to compromise than to stand by one's convictions, as it is for us today. In fact, pressures coming from within and without can serve as an opportunity to reexamine our convictions, adjust them where necessary, and then continue to live by them. Living by compromise is a dead-end street leading into quicksand. Living by conviction is the only way we can consistently stay the course set before by Christ. It is the only way we will arrive at our intended destination and see the will of God done in and through our lives.

The Story of Father's House

Every major city has a variety of communities and ethnic groups, representing a variety of mission challenges. This is certainly true of Portland, Oregon. One of those communities is the downtown district. Several congregations have been planted in the downtown area—with an average life-span of two years. With that reality in mind, Steve and Deborah Trujillo were sent to plant a mission-specific GenX congregation in downtown Portland known as "Father's House."

They were well aware of the challenges facing them and their young church plant team. As is true in many cities, downtown Portland is the center of both local and county governments, as well as most social agencies. It is a regional center for the arts, containing art galleries, performing arts centers, museums, artist repertory theaters, and many clubs. It is an educational center. Portland State University, the largest university in Oregon, is located in the heart of the city. The oldest churches in Portland are also downtown. However, most of them have become centers of new thought.

Their mission was simple: "Touching downtown through serving." Their ministry philosophy was also straightforward: "Small things done with great love will change the world!" Their strategy is to promote community transformation through acts of service. They began by identifying congregations and service agencies that were already there and finding meaningful ways to serve them. They painted the home of the pastor of a youth church called "The Bridge." They packed lunches for homeless youth on behalf of the Love Drop-In Center. They did yard work for the Portland Fellowship, a ministry to gays. They also helped start the downtown House of Prayer, a prayer center in the heart of Portland. In this way they not only served ministries, they also began to network with them for even more effective ministry.

The downtown district is the cultural and business center of Portland. The poorest of the poor also "live" downtown. Steve described the heart of Portland as being like a third world country, "where the poor and rich live side by side. The downtown has the largest concentration of home-less people. In fact, Portland has the largest homeless youth and young adult population per capita in America. But just blocks from the missions and heroin alleys are new, beautiful and very expensive lofts and condos that attract the upwardly mobile. It is an eclectic mix of the artistic, profes-sional, socially active post-modern generation next to those who have the least." The need seemed overwhelming, but the Lord had given Father's House a plan.

Both Steve and Deborah Trujillo grew up in excellent Christian homes. Steve's father is a pastor from Cuba, who moved his family to Portland as refugees in the 1960's. Growing up in a sheltered Christian environment did not seem to prepare Steve and Deborah for the challenges of downtown Portland. However, God had given them a heart of compassion for the outcasts in society. They are also motivated to see miracles, to see the glory of the Lord revealed in impossible circumstances. They needed that faith when they accepted the challenge of church planting in the heart of the city.

When studying the history of Portland Steve discovered deep roots of fatherlessness. When the California gold rush occurred, a large number of men left Portland. The largest pre- Roe v. Wade abortion center in American was located in downtown Portland. This deep fatherlessness and abandon-ment seemed to be feeding into the high number of homeless youth and even the prominence of the gay community. So Father's House began to focus on serving homeless youth. Service evangelism with this displaced, mobile population had to be out-of-the-box to be effective. They wanted to find a way to communicate to street teens that they valued them, so, as Pastor Steve reported, "Armed with back packs and boxes full of colored hair spray bottles, make up, nail polish, glitter and temporary tattoos, they went to the places where street kids hung out and offered them free make-overs." These kids try to find personal worth by looking unique and different. Make-over teams would come up to kids and say, "Hey, how would you like to try polka-dotted hair today, or camouflaged nails?" Most of them jumped at the opportu-nity. What they didn't know is that the Father's House team was praying for them as they served them. The tattoos they applied were Japanese or Chinese characters for "loved," or "beautiful" or "free." As the team served them and prayed for them the young people often opened up about their lives and become very honest. As they experienced the presence of the Lord some wept and hung on to the team members. Others were frightened by it and ran away.

Steve proved to be particularly adept at hair coloring. After awhile the teens began to relax and trust him, and would even introduce themselves with their given name rather than their street name. They felt safe. Although they seldom found their way to worship services some considered themselves a part of the Father's House community. Steve said, "They associated Father's House as their church because it was the church that came to them, that prayed with them on the streets, that gave them socks, toothpaste, band-aides, or anything else they needed. It was the church that did not judge them, but came to them in love."

From the beginning, Father's House clearly understood their redemptive role in the city. According to Steve, "Father's House believes they are the caretakers of the downtown community. They believe that whatever happens there, it is their job to bring it under the authority of Jesus Christ. As a result, they involve themselves in public intercession on behalf of the community." In fact, prayer evangelism is another large part of the mission of Father's House. They spend a significant amount of time "prayer walking" the streets of downtown Portland.

Steve told me a story that illustrates their commitment to prayer evangelism. Every year the city of Portland throws a huge New Year's Eve party at Pioneer Courthouse Square, "Portland's living room." One year there were many problems at the party, including vandalism, assaults, and overall chaos, resulting in several arrests. This was an unusual experience for Portland, so in preparation for the following year's party, the Father's House congregation felt the need to provide "prayer support." Before the actual event members of the congregation gathered on the square to pray. They decided to walk around the square seven times and then pray blessing on the downtown area. At the end of that time, Steve lead them in prayer and declared, "In Jesus name, I speak peace to this square. All chaos is bound, all darkness is bound, let there be peace on New Year's Eve." Later during the party city officials noted there was not even one disturbance, not one arrest made. The local media reported how calm and peaceful the crowd was. Although no one knew of the church's "prayer support," they believe they were able to serve the city as salt and light in that situation. "Culture was impacted, even though the church received no credit for it," Steve said. "It is small acts done with love and obedience to Christ that can bring change. In the end God comes through and you are just glad you where there to see him do His wonders."

At one point Steve felt the need to engage the infrastructure of the city more intentionally. One of the distinctives of Portland is the prominence of neighborhood associations. Through the Office of Neighborhood Standards and Involvement the associations work with the city in deciding what takes place in their neighborhood. Becoming involved in the downtown association seemed to be an important step. At his first meeting Steve noticed that the business community, gay community, law enforcement and social activists were represented, but there were no pastors. So he committed himself to participation in the association and was immediately given responsibility. As a member of the Safety Committee he advises the association on the needs of homeless youth as well as crime problems in the surrounding neighborhoods. As a result, it's not uncommon for members of the downtown association to refer people with needs to Father's House.

Father's House continues to focus on serving the city in small ways. They state their commitment this way: "Transformation and cultural change will not come about if we only focus on building our community and having good services for us. We must get out there where we can impact people's lives with the love of God." Their neighborhood strategies include:

- Surprising employees of nearby businesses with a basket of candy and a card saying, "We appreciate how you serve the community with your business."

- Giving away bottles of chilled drinking water on hot days around the park blocks and the water front park.

- Escorting people on rainy days from parking garages to shopping areas such as Pioneer Place, using large golf umbrellas.

- Setting up tables where they can apply nail polish, have a conversation and make a friend.

Recently the Father's House congregation has moved onto the P.S.U. campus. Pastor Steve told them, "Going to PSU is a logical part of our journey. As we continue to build proper foundations and return the church to its original purpose, the Lord is leading us towards the campus." The Campus Ministry building had been dedicated to the Lord for many years but was largely unused. When that building became available to Father's House they jumped at the opportunity. They now have a specific campus strategy:

- Open the doors for other ministries to have access to the campus.

- Engage in spiritual warfare to bind the strongholds that blind the hearts of men to the gospel.

- Penetrate the campus and become a presence on campus through servant evangelism.

- Target strategic prayer on campus.

In many ways Portland State University, at the heart of the city, represents the city and the spiritual issues of the city. From that center the Father's House congregation is determined to see the grace, love and presence of God released in the city.

CHAPTER SIX:

THE PROMISE OF BEING A CHURCH OF AUTHORITY IN A CITY OF ACCOMMODATION

THE LETTER TO THYATIRA

C hurch planters sent out by the apostolic team in Ephesus faced many dangers. There were dangers from the Roman authorities who considered Christian believers to be stubborn and narrow-minded. There were obstacles put in their path from competing religious communities. There was also the simple need to somehow survive, to earn a living, to support a family in difficult times. That was the challenge facing the team that was sent to Thyatira.

The Story of Thyatira

The city of Thyatira was located on the road from Pergamum to Sardis, 40 miles southeast from Pergamum. It was built on a flat plain surrounded by gently rolling hills. As a simple Lydian village, it may have originally been built around one of the ancient shrines to Artemis. Everything changed when the Greek successors of Alexander took over the area. These former generals fought each other for control of Alexander's conquered territory. In 301 BC the general Lysimachus occupied Pergamum and the general Seleucus I occupied Sardis. As a buffer against Pergamum, Seleucus I built up Thyatira as a military outpost. Thyatira stayed in the hands of the Seleucid dynasty until 262 BC when it was captured by Pergamum. In fact, the outpost of Thyatira experienced continual warfare for the first 100 years of its existence, until its governance finally passed on to Rome in 190 BC.

The city continued to develop as a military outpost under the Romans. Mercenary soldiers from many nations ended up serving there. When their tour of duty was over, some settled down permanently in the city. The *Pax Romana* of Caesar Augustus ended the continual conflict and established peace and prosperity in the area that benefited the small city of Thyatira.

Prior to Augustus's Roman Peace certain craftsmen were attracted to the city to support the work of the army. With the advent of peace and security Thyatira began to develop as an important center of manufacturing and commerce. Soon tradesmen from all the surrounding nations, east and west, found their way to Thyatira. Oriental traders included Egyptians, Persians and Jews. The craftsmen organized themselves into trade guilds that eventually dominated the life of the city. In fact, the prominence of the guilds was the chief characteristic of the city of Thyatira.

Most Greek cities were governed by various "tribes." However, in Thyatira, the guilds were so prominent that they governed the city instead of tribes. One of the chief guilds was the vendors of dyed fabrics (Greek *bapheis*). In the book of Acts, Lydia, "a dealer in purple cloth" from Thyatira was quite probably a member of this guild (Acts 16:14). The other chief guild was made up of the bronzesmiths (Greek *chalkeis*). These talented smiths had invented a special alloy of bronze and zinc called *chalkolibanos*, known only in Thyatira. It was famous primarily for its military applications. Other guilds included bakers, potters, wool merchants, shoemakers, leather workers, linen workers, and even slave traders.

The city was divided into squares, and each square was under the control of a particular guild. The guilds were the center of the social life as well as commerce in the city. Membership in the guilds was mandatory for all tradesmen. Such membership was passed on from father to son. It was impossible to do business in the city without being a member of one of the guilds.

Each trade guild had a patron god or goddess and a temple honoring that god. Guild meetings always occurred in the temple and involved feasts to the deity. Their feasts were essentially religious occasions involving the usual pagan rites, including sexual immorality. To refuse to participate in the guild feasts meant the loss of both goodwill and business in the city.

The patron god of the city was Apollo "Tyrimnos," the sun god and the son of Zeus. Apollo was pictured riding on horseback with a double-sided battle-ax as the embodiment of the spirit of the garrison. In Greek mythology Apollo was the twin brother of Artemis and the father of Asklepios. He was not only a war god but also a god of seers and prophecy. His chief temple was located at Delphi where he functioned as the patron of the prophetic oracle in the temple. He was also pictured as a musician and a patron of the healing arts.

In Thyatira there was also a temple built for Artemis, the twin of Apollo. The two temples were connected, symbolized by the "marriage" of the representative priests and priestesses.

A shrine to an oracle named Sambathe could also be found in the city. "Sibylline Oracles" occupied an important place in Roman society. They were acknowledged as prophetesses and exercised dominant influence in the city that housed their shrines. They claimed they could reveal the thoughts and will of the gods, the secrets of men's hearts, and what the future holds. Political rulers and military generals would go to the shrine seeking counsel and direction. The chief Sibyls were all thought to prophesy under the inspiration of Apollo. We see a picture of the prophetic tradition in Virgil's *Aeneid* (6.35ff). There he tells the story of an oracle demanding the sacrifice of seven bulls and seven ewes, and then entering into an ecstatic state. Virgil reported, "As she spoke neither her face nor hue went untransformed, nor did her hair stay neatly bound: her breast heaved, her wild heart grew large with passion. She seemed taller to their eyes, sounding now no longer like a mortal, since she had felt the god's power breathing near." Later Christians began to believe that the Sibyls spoke in part by the Holy Spirit, and accepted some of their oracles as inspired. Some even patterned their prophetic ministry after the Sibylline Oracles. Sambathe was an Oriental oracle, either Chaldean or Persian. She came to completely dominate the city of Thyatira.

The church in Thyatira was a small congregation attempting to survive in a context that seemed to preclude their survival. In the second century they continued to be small. A fourth century church father, Epiphanius of Salamis, reported that the heretical prophetic movement known as Montanism was particularly strong in Thyatira (*Adversus Haereses*). Evidently the weakness exposed by Jesus in the letter to Thyatira continued to blossom until, according to Epiphanius, there was no church left by the end of the second century.

The Letter to Thyatira

Although we have the least amount of information concerning the city of Thyatira of any of the seven cities, the letter to Thyatira is the longest of the seven. It could be because the concerns Jesus had for that congregation were to be clearly communicated to all the churches.

> *To the angel of the church in Thyatira write: These are the words of the Son of God, whose eyes are like blazing fire and whose feet are like burnished bronze* (Revelation 2:18).

Jesus addresses the church at Thyatira in an unusual way. Instead of referring to a symbol from the vision in chapter 1 he identifies himself as "the Son of God." This title for Jesus is found only here in the book of Revelation. I'm sure this was a meaningful designation for Jesus in a city whose patron was "the son of Zeus." Jesus was not just the son of a god, he was the Son of *the* God. "In the 'Son of God' the church had her true champion, irresistibly arrayed in armour flashing like the refined metal from the furnaces of the city. He was the true patron of their work."[111]

There is also a connection between the letter of Thyatira

Transformers

and Psalm 2. The Psalm begins with "the decree of the Lord," i.e. "You are my Son" (2:7). In the letter of Thyatira John is reflecting the highest possible view of Christ as the unique Son of God. As the Son, Jesus had full authority in the Father's household. Only a Son has a permanent place in the Father's house (John 8:35). As a result, only the Son has the authority to liberate the other members of the house (John 8:36).

"Whose eyes are like blazing fire" comes directly from 1:14. "Whose feet are like burnished bronze" comes from 1:15. Both images are found in Daniel's vision (10:6). The fiery eyes paint a picture of penetrating insight and judgment. Jesus can see through clever manipulations and false motivations. His view is pure and perfect and the standard by which all will be judged.

The glowing feet also draw attention to the fire of Jesus, a fire that has the power to sweep everything away before it. The word for "burnished bronze" is found only in Revelation 1:15 and 2:18, and refers to the bronze alloy invented at Thyatira. The tone of the entire letter to Thyatira is one of judgment. The address and the way it pictures Christ prepares for that theme.

> *I know your deeds, your love and faith, your service and perseverance, and that you are now doing more than you did at first* (Revelation 2:19).

Jesus begins with a generous commendation of the believers in Thyatira. In fact, this is the most complete commendation found in any of the seven churches. He begins by commending their "love." The most important characteristic of the church in Thyatira is their *agape* love. They are motivated at every point by their love for God, their love for one another, and their love for people. This is obviously in contrast to the Ephesians who had lost their "first love." In fact, Thyatira is the only church commended for their love and is their chief distinctive. They were deeply devoted to their Lord and Master.

The church was also commended for its "faith." Their faith refers to their trust in God even in the face of rejection and joblessness. Those in Pergamum had been commended for not renouncing their faith (2:13). The qualities of the faith and the perseverance of the saints are seen again in 13:10 and 14:12. Love and faith constitute the inner strength of the saints.

Paul also delighted in the faith and love of the saints (Ephesians 1:15; 3:17; 6:23; Colossians 1:4; 1 Thessalonians 3:6; 5:8; 1 Timothy 1:5, 14). He taught that faith without love is nothing (1 Corinthians 13:2). The eternal virtues are faith, hope and love, the greatest being love (1 Corinthians 13:13).

The believers in Thyatira are also commended for their "service." Their service is their active life of care toward others, the outworking of their love. It is voluntary service on the behalf of others. Their "perseverance" was also highlighted. Ephesus had also been commended for their perseverance (2:2, 3), as will the church at Philadelphia (3:10). Service and perseverance were the outward results of the believers' love and faith. Paul had encouraged Timothy to pursue faith, love and perseverance (1 Timothy 6:11; 2 Timothy 3:10). He had also encouraged the believers in Corinth to add works to their faith and love (2 Corinthians 8:7). In another place Paul spoke of faith working through love (Galatians 5:6). He commended the saints for their "work of faith" and "labor of love" (1 Thessalonians 1:3). "Underlying all the works there was a principle toward God and man which the Master had declared to be the sum and substance of the law of God. It was a church character. There was no breach, no division, no schism, but a wonderful manifestation of love."[112]

What's more, "You are now doing more than you did at first." Their "first works" were love, faith, service and perseverance. And these had continued to grow through the years, becoming stronger, bearing more fruit. Because all their works were founded upon love, their life never waned. This had also been true of the believers at Thessalonica (2 Thessalonians 1:3). This was again in contrast to the church at Ephesus who was exhorted to repent and "do the first works" (2:5).

Nevertheless, I have this against you: You tolerate that woman Jezebel, who calls herself a prophetess. By her teaching she misleads my servants into sexual immorality and the eating of food sacrificed to idols (Revelation 2:20).

With the sound of this great praise ringing in their ears, the Christians in Thyatira now hear Jesus say, "But, I have something against you." The fiery eyes of Jesus see a fault, a fatal flaw in this church of loving service. "You tolerate that woman Jezebel." The church at Pergamum had some among them who held to the teaching of the Nicolaitans. The Thyatirans have actively tolerated a similar error. The word for "tolerate" is the Greek *aphiemi*, which means "to let go, leave, pardon, forgive; allow, permit, tolerate." This loving church had chosen to forgive a false prophetess in the church whose teaching was deceiving the servants of Jesus. To not tolerate her, to even reject her and her followers, would have seemed harsh to such a loving church. However, even though Ephesus had been rebuked for losing their first love, they had been commended for not tolerating wicked men, false apostles and the practices of the Nicolaitans (2:2, 6).

Whereas the letter to Pergamum had used the example of Balaam, this letter refers to the Old Testament figure of Jezebel. King Ahab had married the daughter of the king of Sidon, who led him into Baal worship, just as Balaam had done (1 Kings 16:31f). When Jezebel had gained sufficient control, she destroyed the prophets of the Lord (1 Kings 18:4, 13) and installed the prophets of Baal and of Ashera, a Canaanite fertility god and goddess (1 Kings 18:19). The resulting pagan religion included involvement in feasts to the gods, and sexual immorality.

"The woman Jezebel" was someone in the church who called herself a "prophetess." She was evidently a leader in the church, not just someone on the fringe who was being tolerated. Her "prophetic" ministry no doubt indicates an emphasis on charismatic ministry in the church at Thyatira. The other leaders were not taking their responsibility to judge her ministry in the light of Scripture. "There can be very little doubt that the woman claimed to be an inspired woman, who had received some new revelation. Some vision or enlightenment had been granted to her, denied to the apostles, and she was promulgating this new teaching."[113]

She was exercising a prophet ministry in the church that was having a very destructive effect. She was being allowed to "teach" in the congregation, and by her teaching, to "deceive" God's people. The word translated "misleads" means "to seduce a person into sin by leading that one into error." Elsewhere in Revelation it is used of Satan (12:9; 20:3, 8, 10), the false prophet (12:14; 19:20) and the harlot Babylon (18:23). This is the only place in Revelation where Christians are being deceived. The ones being deceived are "my servants," or literally "my slaves." The bond-slaves of Jesus are being led astray by a false prophetess and her ecstatic "teachings," and no one is doing anything to stop her. In the place of a weak, tolerant Ahab, there was a weak, tolerant church in Thyatira.

The effect of this prophetic ministry in the church was to justify "sexual immorality and the eating of food sacrificed to idols." This is the same false teaching as that found in Pergamum, only given in the reverse order (2:14). Evidently we are seeing another example of the Nicolaitan movement, only this time led not by a gnostic teacher but by a false prophetess. In addition, while the motivation to compromise in Pergamum was political and religious, in Thyatira it was primarily economic. Participation in the guild feasts was a necessary component of the economic life of the city. "Jezebel probably 'taught' that there was nothing wrong with a Christian taking part in the guild feasts and celebrations, for it was merely civil. Since idols were nothing, Christians would not destroy their faith by participating."[114]

Sambathe, the Sibylline Oracle in Thyatira, was dominating the city spiritually. Because of their tolerance, the church had absorbed the spirit of the Oracle and was now being dominated by "Jezebel."

> *I have given her time to repent of her immorality, but she is unwilling. So I will cast her on a bed of suffering* (Revelation 2:21, 22).

For some time Jesus had been giving the false prophetess time to repent. It could be that at a certain time in the past someone in authority, perhaps even John himself, had exposed the error of "Jezebel" and called her to turn from it. She was not only to turn from her false spirituality and her false teaching, but the immoral consequences (and perhaps motivations) for her prophetic "ministry." Her deception had implications both for people's covenant relationship with the Lord and for their lifestyle choices, especially as it pertained to their participation in the local trade guilds.[115]

However, Jezebel had been consistently unwilling to repent. She refused to acknowledge either the error of her ministry or the many errors it led to. As a result, Jesus is now coming to her with judgment. He is going to "cast her on a bed of suffering." The word translated "bed of suffering" is the Greek *kline*, which can refer either to the couch used in banquets, a sick bed, or even a funeral bier. It's perhaps intended to communicate the irony that the intent of Jezebel's ministry was to justify participation on the "banquet couch" of the guild feasts, but its actual result will be a "sick bed," and even a "funeral bier." The temporary pleasures and benefits of membership in the guilds and the accompanying participation in their pagan feasts will only lead to suffering and death.

> . . . and I will make those who commit adultery with her suffer intensely, unless they repent of her ways. I will strike her children dead (Revelation 2:22, 23).

Evidently there were three groups of people in the church at Thyatira: (1) Those who accepted both the content and the implications of the ministry of Jezebel but were not fully engaged in it; (2) those who were actively living out and propagating her deception; and (3) the rest who did not accept her ministry personally but who nevertheless refused to censor her.

The first group is classified as "those who commit adultery with her." Their acceptance of the message of Jezebel constitutes an ongoing spiritual adultery. They are growing in their unfaithfulness to the Lord. Their hearts are turning from a simple loyalty to Jesus to a pagan pursuit of self-gratification. These supporters are being given a specific opportunity to repent of the works—the corrupt consequences—of the ministry of Jezebel. If, like Jezebel, they refuse to repent, they will be cast into intense suffering, or literally, "great tribulation."[116] They will experience tribulation at the hands of Jesus, an attempt to discipline them, to get their attention, to convince them to repent. This action will not constitute the judgment of God but will instead be the discipline of a Father who loves them and seeks to restore them (see Proverbs 3:11, 12; Hebrews 12:5, 6). Restoration for this group is still possible, if they will truly repent.

The second group is designated as "her children." They are more than advocates or even followers. They are active partners with Jezebel. As "children" they reflect her DNA in every way. They have fully accommodated the false teaching and the adulterous works of Jezebel. They have moved beyond the possibility of discipline leading to restoration. Like their spiritual "mother," they have been given an opportunity to repent and have refused. Like Jezebel the only thing that awaits them is judgment. "Strike dead" is a Hebraic phrase that literally means "kill them in death," two different words for death being used together for emphasis. It is similar to the phrase "you will surely die" in Genesis 2:17. "Dying you will die."[117] "Jezebel and her children [are] facing a strict judgment of sickness and death, while those who have not yet been totally converted face 'great suffering' only if they too refuse to repent."[118] In the same way, the Jezebel of the Old Testament was judged by the Lord according to the word of Elijah (2 Kings 9:33–37) and all her children with her (2 Kings 10:6, 7).

> Then all the churches will know that I am he who searches hearts and minds, and I will repay each of you according to your deeds (Revelation 2:23).

The problem in Thyatira was so serious and the resultant judgment so severe it was necessary for all the churches to be aware of it. All churches must be very clear about the fact that although God is love and Jesus is full of grace, God is also the righteous Judge and Jesus is the all-knowing Prosecutor.

Jesus communicates himself in an "I Am" statement. In the past he had revealed himself as "I am the bread of life" (John 6:35), and "I am the light of the world" (John 8:12), "I am the good shepherd" (John 10:11), and "I am the resurrection and the life" (John 11:25). Here Jesus reveals himself as "I am he who searches hearts and minds." He is the one who is examining carefully the souls of men. Paul used this word to refer to "searching the heart" (Romans 8:27) and the Spirit searching "the deep things of God" (1 Corinthians 2:10). In this case, Jesus is searching the hearts and minds of people. The word translated "hearts" is borrowed from the Old Testament and literally means "kidneys" and is used for the will and emotions. The second word is used for human thought. The two together refer to the entire inner person. Jesus is aware of every thought, every emotion, every motivation. Therefore when he judges, he does so with perfect knowledge and complete justice.

Jesus then promises a gift to those being examined and judged. "I will give each of you according to your deeds." This is the Roman legal principle known as the Law of Retribution (Latin *lex talionis*), "which means that each person receives judgment on the basis of what each has done."[119] We see this principle occurring again in the book of Revelation when Babylon is judged and given "back to her as she has given" (18:6). On the final day of judgment, those whose names are not written in the book of life are judged "according to what they had done" (20:12, 13). The first "works" of the church at Thyatira were recorded in verse 19: love, faith, service and perseverance. The works of Jezebel and her followers were immorality and adultery. The works of both would be examined and judged.

In the Old Testament the Lord revealed himself in a similar way: "I the Lord search the heart and examine the mind, to reward a man according to his conduct, according to what his deeds deserve" (Jeremiah 17:10). Our deeds have consequences for eternity.

The idea of the judgment of God can be uncomfortable.

"Judgment" simply means "separation" and paints a picture of the separation of sin from humanity, and ultimately from all creation. Our God is a moral God ruling over a moral universe. As such, he cannot allow sin to just continue unchecked. At some point a line must be drawn and sin told, "This far and no farther." Even under grace a point can be reached at which God's moral judgment against sin is necessary. That's the point the church at Thyatira had reached.

> *Now I say to the rest of you in Thyatira, to you who do not hold to her teaching and have not learned Satan's so-called deep secrets (I will not impose any other burden on you): Only hold on to what you have until I come* (Revelation 2:24, 25).

Jesus now addresses the third group in the church. "The rest" of the members of the church who do not hold to the teaching of Jezebel and her children are now corrected. Although they do not believe the teaching nor practice the deeds of this false prophetic movement in the church, they have nevertheless allowed for it. They have refused to respond with the necessary church discipline that would have spared the congregation so much suffering. G. Campbell Morgan observed,

> The church's wrong was that this woman had been permitted. Some of the children of God had been seduced, and yet no protest had been raised. It was a false charity, permitting the teaching of the woman, somewhere and somehow under the patronage of the church itself. The whole church was not contaminated with the doctrine. But in false charity the woman Jezebel had been suffered.[120]

The rest of the church is commanded to "hold on to what you have." While rejecting the false ministry of the Jezebel party, they are to make a clear decision to reestablish the importance of what they have received. "What you have" is no doubt a reference to the apostolic traditions and teachings handed down to them, truths that were being undermined and even displaced by a false prophetic movement. To "hold on" to it refers to a specific choice to strengthen their grip and their commitment to the authority of those apostolic teachings in their lives. They are to persevere in those truths as a way of life. "[It] refers to the body of accepted Christian doctrine in contradistinction from the heretical teachings they must oppose. In short, the true believers in Thyatira are commanded by the Lord to maintain a firm grip on the truths of the faith against the false teachings of Jezebel."[121] "What they have" may also refer to the apostolic instructions they had already received to reject the ministry of Jezebel and remove its influence from the church.

While observing this word of correction we get more information about the teaching of Jezebel. The rest of the church is commended for not knowing "Satan's so-called deep secrets," literally "'the depths of Satan,' as they say." Most commentators agree that Jesus is referring sarcastically to Jezebel's claims to know "deep secrets" or even "the deep things of God."[122] In fact, Paul used this same word to speak of "the depth of the riches of the wisdom and knowledge of God" (Romans 11:33), and to "the deep things of God" (1 Corinthians 2:10). This reference to a special, secret knowledge confirms that we are seeing another expression of the Nicolaitan heresy. As such, Jezebel and her children would have been claiming to be special enlightened ones, in this case enlightened prophets, who had the power to initiate their followers into secret mysteries. Gaining knowledge of these "deep things" would empower them to participate in the local guild feasts without being hurt by them. However, the perspective of Jesus was that this "deep knowledge" was Satanic in origin. Again G. Campbell Morgan:

> This new revelation by inspiration, the end of which was to show how in the heathen systems were deep philosophies, and the result of which was to seduce the servants of God into complicity with the outward corruptions of heathendom, Christ characterizes as the "deep things of Satan." Here was an attempt made to fathom deep and underlying and unrevealed mysteries of life, and to make application of them under the name and sanction of the church, and the issue of the whole business was corruption.[123]

As a gnostic, Jezebel "denied the sinfulness of sin, affirming that within the things that seem to be evil are things of good. It was a practical denial of evil, in that it advocated union between the deep things, or mysteries of the outside world, and the mysteries which are the revelations of the Christian church."[124] The Nicolaitans denied the reality of sin, looking instead for salvation by enlightenment. This both removed the need for repentance and justified any lawless lifestyle. This is the very error John was exposing when he wrote, "If we claim to be without sin, we deceive ourselves and the truth is not in us" (1 John 1:8), and "If we claim we have not sinned, we make him out to be a liar and his word has no place in our lives" (1 John 1:10).

While allowing this false knowledge to spread in the church, the rest of the congregation had not allowed themselves to be initiated into these deep mysteries. So Jesus tells them, "I will not impose any other burden on you." This seems to be a parenthetic remark in the context of the "depths" offered by the Nicolaitan party. The rest of the congregation had been under considerable pressure to submit to the prophetic ministry that would initiate them into the secret knowledge. Their very salvation may depend on their ability to attain a certain level of enlightenment. But Jesus comes to them and promises, "I will not cast a burden on you."[125] Jesus is not going to pressure them with any such demands. Nor is he going to bring them into judgment, if they respond by getting a fresh grip on the apostolic instructions that had been given them.

> To him who overcomes and does my will to the end, I will
> give authority over the nations—"He will rule them
> with an iron scepter; he will dash them to pieces like pot-
> tery"—just as I have received authority from my Father
> (Revelation 2:26, 27).

Jesus now gives a promise to the overcomers in the church. Once again we must ask what it is they must overcome and what being an overcomer in the city of Thyatira would look like? Thyatira is a city of mercenaries, both military and commercial. The city exists for pragmatic reasons only, either to serve as a military buffer to more important cities, or to promote trade. We would think of it as a "blue collar" city. Living successfully in Thyatira would require doing whatever was necessary to function in that economy, to make a living.

The church in Thyatira was a loving, serving church. The people were faithful and growing in their service of their community. But the spirit of accommodation in the city was also in the church. I'm sure they were convinced that exercising authority and disciplining the heretical party would have been harsh and unloving. As followers of Christ they were there to love and serve, not judge and discipline, even if they were under apostolic instruction to do so. To overcome would require them to model appropriate authority and appropriate discipline in the midst of a mercenary atmosphere of accommodation.

The promise is not only given to the overcomers but also to "the ones keeping my works until the end," or until they are complete. It's not only important to overcome the tendency to accommodate dangerous and destructive ministries in the church, it is also vital that the believers positively reaffirm their commitment to the truth and to true authority. Their commitment is for the sake of the fulfillment of the works of Christ in their midst. The ability to fulfill their mission in Thyatira depends on their ability to submit to the authority of Christ, even when it involves seemingly strict and harsh positions.

The promise to the overcomers and the keepers of Christ's works is now given: "I will give authority." It is authority they had refused to exercise in the church. Jesus not only wanted to give them authority over the Jezebel party, but he also intended to give them authority "over the nations." They need to remember that in the end, the saints will participate with Christ in judging the nations and ruling the nations. Jesus had told his twelve disciples that "when the Son of man sits on his glorious throne, you who have followed me will sit on twelve thrones, judging the twelve tribes of Israel" (Matthew 19:28).

When the Corinthian believers were bringing their conflicts to court, Paul reminded them "that the saints will judge the world" (1 Corinthians 6:2). Later the book of Revelation paints a picture of the victory of the Lamb, "and with him will be his called, chosen and faithful followers" (17:14).

Being intolerant in a very tolerant, diverse, pluralistic city like Thyatira would have been very unpopular. In fact, it could result in long-term unemployment. But hadn't Jesus predicted such a dilemma? "All men will hate you because of me, but he who stands firm to the end will be saved" (Matthew 10:22). Paul gave it poetic expression: "If we endure, we will also reign with him. / If we disown him, he will disown us" (2 Timothy 2:12). "It was, certainly, hardly possible for a tradesman to maintain his business in Thyatira without belong to the guild of his trade. The guilds were corporate bodies, taking active measures to protect the common interests, owning property, passing decrees, and exercising considerable powers. It was therefore a serious thing for a Thyatiran to cut himself off from his guild."[126]

To reinforce the promise Jesus once again refers to Psalm 2. In verse 8 the Lord said, "Ask of me, and I will make the nations your inheritance, the ends of the earth your possession." Ultimately the redemption of the nations, the people of the earth, was at stake. Verse 9 then promises, "You will rule them with an iron scepter; you will dash them to pieces like pottery." The word translated "rule" literally means "shepherd." The Lord is going to judge the nations but redemption is the motivation. God wants to rescue anyone who is willing, but ultimately "the kingdom of the world" must come to an end.

The "iron scepter" is literally a "rod of iron." The shepherd's rod was a large club with an iron tip designed to fend off predators. King David used this shepherd's rod as the symbol or scepter of his rule. The royal scepter of Jesus is also the shepherd's rod, an iron rod he has shared with the church and expects them to use when necessary.

The rebellious nations will finally be "shattered," a picture of a potter throwing his jar on the floor to break it. In ancient cultures, "earthen pots were often inscribed with the names of a nation's enemies and then ritually smashed to symbolize the future victory of the king. This depicts the

Transformers

absolute devastation of the hostile nations by the Messiah and his people."[127]

"Just as I have received authority from my Father." Jesus received his authority and he is delegating his authority to the church. Therefore when the church exercises spiritual authority, they are using delegated authority from the Father. And when that authority is used appropriately at the initiative of the risen Christ, there are real consequences. On the other hand, to refuse to exercise authority also has consequences—in the case of Thyatira, devastating consequences.

I will also give him the morning star (Revelation 2:28).

A second gift is promised the overcomers in Thyatira. The "morning star" is a reference to the planet Venus. The planet Venus had been used by kings and emperors as a symbol of their authority from ancient times. In fact, all the Roman emperors claimed descent from the goddess Venus. It symbolized sovereignty and immortality. It's interesting that one of Balaam's Old Testament prophecies predicted, "A star will come out of Jacob; a scepter will rise out of Israel. He will crush the foreheads of Moab" (Numbers 24:17). The Jewish Rabbis accepted this as having Messianic import. The Messiah would be the morning star and the scepter that would judge the nations. Peter pointed out that the prophets shone like a light in a dark place, "until the day dawns and the morning star rises in your hearts" (2 Peter 1:19).

At the end of the book of Revelation Jesus himself claims, "I am the Root and the Offspring of David, and the bright Morning Star" (22:16). Jesus is not only giving the overcomers his authority, he is ultimately giving them himself.[128] Participation in the guild feasts promised only temporary economic benefits. Participation in the Messianic feast promised eternal rewards, and ultimately Christ himself.

He who has an ear, let him hear what the Spirit says to the churches (Revelation 2:29).

True discernment of the voice of the Holy Spirit is called for. It cannot be assumed that a prophetess faithfully represents that voice just because she says, "Thus says the Lord." The church as a whole must take the time to listen, to judge, and to obey the word of the Lord. Indeed, all the churches must listen to this word spoken to Thyatira. The consequences will be eternal.

The Key of Perseverance

One of the chief things the church at Thyatira was commended for was their "perseverance." Unfortunately, their perseverance did not extend to their commitment to apostolic authority and to the exercise of that authority.

The word translated "perseverance" is the Greek noun *hupomone*. It is a compound word made up of the preposition *hupo*, meaning "under" and the noun *mone* meaning "an abiding place." It literally means "to abide under" and gives us a picture of someone under pressure who refuses to give up or run away. It tells the story of someone who has conquered certain territory and refuses to give any of it up. It is the courage to refuse to give up, even under severe pressure. Perseverance can be thought of as peace under pressure. Perseverance "is the capacity for being still when all around is tempest-tossed. It is that peace of heart under pressure of life which is so fair and fragrant a thing to us, and ever seems to give the heart of the Lord satisfaction and joy."[129] It is also translated "patience" and "patient endurance."

It seems as though the key to overcoming should seem more triumphant, but perseverance is the key characteristic of the "overcomer" who remains true to God. In his prologue to the book of Revelation John acknowledges that he is their companion in "patient endurance" (1:9). The Ephesian church was commended twice for its "perseverance" (2:2, 3). The church at Philadelphia will be commended for keeping the command to "endure patiently" (3:10). The picture of tribulation in chapter 13 "calls for patient endurance" (13:10). Another picture of the beast kingdom "calls for patient endurance on the part of the saints" (14:12). More than any other personal exhortation in the book of Revelation, the saints are encouraged to "persevere" in every situation, no matter how difficult.

Perseverance produces abundant fruit. In the parable of the sower and the seed Jesus taught that the seed falling on good soil stood for those who "by persevering produced a crop" (Luke 8:15). Paul instructed that the older men in the congregation should be "sound in faith, in love and in endurance" (Titus 2:2). The ability to stand strong in the midst of adversity guarantees a life of fruitfulness over time, even if there are apparent temporary setbacks.

Perseverance is the key to our spiritual formation. Paul placed a high value on patience. He taught that suffering produces perseverance and that perseverance produces character (Romans 5:3, 4). Just refusing to give up under pressure will form Christ-like character in us. Christian character is noted by being joyful in hope, "patient in affliction," and "faithful in prayer" (Romans 12:12). We grow in hope through "endurance" and the encouragement of Scripture (Romans 15:4). Paul prayed that the God "who gives endurance" and encouragement would give the saints a spirit of unity (Romans 15:5). Love "always perseveres" (1 Corinthians 13:7). Paul prayed that the saints' hearts would be directed into "Christ's perseverance" (2 Thessalonians 3:5). Paul exhorted Timothy to pursue "endurance" (1 Timothy 6:11). The primary value of trials is the extent to which it can produce "patience" (James 1:3, 4). The pattern of our spiritual development includes adding "perseverance" to self-control and godliness to perseverance (2 Peter 1:5–8). Perseverance is not only the key element in our ability to overcome, it is also the key element in our spiritual growth.

Perseverance increases our capacity for compassion and comfort. When we suffer, we grow in perseverance, which enables us to encourage others to persevere (2 Corinthians 1:6). Paul prayed that he would be strengthened by the power of God so he could encourage the saints to have "great endurance and patience" (Colossians 1:11). We are willing to "endure everything" for the sake of our brothers and sisters (2 Timothy 2:10). Perseverance, as an expression of a softened heart, empowers us to be more effective in our care of others.

The New Testament believers were consistently commended for their perseverance. The Thessalonian believers were remembered for their "endurance inspired by hope" (1 Thessalonians 1:3; 2 Thessalonians 1:4). The Hebrew believers were reminded of their ability to stand their ground in the face of suffering (Hebrews 10:32). Blessing comes to those who have "persevered" (James 5:11). Suffering for doing good, with endurance, "is commendable before God" (1 Peter 2:20). From God's perspective, perseverance is to be highly valued.

Perseverance increases the effectiveness of our service of the Lord. Paul testified that the signs of an apostle were done among them "with great perseverance" (2 Corinthians 12:12). Paul's own lifestyle was known for the quality of "endurance" (2 Timothy 3:10). As with Jesus, if we are to win the race, we must run it with patience (Hebrews 12:1–3). Learning how to "endure hardship" is a valuable discipline for the development of our ministry (Hebrews 12:7). Especially during times of "pruning," a steadfast endurance will release us to a new level of fruitfulness.

Persevering "to the end" is the final key to overcoming. In his "Olivet Discourse" Jesus taught on the circumstances of the "church age" and of his return. After describing a time of tribulation Jesus told his disciples, "He who stands firm to the end will be saved" (see Matthew 10:22; 24:13; Mark 13:13; Luke 21:19). This is the last word of Jesus in his teaching concerning the last days. Paul also taught that eternal life would come "by persistence" (Romans 2:7). If we are to receive what Jesus has promised, we "need to persevere" (Hebrews 10:36). To overcome we must persevere. The one who "perseveres under trial" is the one who will "receive the crown of life" (James 1:12). We are called to be victors at the end of it all. The key to that final victory is the grace to persevere on the journey.

The Message of the Letter to Thyatira

The church at Thyatira faced a cluster of issues we might easily face in our own day. Unfortunately they didn't handle them well. In fact, the record of church history would indicate that they did not heed the words of Christ in this letter and eventually ceased to exist altogether. Perhaps we can learn from their issues and their mistakes and grow as overcomers in our specific context.

The Challenge of Financial Pressures

The daily concrete challenge in Thyatira was the simple need to survive. It was a blue collar town made up of hardworking citizens trying to support their families. I'm sure there were a few exceptionally wealthy tradesmen but most were simply laborers. Unfortunately, to function they needed membership in a trade guild, and that membership would require them to compromise their dedication to Christ.

Faith for financial provision can be a severe test. Financial pressures are often some of the most severe pressures we face in life. What if our faith in Christ forced us into a situation where we lost our job? Would we still have the grace to persevere in that situation?

It's helpful to remind ourselves of the Lord's commitment to us. Jesus taught us to pray, "Give us this day our daily bread" (Matthew 6:11). The laborers in Jesus' day literally worked one day at a time, picking up their wages at the end of the day. They were then able to buy food and supplies on the way home for them and their families to live on that night and the next day. They had to have daily faith for their daily needs. In that context, Jesus assured his followers that the Father was well aware of their needs (Matthew 6:8, 32) and that if they sought after the Kingdom of God as their first priority, all their needs would be taken care of (6:33).

In the parable of the "friend at midnight" Jesus taught that a needy person's persistence, even at an awkward moment, would result in him receiving "as much as he needs" (Luke 11:5–8). As a result, Jesus taught us to "ask and it will be given to you; seek, and you will find; knock, and it will be opened to you" (11:9). If we keep on asking, seeking and knocking, we will receive what we need from the Lord.

The New Testament church had the grace and compassion to care for one another during times of extreme need. Even if it meant selling personal property and sharing the proceeds, they were willing to do so (Acts 2:45; 4:35). Indeed, some in the church had the ministry of "contributing to the needs of others" (Romans 12:8).

The church at Philippi lived in almost identical circumstances to those in Thyatira. Yet this same Macedonian church built a reputation for the extent of their generosity, giving sacrificially to others in need (2 Corinthians 8:1-7). "Out of the most severe trial, their overflowing joy and their extreme poverty welled up in rich generosity" (8:2). Extreme affliction and poverty positioned them to be compassionate and generous to others. They did not give in to the pressure and decide to accommodate themselves to their economic circumstances.

The normal Christian life involves sharing "with those in need" (Ephesians 4:28). We know how to be content "in want" because, as Paul wrote, "I can do everything through him who gives me strength" (Philippians 4:12, 13). We are convinced that "my God will meet all your needs according to his glorious riches in Christ Jesus" (Philippians 4:19). It's easy to get discouraged under prolonged financial pressure and in our desperation be willing to do whatever it takes to see our needs met. During those times it is very important to remind ourselves of the Father's commitment to our lives and persevere in our trust of him. "Let us then approach the throne of grace with confidence, so that we may receive mercy and find grace to help us in our time of need" (Hebrews 4:16).

The Challenge of Subjective Experiences

Christian faith is all about personal relationship with Jesus Christ. It is appropriate to seek a personal encounter with God in our worship. Christianity is not primarily a superior morality or a superior philosophy, it is the reality of true life in Christ. There is a legitimate role for personal experience and human emotion in Christian spirituality.

There are also objective ways of looking at and thinking about our subjective experiences. The Thyatiran believers were a loving, serving people, but they did not sufficiently value the authority of the tenets of the faith. If someone in the congregation claimed to have a vision or to have heard the voice of the Lord, they did not take the time to judge it but were all too quick to accept it at face value. As a result, they were open to all kinds of deception.

I've often heard the view that what the church needs today is more of the supernatural, more miracles, more signs and wonders. But if all we want is to see something supernatural, we are vulnerable to deception. For instance, later in the book of Revelation the "false prophet" is able to deceive all the inhabitants of the earth "because of the signs he was given power to do" (13:14). Every miracle of God is pointing to a revelation, a specific word, usually a word about Jesus. Jesus himself fed the crowd with loaves and fishes and then taught, "I am the bread of life." He opened the eyes of the man born blind and declared, "I am the light of the world." Jesus raised Lazarus from the dead and revealed, "I am the resurrection and the life." Every miracle must be interpreted. It is the content of the revelation that is primary, not the visible, supernatural sign that drew attention to it. We will avoid deception if we interpret our subjective experiences in the light of God's objective revelation and not the other way around.

The Challenge of Charismatic Manifestations

A specific situation of the need to interpret subjective experiences is spiritual gifts or charismatic manifestations. The source of "Jezebel's" authority was her claim to be a "prophetess." As someone with a highly developed prophetic gift she could be trusted to accurately hear the voice of God and faithfully proclaim his word — at least, that's what they thought.

Paul told the Corinthians, "You can all prophesy" (1 Corinthians 14:31), but not without appropriate checks and balances. Two or three prophets could speak in a service, but the rest were to carefully discern what the Holy Spirit was communicating to the church (14:29). The involvement of the church in the discernment process was especially important in light of the fact that "we prophesy in part" (1 Corinthians

13:9), meaning that at our most spiritually sensitive we prophesy with less than complete spiritual accuracy. Fortunately, we have God's Word to guide us in our discernment of the prophetic word.

Christian prophets did not speak "ecstatically," that is, apart from their conscious involvement, for "the spirits of prophets are subject to the control of prophets" (14:32). The result of charismatic manifestations was to be edification (14:26) and peace (14:33). Spiritual gifts were to be encouraged in the congregation, but "in a fitting and orderly way" (14:40).

Spiritual gifts are important spiritual tools for building up the Body of Christ. In fact, spiritual gifts have no legitimate function apart from "the common good" (1 Corinthians 12:7). The only helpful motive for seeking to participate in the charismatic manifestations of the Spirit is love (1 Corinthians 13).

The believers in Thyatira would have saved themselves the judgment of Christ if they had taken the time to judge the ministry of Jezebel and her followers. It would have helped them if they had some kind of theology of spiritual gifts. Spiritual gifts are vitally important to the life of the church, but they must be seen in the light of Scripture.

The Challenge of Cultural Accommodation

Economics, religion and culture were all wrapped up together in Thyatira. The guilds were the primary means of protecting the common interests of their members. They controlled the ownership of property in the city, sponsored relevant laws, and in most ways controlled the city.

The guild feasts were at the center of the community. They met for business, "worship," and social discourse, all at the same time. It was almost impossible to function in the city without faithfully attending the celebrations of the appropriate guild.

The pressure on the church to accommodate the practices of the guilds must have been enormous. The message of the Jezebel party offered a "spiritual" way of doing so. But that accommodation would have resulted in idolatry and spiritual adultery. It would have ended in breaking their covenant with the Lord.

It's so easy to become desensitized to elements of our own culture. Things that used to violate our conscience are now completely acceptable. While culture changes and cultural norms change, our sense of faithfulness to the Lord should not change. Yet much of the time our Christian standards change with the culture. "I fear that the voice of Jezebel is yet tolerated, and that the children of God are being seduced. Things at which our fathers shuddered are today being introduced as necessary to the social and financial success of the church."[130]

Today cultural accommodation is usually preached in the name of "tolerance" and "diversity." There are ways in which we want to "celebrate diversity." We celebrate the multiplicity of ethnic groups and cultures in our midst. We celebrate the diverse gifts and personalities among us. We don't insist that everyone be alike. But if our tolerance causes us to violate our covenant commitment to the Lord and to his will for our lives, surely a line must be drawn. No manner of apparent spirituality can offset true discipleship. As David Ravenhill has written:

> The sin for which this church was being corrected was having a tolerance for what should not have been tolerated. We, too, err when tolerance takes priority over holiness. We think that tolerating all manner of things is a virtue. So while we in the Church are out hunting for the enemy that we might 'wage spiritual warfare' against him, the enemy has silently infiltrated within us by breaching the walls of our own souls.[131]

The Challenge of Spiritual Authority and Church Discipline

It appears as though those in authority had already judged Jezebel, and the Thyatiran congregation had chosen to ignore their judgment. They both resisted spiritual authority and refused to exercise spiritual authority in bringing discipline to the situation. A loving, serving congregation may have found it difficult if not impossible to take "harsh" actions against unrepentant sinners, even proven heretics, in their midst. Perhaps they needed to consider the fact that refusing to exercise authority and discipline would result in serious harm to the members and the eventual destruction of the congregation.

Paul faced a similar dilemma in Corinth. There was actually a man in the church who was sleeping with his step mother, a thing even the pagan Romans would not allow. Instead of being alarmed and taking the appropriate action the Corinthians were "proud"! (1 Corinthians 5:1, 2). Perhaps they too were proud of their "love" and their "grace" and their commitment to tolerate diversity in their midst. Paul responded by "passing judgment" on the man, and commanding the congregation to "hand him over to Satan," which means to remove him from the fellowship of the church (5:3–5, 11). He reasoned with them that sin was contagious, and allowing it to go unchecked in the church would eventually contaminate the entire congregation (5:6–8). If they truly loved the church and the offending member, they would exercise appropriate discipline leading to eventual restoration (5:5).

Paul instructed the Ephesian believers to "speak the truth in love," and that if they would, they would grow up (Ephesians 4:15). The apostle John encouraged the believers to "love in truth" (1 John 3:18). If we truly love people, we will hate sin, because it is sin that is killing humanity. God demonstrated the full extent his love for us by providing us with the final solution to the sin problem—Jesus Christ. Refusing to deal with sin in the name of love is no love at all (except perhaps the love of self).

The Story of Mt. Zion Ministries

The economy in the Mohawk Valley in upstate New York was in transition. The needs of the poor seemed to be growing exponentially. In Utica the number of needy families was increasing while the resources available to food pantries were decreasing. By mid-year 1999, the feeding centers in town were all out of food and the poor had to simply go without.

Mike and Barbara Servello had been pastors in Utica for almost twenty years. The congregation of Mount Zion Ministries had been growing steadily and Pastor Mike was praying about new ways to serve the city. As he testified, "I have always had a deep burden to see our city and region won to Christ." As he was praying he was also reading the local newspaper and became aware of the crisis facing many poor families in the community. He said, "My heart broke as I heard the story of family after family being turned away because there was just no more food to give. I knew we had a mandate from the Lord to do something about it."

During the next several weeks Mike and his pastoral team became increasingly convinced they were to serve their city by serving the poor of the city. They became convinced they had a biblical mandate to do so. In prayer Mike meditated on Job 34:28: "The cry of the poor comes to God; He hears the cry of the needy" (NCV). Their study of Scripture highlighted the need to actively embrace ministry to the poor. "I am commanding you to share your resources freely with the poor and with others in need" (Deuteronomy 15:11). "Share your food with everyone who is hungry; share your home with the poor and homeless. Give clothes to those in need . . . . Give your food to the hungry and care for the homeless. Then your light will shine in the dark" (Isaiah 58:7, 10 CEV).

Their first assignment from the Lord was, "Get a large warehouse, fill it with food and feed every needy person in your city." It seemed like a daunting task for a local church, one that all the social services in town together were not able to accomplish. Yet it was impossible to deny the mandate from the Lord.

In early 2000 they found just the right building with over 30,000 square feet of floor space. Through a series of supernatural events, the owner of the building ended up donating it to the church for $1.00, and the Compassion Coalition was launched. This was a sure confirmation that they were heading in the right direction. Pastor Mike and the Mt. Zion Ministries congregation had been praying for miracles, and now they were beginning to see them as they served the poor. "I have never been involved with anything as consistently supernatural as this ministry of helping the needy."

They took possession of the building and set their vision. Their first goal was to distribute one tractor-trailer load of food every two months, or six loads per year. They met that goal quickly, and within six months they were distributing one load per week. By 2004 they were distributing ten loads of food to the poor every week.

It wasn't long before the local government began to take note of the work of the congregation. Mike made an appointment with the mayor and simply asked for input on how to best serve the poor of the city. They were amazed that anyone actually cared. Soon a close, personal relationship developed between Mt. Zion Ministries and the various local government agencies, resulting in far-reaching influence in the city.

Transformation in the community is now the natural result of consistently serving those on the margins. To Mike Servello the key was tapping into God's heart for people. His conclusion was clear: "God promises to bless those who will carry out His desires. He promises to bless those who bless the poor (Ps. 41:1–3; Pr. 22:9; 28:27; 19:17). God will help them out of their troubles (Ps. 41:1; Job 5:20). He will protect them (Ps. 37:19). He will destroy the power (plans) of their enemies (Ps. 41:2; Job 5:1). God will heal them (Ps. 41:3; Is. 58:7–8)." God places such a high priority on serving the poor and powerless, identifying with his heart simply results in the blessing of the Lord. And that has certainly been the experience of Mt. Zion Ministries.

The members of the congregation have been newly energized by their compassion ministries. The church did well before, focusing on the usual congregational goals. Now they are aware of a more important focus outside of themselves, on the community around them, and as a result, they have far more spiritual passion and motivation for ministry. They are learning what it means to be a New Testament church.

Mike Servello gives specific words of advice to pastors and local churches who may want to embrace ministry to the poor in their area:

1. Begin by praying. Ask the Lord for a burden and a vision to help the poor.

2. Realize this is a ministry the Lord desires His church to embrace. It is a biblical mandate given to every local church in every city. It is central to the purpose of God for the church.

3. Learn how to discern needs in your area. Read the local newspaper. Prayer walk the streets of the city and ask the Lord to open your eyes to the needs around you.

4. Contact your local government and social service leaders. Ask your government officials about the needs of the city as they see them, and ask for their advice in how best to meet them. They will be shocked!

5. Don't despise small beginnings. Start where you are able and grow from there. Let the Lord bring increase according to his purpose and timing.

6. Enlist the help of local businesses and suppliers. Communicate your vision to serve the city. Offer the help of volunteers from the congregation. Ask them to donate goods, services, and finances. You might be surprised at their response.

7. Have faith and be generous. The Bible says that God "will take care of the helpless and poor when they cry to him; for they have no one else to defend them" (Ps. 72:12 TLB). Pastor Mike advises, "Jesus used five loaves of bread and a few small fish to feed 5,000. He will use your efforts to bear abundant fruit in your city."

During 2004, Mt. Zion Ministries laid the plans for a children's feeding center. A couple in the church encountered very needy children in a housing project and began bringing them boxes of juice and snacks. It wasn't long before the vision began to spread in the congregation. At one point Mike and members of his leadership team met with the mayor and the commissioner of social services. They were so supportive the Mayor turned a building owned by the city over to the church for use in feeding children. The commissioner immediately helped to get a financial grant for the service.

As a result, the food center, Compassion Kids, was opened in July, feeding thirty to forty children per day. Within two weeks they were feeding over a hundred children every day. As of 2005, Compassion Kids is feeding over one thousand children every day in seven schools.

It soon became apparent that the compassion ministries launched by Mt. Zion Ministries was too big a task for one congregation. This realization led to the promotion of a growing network of various congregations in the area, resulting in new expressions of Christian unity. They have also begun to serve the business community by sponsoring training events and marketplace consultations.

It's one thing to have a vision for transforming a city. It's another thing to see practical expressions of the gospel that will result in transformation. If Jesus was a Pastor in Utica, New York, how would he work for community transformation? I'm sure he would do so in the same way he did during his earthly ministry: by showing the love of God to those inhabiting "the highways and byways" of the city. Community transformation is possible, not by seeking power but by serving the powerless. That is the lesson of Mt. Zion Ministries, and many other like-minded congregations.

CHAPTER SEVEN:

THE PROMISE OF BEING AN ALERT CHURCH IN A CITY ASLEEP

THE LETTER TO SARDIS

I magine the task of establishing an effective Christian congregation in the oldest, most famous city in the area. In the US it might be Boston or Philadelphia or even New York City. A city with a rich history, a cultural center for many generations. That was the task of the believers who first went to Sardis. However, in the case of that ancient city, their greatest claim to fame was their history.

When the Christian church was established in Sardis it was a proud city but a city in decline. That congregation had the opportunity to establish a dynamic community, a living representative of Jesus in a declining city. How well they did is the subject of the letter to that church.

The Story of Sardis

When John sent his letter from Patmos, Sardis had been in existence for at least 1,300 years. It may have started out as a Hittite village but gained its fame as the capital of the Lydian kingdom. As the Lydian capital Sardis became known as one of the greatest cities in the ancient world. It was known as "the First Metropolis of Asia" and was the one great enemy of the invading Ionian Greeks. Eventually the Greeks considered it the greatest of all cities.

Sardis was built on a spur of Mount Tmolus. The mountain rose to a height of 7,000 feet and the spur connecting to it was 1,500 feet above the valley below. The structure of the mountain was alluvial, made up of compacted mud which easily broke off. This resulted in extremely steep, smooth sides, making the city "impregnable."

The Hermus River ran north of the city. The Pactolus River flowed out of Mount Tmolus through the west side of the city and then joined the Hermus. The valley was very fertile and a source of great riches. The main trade routes in Asia—the north-south route from Pergamum in the north, and the east-west route ending at Smyrna—intersected in Sardis.

Sardis had an upper and lower city. The lower city filled most of the river valley surrounded by the Hermus and Pactolus rivers. The acropolis and royal residences were on the fortified spur while most of the people lived in the city built in the valley. The only access to the city above was a narrow "saddle" where the spur joined the mountain. Only the defenders in the city who knew where the pass along this saddle was located could gain entrance. When being invaded the citizens of the lower city took refuge in the fortress above.

The city of Sardis was a part of ancient mythology. The famous Phrygian king Midas was supposedly given the ability to turn anything he touched into gold. When this meant he couldn't eat anything he was given permission to wash in the Pactolus River, resulting in gold being found in the river that ran through Sardis. And there was in fact gold in the Pactolus, making Sardis the richest city in the ancient world.

King Gyges was one of the most famous of the ancient Lydian kings of Sardis. He successfully mined the gold from the Pactolus and was the first person in history to mint gold coins. Gyges is known as "Gugu" in Assyrian literature and "Gog" in the Old Testament. When the Cimmerian raiders passed through Asia Minor King Gyges was killed in battle in 657 BC.

The son of Gyges was King Croesus, the most famous of all the Lydian kings. Croesus was known as the richest man in the world. During his reign Sardis was a wealthy, powerful city. Because of their feeling of security, the people of Sardis had a tendency to become complacent. According to the Greek historian Herodotus, "Croesus the king had been vainly warned by the wise Greek, Solon the lawgiver, when he visited Sardis, to beware of self-satisfaction and to regard no man as really happy until the end of life had set him free from the danger of sudden reverse. [Solon] augured ruin because he had rightly mistrusted material wealth and luxury as necessarily hollow and treacherous."[132] Croesus had been careless in repairing the fortifications of the only access to the city, but he was still confident that his fortress was insurmountable.

Cyrus the Persian was a rising star in the eastern part of Asia Minor during the reign of Croesus. When King Croesus consulted the Oracle at Delphi he was told that if he crossed the Halys River to the east the result would be the destruction of a great kingdom. Croesus interpreted that to mean that the Persians would be defeated if he attacked them, so he raised his army and went to war against Cyrus. Unfortunately Croesus was defeated in battle and had to return to Sardis to take refuge in his impregnable fortress, assuming Cyrus would not follow him. But Cyrus did follow him and laid siege to Sardis.

On the fourteenth day of the siege, 549 BC, a Persian soldier named Hyroades saw a Sardian soldier drop his helmet over the wall of the fortress. Thinking that no one was watching, the helmetless guard snuck down the secret pass to the city. Of course, the Persian saw this drama and alerted the other troops. Later that night they entered the city and took it without a fight. According to the Greek historian Herodotus, "An enemy succeeded in climbing to an unguarded point, where no guard was stationed, for there was no fear that it would ever be captured at that place, for the acropolis is sheer and impregnable."[133] This so astounded the Greek world that the phrase "capturing Sardis" became a saying for achieving the impossible.

According to the Greek historian Bacchylides, Croesus responded by immolating himself, that is, setting himself on fire. In Lydian culture self-immolation was not just suicide. The fire released the spirit from the body, guaranteeing immortality. This story tells us something about the religious culture of the area. "In the difficult subject of the local religion of Sardis there are at least clear hints of a preoccupation with death and renewed life."[134] This practice was called "Apotheosis" and symbolized as well as achieved life after death.

Sardis then became the capital of the Persian governor (satrap). The defeat of Sardis changed the course of Greek and Persian history, bringing the Persians to the shore of the Aegean Sea and giving them the confidence to begin a series of wars against the Greeks. Xerxes used Sardis as his military base for his invasions of Greece. However, the citizens of Sardis were never comfortable under the Persians. The Lydians revolted a few years later and the lower city was burned by the Ionians in 499 BC. When Alexander the Great was approaching Sardis with his army, the people gladly opened the gates to him.

Sardis was under the rule of the Seleucids at first and then fell to the Attalids in Pergamum. In 218 BC Antiochus III sought to reconquer the city to restore it to Seleucid control. According to the Greek historian Polybius, one of the Greek soldiers named Lagoras discovered the hidden pass into the fortress in much the same way the Persian soldier had done over three hundred years earlier. Lagoras passed into the city himself and opened the gates to the Greek army. Sardis then became Antiochus' base in his struggles against the Romans. However, under the Seleucids Sardis was of secondary importance to Pergamum.

The Romans eventually defeated Antiochus III in battle in 190 BC. They gave Sardis to the kings of Pergamum who eventually gave it back to Rome in 133 BC.

One of the worst earthquakes in ancient history struck the province of Asia in AD 17. The Roman historian Pliny described it as the greatest disaster in human memory. Twelve cities were seriously damaged. According to Tacitus, Sardis received the most severe damage. "This was nothing less than the sudden collapse of a great part of the mountain and the consequent disappearance of much of the very site of the original fortress-city."[135] The lower city was rebuilt thanks to the generosity of the emperor Tiberius, who among other

Transformers

things remitted all local taxes for five years. However, the city was never the same again. When Sardis applied for the privilege of building a temple to the emperor in AD 26, the honor went to Smyrna instead.

As in Smyrna, the principle deity of Sardis was the earth-mother goddess Cybele. She was a death-goddess who reflected an older, underlying Hittite and Anatolian fertility religion. She was the goddess of caverns and personified the earth in its primitive state. "Its essence lies in the adoration of the life of Nature—that life subject apparently to death, yet never dying but reproducing itself in new forms, different and yet the same. The mystery of self-reproduction, of eternal unity amid temporary diversity, is the key."[136] Cybele was worshiped on the tops of mountains and was thought to rule over wild animals. She was shown wearing a turreted crown, seated on a throne flanked by two lions. Her emblem of power was a whip decorated with knucklebones. Religious rites included priests who danced convulsively to the sound of lute, drums and cymbals while clashing their shields with their swords, flagellating themselves with whips on which were tied knucklebones.

Various gods served as consorts to Cybele, principally Attis. The god Attis was known as Tammuz in Babylon (see Ezekiel 8:14). The annual death and resurrection of Attis was the focal point of the Cybele cult. The worship of Cybele-Attis involved the rite of the "tarobolium," by which the worshiper was rejuvenated with the life-force of a bull. The worshiper went down into a pit, a bull was slain over him or her and he bathed in the blood of the bull. Cybele and Attis were considered to be the guardians of the gates of the underworld, and life after death was thought to be a reunion with the Earth-Mother. Serpents, a common symbol of death and resurrection, were also involved in the worship of Cybele-Attis.

The more Asian worship of Cybele was eventually combined with the worship of Artemis and Zeus. A large temple to Artemis was begun but never completed. Even in its incomplete state it was one of the seven largest temples in the ancient world, containing 78 columns. The earthquake of AD 17 did serious damage to the Artemis temple.

Sardis was one of the original Jewish colonies in Asia Minor. Evidence of this ancient connection with Israel can be seen in the Hebrew word for Sardis, "Sepharad," in Obadiah 20, and the Hebrew word for Lydia, "Lud," in Ezekiel 27:10 and 30:5. According to Colin Hemer, "Commercial expansion may have induced some voluntary dispersion of Jews even before kings of Assyria and Babylonia initiated compulsory transplantation of population."[137] The Persian king Artaxerxes I favored the Jews during his reign. According to Josephus (*Antiquities* 16.171) Antiochus III established 2,000 Jewish families and colonists in the area of Sardis. Many of them worked as goldsmiths and shop-keepers. The Jews favored by the Seleucids were significantly Hellenized, reflecting a mixture of Hebrew and Greek culture. These colonists were given citizenship rights which continued under the Romans. There is no evidence that there was ever a conflict between the Jews and the Gentiles in Sardis.

The largest synagogue in history has been discovered in the ruins of Sardis. It was built after the earthquake of AD 17, in part to honor the wealthy Jewish citizens for their help in rebuilding the lower city. The list of members of the synagogue included Jews with Greek names. Nine members of the synagogue were also listed as city councilors. A large table has been found in the synagogue with carvings of an eagle, the symbol of Rome. On either side of the table are pairs of lions, the symbol of Cybele. The large fountain in the courtyard of the synagogue was listed in the city as a "public fountain" for common, public use.

The synagogue was built as part of a large gymnasium complex. The gymnasium included a school and a bath house as well as the court of the emperor. The Greek gymnasium was the focal point of culture in the city. "The evidence for the acceptance of a Jewish community in a pagan society seems to be unique [to Sardis]."[138]

At the time of the writing of the book of Revelation, Sardis had a population of around 100,000 and was a shadow of its former glory. However, due to its location on the trade routes it continued to be a prosperous commercial center. The Roman historian Strabo was still able to characterize

Transformers

Sardis as "a great city." According to the Roman historian Pliny the Sardians had invented a process for dying wool and continued to enjoy the wealth that came from that industry. They also invented commercial uses for chestnuts, also called the "nuts of Sardis." Sardis also had the distinction of being the first marketplace to include shops for the slave trade.

The church in Sardis was no doubt planted during the time Paul was residing in Ephesus. It must have had a very successful beginning. There is no evidence of either conflict with the Jewish synagogue or with the city as a whole. Archaeological evidence shows that the church met in a side room of the Artemis temple. Shops in the marketplace have been uncovered, many of them with a sign with a Jewish menorah and a Christian cross. However, these Jewish and Christian shops also displayed pagan symbols.[139] Both the synagogue and the church succeeded in finding a way to peacefully co-exist with the population of Sardis. But at what cost?

The Letter to Sardis

To the angel of the church in Sardis write: He who has the seven Spirits of God and the seven stars, says this: (Revelation 3:1).

Jesus begins his address to this church by identifying himself as "the one having the seven Spirits of God." This reminds us once again of the vision in 1:4 that refers to "the seven spirits before his throne" (see also 4:5; 5:6). Zechariah's vision pictured a lampstand with "seven lights on it" which are later said to be the seven "eyes of the Lord" (Zechariah 4:2, 10). The symbol of the "sevenfold spirit" communicates to us the fullness of the Holy Spirit, the full life and power of the Spirit, sufficient for the churches, sufficient for Sardis.

Jesus also points out that he has "the seven stars." Chapter 1:16 showed Jesus holding the seven stars in his right hand, and in 1:20 Jesus explained that the seven stars were the angels of the churches. Once again we see the connection between heaven and the church on earth, and the fact that Jesus is in control of both.

*I know your deeds; you have a reputation of being alive,
but you are dead* (Revelation 3:1).

Usually all looks positive whenever Jesus acknowledges the deeds of the church. However, in this case their deeds, the product of their labor, is simply a reputation, and a false reputation at that. They have been given a name: "Life." They are known for being a vibrant, living church. But Jesus has a very different point of view. From his perspective, the name of the church in Sardis is "Death." Their life is only visible, on the surface. At the center, at the level of the human heart, they are dead.

In this case the strength of Sardis, their reputation, has become their weakness. Their name has caused them to believe they are a vital representative of Jesus, a life force to be reckoned with. In relying on their reputation they have become increasingly unaware of their spiritual decline, until death has filled their assembly. "Nothing is lacking as to external manifestation, and yet Christ says, 'And thou are dead.' He Who seeks first for the inward life, finds nothing to satisfy His heart in this church."[140]

The culture of the city of Sardis was fixated on death. Just outside of the city limits was a world-famous necropolis, or cemetery. For all its reputation, an accumulating death was its present reality. The same is also true of the church.

It's possible to see the Sardian church, meeting together in the Artemis temple precinct, as a church successfully contextualizing the gospel in their surrounding culture. They had created a community where everyone was welcome and everyone felt at home. As a result, they weren't experiencing conflict with the synagogue (that modeled the same user-friendly environment) or persecution from the city. They were a "successful" church; they looked good. But they weren't aware of their growing spiritual slumber and insensitivity. "It was such a model of inoffensive Christianity that it was impossible to distinguish it from its worldly pagan neighbors."[141]

Wake up! (Revelation 3:2).

But there is still hope for the church in Sardis. As we will

Transformers

see, there is a faithful remnant who have not died spiritually. They are the hope for revival in the church. But that revival will require an obedient response to five commandments. The first one is, "Wake up."

This commandment could be translated "be watchful" or "show yourself to be watchful" or "show that you are the ones who are awake." The verb for "awake" is the Greek *gregoreo*, and it means, "to have been roused from sleep, to be awake; to watch, to give strict attention to; to be cautious, active, watchful; to be alive." The opposite meaning is to be asleep, to be caught napping. The opposite refers to a lack of alertness and attention.

In his Olivet Discourse Jesus used this word as the conclusion to his teaching on his return. "Therefore keep watch" (Matthew 24:42; 25:13; Mark 13:35). "What I say to you I say to everyone: 'Watch'!" (Mark 13:37). In Luke's account Jesus communicated this message a bit differently: "Be dressed ready for service and keep your lamps burning" (Luke 12:35). Spiritual attentiveness and sensitivity are absolutely essential for the servants of the Lord.

This was also a common theme in Paul's letters. "So then, let us not be like others, who are asleep, but let us be alert and self-controlled" (1 Thessalonians 5:6). It's interesting that Paul joins spiritual alertness to self-control. Perhaps the opposite is a connection between spiritual slumber and self-indulgence. For the church in Sardis to be revived, they must reignite their vigilant attendance upon the Lord.

> Strengthen what remains and is about to die, for I have not found your deeds complete in the sight of my God (Revelation 3:2).

The second commandment is to "strengthen what remains." They are to take immediate steps to establish the things (or people, issues and truths) that have not died. The word for "strengthen" is the Greek verb *sterizo*, "to make stable, place firmly, set fast, fix; to strengthen, make firm; to render constant, confirm." The people in Sardis who are not spiritually asleep are to actively reestablish their firm foundation and then continue building on it.

This was an important word for the apostle Paul. He referred to the establishing of the saints in Rome by the gospel he preached (Romans 16:25). He sent Timothy to Thessalonica to establish the faith of the believers there (1 Thessalonians 3:2). The strengthening of their faith would enable them to be blameless and holy before the Lord (1 Thessalonians 3:13). He prayed that they would be encouraged by the Lord and strengthened in every good deed (2 Thessalonians 2:17). The faithfulness of the Lord would strengthen and protect them (2 Thessalonians 3:3).

James exhorted the believers to be patient and "stand firm" as they anticipate the Lord's coming to them (James 5:8). Peter promised the saints that after they suffered for a little while the Lord would restore them and make them strong (1 Peter 5:10). He also commended them for being established in the present truth (2 Peter 1:12). The objects of this strengthening or establishing included faith, encouragement, patience and good works. All these required an occasional refreshing from the Lord.

In the case of Sardis, the things that needed to be strengthened were "about to die." If the remnant in the church was going to see revival and restoration, there was no time to lose. "This process of dying had been going on for some time and the culmination (their death) was around the corner. There was hardly any time left, and they had to act quickly or die."[142] It was as though the Lord was saying, "Act fast or die!"

What was specifically at stake was the inadequacy of their works. At some point in the past they had stopped fulfilling their mission before the Lord, and the effects of that lack of fulfillment had lead to a growing decay and death. "I have found" can relate to the conclusion of an investigation into the facts. Jesus had weighed the deeds of the Sardian church in the balance and found them wanting. They are incomplete, unfulfilled. In the beginning the church had begun with a clear vision and sense of mission and purpose. At some point in time they lost sight of that vision and became distracted from their assignment in the city. Others may consider them to be an active, growing, successful church, but "in the sight of my God" they had left their work incomplete and were now dead and dying.

Paul had warned Timothy about those who would have "a form of godliness but denying its power" (2 Timothy 3:5). Because the church in Sardis still had the forms of their original life, they still looked good. "The forms were not wrong. They needed to be filled with power. The dry bones were necessary, but they needed to be clothed with flesh, and become instinct with life. The organization must not be neglected, but it should act in the power of vital force."[143]

It's interesting to remember that the church met in the temple complex of Artemis, a temple that was never completed. As with the city, the church was largely unfulfilled promise, unrealized potential, appearance without reality. At some point they had taken their eyes off of the vision and without knowing it, had become blind. G. Campbell Morgan drew this conclusion:

> There was great promise, but no result, that is, nothing fulfilled before God. Outward forms, ceremonies, organization; but death reigned. There were many things fulfilled before men; indeed, the church had come to the place where it lived before men rather than before God, more anxious in all probability about their reputation in Sardis than their reputation in heaven, more desirous for the good opinion of neighboring churches, than for the commendation of the Head of the church.[144]

Remember, therefore, what you have received and heard (Revelation 3:3).

The third command to the potential revivalists in Sardis is to "remember," the same exhortation given to Ephesus (2:5). They are to engage in an ongoing process of remembering the vision, the mission given them in the beginning. As with Ephesus, remembering "demands a continual recall and actualization of the past truths they had been taught. It is not just bringing these realities to mind but putting them into practice in their lives."[145] They had "received" an assignment from the Lord, one that was still in effect. The things received are the apostolic instructions given to them when they were sent out to plant the church. They had "heard" words of instruction, perhaps even prophetic words of confirmation, and now they were to obey them. They are to renew their commitment to hear and obey, to believe and act on the word given to them.

Obey it (Revelation 3:3).

The fourth command from the Lord is to begin a new life of obedience to all they have heard from the Lord. After they have clearly recalled the word of the Lord they need to reestablish an active lifestyle of obedience. Once again John uses his favorite word for "obey," the Greek verb *tereo*, meaning "to hold fast, to watch over, to keep." They are to dedicate themselves to obeying the Lord. Jesus does not tell them specifically what to obey. He simply tells them to be obedient, to live a new life of dedication to God's will.

. . . and repent (Revelation 3:3).

The last word to the remnant in Sardis is "repent." They are to make a clear decision to turn from their spiritual laziness and stupor and return to a life of dedication to Jesus and his mission in Sardis. They are to bring a halt to their backsliding and return to a life of dynamic obedience to Christ. As with "remember," "repent" calls to mind the word to Ephesus.

> *But if you do not wake up, I will come like a thief, and you will not know at what time I will come to you* (Revelation 3:3).

Jesus now returns to the theme of spiritual alertness. If they don't rouse themselves from their sluggish state, if they don't snap out of it, instead of revival they will experience judgment. The lack of preparation and alertness in Sardis's past had resulted in their defeat on two different occasions, at the hands of Cyrus and Antiochus III. Both had been able to enter the city "like a thief" and carry off the spoils.

Jesus had used the imagery of coming like a thief in his teaching on his return. Those who were not alert and prepared would be unaware of his imminent return and would suffer the consequences. The Son of Man is going to "come at an hour when you do not expect him." As a result, the wise will be ready and alert at all times (see Matthew 24:42–44; Luke 12:39, 40). Paul referred to the fact that Jesus is going to return "like a thief in the night," but that the spiritually alert would not be caught unprepared (1 Thessalonians 5:1–4; see also 2 Peter 3:10).

While Jesus and Paul were referring to the return of Christ at the end of the age, his coming to Sardis probably referred to a coming to them in judgment in their own day if they allowed everything to die. "You will not know" gives a picture of the stealth of a thief. Jesus will come to them without warning, making constant alertness a necessity. "What time" is literally "what hour," implying a sudden, unexpected coming. As they nap Jesus will come to them, and they will be completely unprepared.

> *Yet you have a few people in Sardis who have not soiled their clothes* (Revelation 3:4).

Now the righteous remnant in Sardis is addressed personally. They are only a "few," probably a minority of the members in the congregation. John literally comments on a "few names" of the faithful in the city. The church as a whole had a "name" and a reputation for spiritual life. There were, in fact, only a "few names" of those who had remained faithful in an otherwise lifeless church.

These few are described as those who have "not soiled their clothes." Their garments are unwashed, i.e. they have not made the kinds of lifestyle decisions that would have brought corruption into their lives. The presence of a world-famous woolen industry in Sardis would make this image of speech easy to understand. "The few" in Sardis are still alive because they have avoided the moral compromises others have given in to.

This commendation clearly implies that spiritual insensitivity, a lack of spiritual attentiveness, if not repented of, leads to moral compromise. To use the analogy, if they are unaware of the need to keep their garments washed, they will eventually become dirty. "Here the reference is doubtless to heathen impurities into which the Sardians had plunged, spiritual deadness having issued in indifference to moral evil."[146] References such as Jude 23 confirm the meaning of "clothing stained by corrupted flesh." Getting too close to Sardian culture had resulted in insensitivity and eventual compromise with the famous Sardian immorality. Spiritual slumber will lead to moral corruption, and that defilement will lead to spiritual death.

They will walk with me, dressed in white, for they are worthy (Revelation 3:4).

In the address to the church at Ephesus Jesus introduced himself as the one who "walks among the seven golden lampstands" (2:1). It gives a picture of Jesus walking about in personal fellowship, identification and solidarity with the church. To the faithful in Sardis Jesus promises the same kind of fellowship. They will be given the privilege of walking about with him, sharing in his life in a personal way. In the Old Testament we read of God coming to walk in the garden with Adam and Eve (Genesis 3:8). Both Enoch (Genesis 5:22, 24) and Noah (Genesis 6:9) were also said to have "walked with God." Such a level of ongoing intimacy is rare in the human story, but it is here promised to the remnant in Sardis.

As they walk with Jesus they will be "dressed in white." Rather than defiled garments they will walk in clean, pure garments. The saints being "clothed in white" is a repeated symbol in the book of revelation (cf. 4:4; 6:11; 7:9, 13; 19:14). Their clothes are white because they have been washed in the blood of the Lamb (7:14). The white clothes are garments of righteousness (see Isaiah 61:10). They are garments of purity and holiness. White garments were also worn by people attending the triumphal procession of a Roman general. They were garments of victory, the clothing of the overcomers. "Those who on earth did not defile their garments, shall finally walk with Him in white. They shall come to the time

Transformers

when there shall be manifested in outward glory their inward loyalty to Christ."[147]

"For they are worthy." In the rest of the book of Revelation only God and Christ are said to be worthy (4:11; 5:2, 4, 9, 12). However, here the saints are said to be worthy. Saying they are "worthy" simply means that it is fitting or appropriate for them to walk with Christ, dressed in white. It is the appropriate reward of their faithfulness to Christ in the midst of a dying church. Jesus spoke of those who would be worthy to participate in the resurrection (Luke 20:35). Paul commended the Ephesians for living a life worthy of their calling (Ephesians 4:1; see also Philippians 1:27; 1 Thessalonians 2:12). Those who live in a worthy manner will receive an appropriate reward from the Lord, and the best of all rewards is intimacy with him.

> *He who overcomes will, like them, be dressed in white* (Revelation 3:5).

The church in Sardis has a need to win a victory. They need to overcome the tendency to be entirely too impressed with their reputation and with past glories. Establishing a "good name" in the community, although significant (see 1 Timothy 3:7), putting too high a value on one's reputation can create a false impression of spiritual vitality. Just "looking good" is not the same thing as being spiritually alert and alive. The church needs to triumph over their spiritual sleepiness and laziness that has come as a result of their deceptive appearance. They need to overcome their spiritual insensitivity that has led to moral insensitivity and has threatened their very lives.

The promise given to the overcomers makes clear that there are already overcomers in Sardis. Like "the few" already identified, they will be clothed in white garments. They will refuse to soil their garments with the corrupting influences of the surrounding culture. They will participate in Christ' triumphal procession, both in their generation and at the end of the age.

> *I will never blot out his name from the book of life* (Revelation 3:5).

All Greek cities had an official register containing the names of living citizens. No one's name was erased from the register unless they had been convicted of a crime or had died. There was also a register of the citizens of heaven. The spiritually alive citizens of the Sardian church were still recorded in heaven's "book of life." Their names had not be erased. Moses referred to "the book" God had written (Exodus 32:32, 33; see also Daniel 12:1). Malachi refers to "a scroll of remembrance" in the presence of the Lord (Malachi 3:16). "The book of life" is also mentioned in Psalm 69:28; Philippians 4:3; Revelation 13:8; 17:8; 20:12, 15; 21:17. The "Lamb's book of life" contains the names of those who have a living faith in Jesus. To expunge someone's name from the Lamb's book of life surely implies a radical disconnection from Christ resulting in spiritual death. "The 'few names' in Sardis which are distinguished by resisting the prevalent torpor of spiritual death find their reward in finally retaining their place among the living in the City of God."[148]

Sardis was the depository of the royal archives extending back to the Greeks and Persians. Those archives contained the official lists of the royal families and the chief citizens of those kingdoms. The city of Athens had begun the practice of deleting from such archives the names of condemned prisoners before their execution. To say that the overcomers in Sardis would not have their names deleted is to say that they will not be subject to judgment. When Jesus comes like a thief, they will be prepared.

> . . . but will acknowledge his name before my Father and
> his angels (Revelation 3:5).

For the second time the word "name" is used in verse 5. The church in Sardis, as the city itself, had a "name" before the world. However, the few "names" of those who have remained faithful in the city will not be judged but will be acknowledged by Jesus. "I will acknowledge" is literally "I will confess," a phrase that refers to the judge and jury pronouncing the word of acceptance or rejection. To the faithful overcomers in Sardis Jesus promises to bear witness to them in heaven just as they have borne witness to him on earth.

184   *Transformers*

Jesus had made this promise to the twelve disciples. "Whoever acknowledges me before men, I will acknowledge him before my Father in heaven" (Matthew 10:32). However, Jesus went on to promise, "Whoever disowns me before men, I will disown him before my Father in heaven" (Matthew 10:33; see also Luke 12:8, 9; Mark 8:38.) Evidently the majority of the members of the church in Sardis had proven to be "ashamed" of Jesus in their state of spiritual slumber.

On the other hand, the faithful few had paid the price to consistently confess Jesus before men. Their "name" will be recorded in heaven, and their "name" will be personally confessed by Christ at the last day. "The church as a whole is dead; but a few, who form bright and inspiring exceptions, shall live as citizens of the heavenly city."[149] Even in the midst of spiritual death, the last word of Christ is one of hope.

> *He who has an ear, let him hear what the Spirit says to the churches* (Revelation 3:6).

Every church needs to hear what Jesus had said by the Spirit to Sardis. Every church has the potential of gradually declining into a state of spiritual sleepiness, riding on their reputation and past accomplishments. Only those who maintain a lively dependence on the Spirit of God will have the grace to stay awake and be prepared for anything.

The Key of the Power of the Holy Spirit

In the address to Sardis the risen Christ drew attention both to the problem in the church and the cure. Something had gone wrong with the church's relationship and partnership with the Holy Spirit. The reference to "the seven spirits of God" brought to mind Zechariah 4:2, 10. The middle of that vision in Zechariah, in fact the theme of the vision, is verse 6: "Not by might nor by power, but by my Spirit, says the Lord Almighty." All that God does in and through the church is done in the context of a living relationship with the Spirit of God.

Sardis was a very successful church on the outside but dead on the inside. They were going through all the right motions but had lost sight of the need for the power of the Holy Spirit at every point. The only way they could be revived from their state of death would be for them to reconnect to the life of the Spirit, to become a Spirit-filled church once again. To do so, they needed to be reminded of the importance of the person and work of the Spirit.

The Holy Spirit is a person, not an impersonal force. All too many Christian believers look at the Spirit of God as a force to be used, as an impersonal "anointing," rather than the third person of the Godhead sent to teach us, guide us, and empower us to be God's kingdom community in our time and place. The Holy Spirit guides us into all truth (John 16:13), helps us pray (Romans 8:26), releases us to ministry (Acts 13:2), and offers us personal fellowship (2 Corinthians 13:14). The Holy Spirit can be personally resisted (Acts 7:51), grieved (Ephesians 4:30) and insulted (Hebrews 10:29), and therefore must be thought of as a Person. The Holy Spirit is our "Paraclete," our advocate, counselor, comforter. Relationship with the Holy Spirit is the key to our "life" in God.

Our life in the Spirit empowers us to serve Christ and to become more like Christ. The love of God is poured into our hearts by the Holy Spirit (Romans 5:5). Righteousness, peace and joy rule in our hearts by the Holy Spirit (Romans 14:17). We are able to have hope by the power of the Holy Spirit (Romans 15:13). We are able to guard the word of the Lord in our hearts by the Holy Spirit (2 Timothy 1:14). It is the presence of the Holy Spirit in our lives who causes the "fruit" of God's love to grow in our hearts (Galatians 5:22, 23). It's the one who "sows to the Spirit" who will reap a harvest of life (Galatians 6:8). Indeed, our lives are renewed in every way by the Holy Spirit (Titus 3:5). Our life flowing out in lasting fruit is only possible because of the presence of the Holy Spirit.

The person of the Holy Spirit is the life of the church. Jesus made it very clear that it is the Spirit who gives life (John 6:63; see also 2 Corinthians 3:6). Paul taught that it is the law of the "Spirit of life" that sets us free from the law of sin and death (Romans 8:2). Paul corrected the Galatian church for thinking that they could begin with the Spirit and then continue in their own strength (Galatians 3:2, 3) In the end, we are being built together as a church in order to be "a dwelling in which God lives by his Spirit" (Ephesians 2:22). "A dead church is one that has lost its life, or perhaps never had this vital connection to Christ by the Spirit to begin with."[150]

The Holy Spirit is carrying on the mission of Christ in and through the church. The church was birthed by the Holy Spirit on the Day of Pentecost (Acts 2:1–4). Without the presence and power of the Spirit, the church would not be the church, but would be just another human agency. Jesus had promised the coming of the Spirit from the earliest days of his ministry (Matthew 3:11) and again before his ascension to the throne of the Father (Acts 1:5). It was the power of the Holy Spirit that was to enable the church to be witnesses (Acts 1:8). When the church began to experience persecution they were once again filled with the Spirit and empowered to preach God's Word with boldness (Acts 4:31). The believers partnered with the Holy Spirit in bearing witness to Christ (Acts 5:32). Every step in the advancement of the gospel was marked by an outpouring of the Spirit (Acts 8:17; 10:44, 45; 19:6). It is the Holy Spirit who gives certain "spiritual gifts" or "manifestations" that make possible the building up of the local church (1 Corinthians 12:4–11). Without the presence of the Holy Spirit in the church it would be powerless to faithfully carry on its kingdom assignment.

The church is a community of power, love and truth. The kingdom of God is not just a matter of words; it is a kingdom endued with the power of God (1 Corinthians 4:20). The gospel was preached by the power of the Spirit (Romans 15:19). Paul did not attempt to convince people to believe in Jesus because of the persuasiveness of his arguments but by the power of God (1 Corinthians 2:4; 1 Thessalonians 1:5). The church was also to be known for its love (Colossians 3:14) and commitment to the truth—all by the power of the Holy Spirit (2 Corinthians 6:6, 7).

God has given us power, love and a mind ordered by the word of God (2 Timothy 1:7). Whenever people encounter the church of Jesus Christ, they are to have a power encounter, a love encounter, and a truth encounter. Instead, all too often people encounter programs, budgets and facilities. Those things are not evil, but they are lifeless. Only the life of the Holy Spirit can animate the church and make it what it's designed by God to be. David Ravenhill has drawn this conclusion:

> How easily we become attenders of church, rather than abiders in Christ. How quickly program and routine replace relationship. Soon the machinery is running smoothly, and we compare ourselves among ourselves, all the time becoming numb to the life of the Spirit. Before we know it, we are no different from any worldly organization with "a great program to offer."[151]

The Message of the Letter to Sardis

How embarrassing would it be for Christ to pronounce over any of our congregations, "You are dead"? We would be tempted to rebuke the devil for such a faithless, discouraging word. But what if it were simply true? Our Christian faith is more of a relationship than it is a religion. It is more a matter of life and death than it is right and wrong. We must have the ability to discern the smell of death in the church if we are to remain a living force in the world. The letter to the church at Sardis contains a cautionary word to us all.

The Challenge of Being in the World but Not of the World

The "high priestly prayer" of Jesus (John 17) contains a description of his followers that have challenged them ever since. He spoke of certain ones "whom you gave me out of the world" (John 17:6). Jesus spoke the Father's word to them and as a result, "the world has hated them." Why? Because "they are not of the world any more than I am of the world" (vv. 14, 16). Jesus then prays that these followers be sanctified by the truth of God's Word (v. 17). He will then send them back into the world to continue his mission (v. 18).

In other words, the disciples of Jesus are to be called out of the world, sanctified by Christ and his Word, and then sent back into the world to represent Christ. As a result, their status will be those who are "in" the world, but not "of" the world. They will reside in the midst of the world, bearing the love God has for the world, but they will have been separated from the fallen values of the world.

How to do this has puzzled the Christian church throughout our history. Most believers in Jesus either drop out of the world permanently, building high and strong walls around themselves to keep the world out, or they identify themselves fully with the world, absorb the world's values, and eventually become indistinguishable from the world. Neither fulfills the prayer of Christ and the heart of the Father.

It seems as though the church in Sardis had bent over backward to reach out to their community by identifying with them, even to the point of assembling together in the Artemis temple complex. I'm sure they were a very "seeker friendly" congregation, and that in itself can be a very good thing. But when is close too close? When the community can no longer see our Christian distinctives, haven't we lost ground?

The Old Testament story of Lot is illustrative. After choosing to keep his flocks in the rich valley along the Jordan River we are told that Lot "pitched his tents near Sodom" (Genesis 13:12). Some time later we are told that Lot was "living in Sodom" (Genesis 14:12). Finally, we see Lot "sitting in the gateway of the city" of Sodom as a city elder (Genesis 19:1). He moved from being "near" Sodom to being "in" Sodom to being a leader of Sodom. Perhaps Lot went wrong at the very beginning when he found the fertile valley of Sodom too attractive (Genesis 13:10). He didn't go to Sodom in a sense of God's will; he went there because he found it very much to his liking.

At what point does the church simply cease being the church? James William McClendon, Jr. has written about the pull of the world on the church:

> The strength of this worldly appeal lies in its claim to the universal—an appeal which faith must also make somehow. Its vice is that in its approach to universal truth it

abandons the truth available to Christians, which is that the church is not the world, her story not the world's accepted story, her theology not the world's theology. If we yield this point, conspiring to conceal the difference between church and world, we may in the short run entice the world, but we will do so only by betraying the church.[152]

While we seek an appropriate "cultural relevance," perhaps we should ask ourselves whether or not we are inappropriately attracted to elements of our culture. Are we in the world representing Jesus, or are we there because the world is still in us? If so, we run the risk of becoming irrelevant from God's point of view. Like Sardis, we will experience the process of growing spiritual insensitivity leading to ever-increasing moral corruption.

The Challenge of Being Salty

In his great Sermon on the Mount Jesus taught his disciples, "You are the salt of the earth" (Matthew 5:13). As so many have pointed out, being "salt" implied being a preservative. It also implied having a distinctive flavor, of being salty. In reality, most people put salt on their food because they like how it affects the taste of the food.

For that reason, after making a short statement about being salt, Jesus made a much longer statement about the dangers of losing one's saltiness. "If the salt has become tasteless, how can it be made salty again?" If the salt has lost its distinctive flavor, it becomes tasteless and useless. "It is no longer good for anything, except to be thrown out and trampled under foot by men." Luke's account adds this statement: "It is fit neither for the soil nor for the manure pile; it is thrown out" (14:34, 35). A tasteless salt isn't even relevant to manure. Instead of being a tasty preservative in the community of men, it will become despised. It's interesting how some churches, in the name of becoming more inclusive, lose their distinctiveness and become more despised.

Perhaps the issue begins in the human heart. In another place Jesus said, "Have salt in yourselves" (Mark 9:50). The

Transformers

power of the sanctifying work of the Holy Spirit produces an inevitable flavor in the human heart, both individually and corporately. This command could also be translated, "Have salt among yourselves." The members of the Christian community are to be salty in their relationship with each other. "Be at peace with each other" (Mark 9:50). As a community they can then function as salt in their culture.

The distinctive saltiness of the Christian community begins and ends with grace. A grace-filled lifestyle is "seasoned with salt" (Colossians 4:6). It is a life that brings flavor to everything it touches. Not everyone may like the taste of salt, but at least it never loses its power.

The Challenge of Spiritual Awareness

The primary challenge to the Sardian church was to "be awake." Their error was becoming increasingly sleepy spiritually. At some point they became lazy and insensitive to issues around them. This state grew worse and worse until they fell asleep spiritually, compromised morally, and then died.

My experience leads me to believe that our natural inclination as human beings is to become lazy and sleepy unless we work at remaining alert and focused. Just as our minds tend to wander, so our hearts tend to wander from the place of intimacy with Christ. The resultant desensitization is so gradual it's barely discernable. We wake up one day aware that we are unaware of God's presence and are deaf to his voice, but that condition had been building for some time.

At the end of his life Moses rebuked the people of Israel for not having "a heart to know, nor eyes to see, nor ears to hear" what the Lord was saying to them (Deuteronomy 29:4). This was a major theme for the prophet Isaiah. His ministry was to a generation whose "ears were dull" (6:10; cf. Matthew 13:15; Mark 8:18; John 12:40). Jeremiah also confronted a people "who have ears but do not hear" (5:21; 6:10; see also Ezekiel 12:2). In the same way, Jesus often called for people who had "ears to hear" to listen to the voice of the Spirit (cf. Matthew 11:15; 13:9, 43; Mark 4:9, 23; Luke 8:8;

14:35; etc.). Having "ears to hear" is not a given. It requires a conscious spiritual focus, an intentional attentiveness of the heart, on Jesus.

In the "Parable of the Sower" (Matthew 13:3–9, 18–23) Jesus taught about four possible heart conditions. The first is a heart with no understanding. The implication is of a hard heart with no desire to understand. When the seed of God's Word comes, there is no penetration and the evil one simply snatches it away. The second is a shallow heart. This heart is also hard and rocky but with a shallow layer of top soil surrounding it. When the word comes, there is an apparent enthusiasm for it, but as soon as the word is tried, it is rejected.

Jesus then taught about a distracted heart. This person also receives the Word of God with an initial faith and commitment, and not a shallow commitment. There is no hardness under the surface. Instead, when weeds begin to grow, as they always do, the life of the original seeds begins to slowly wane. Other seeds have been allowed to grow in the soil, and soon "the worries of this life and the deceitfulness of wealth choke it, making it unfruitful" (Matthew 13:22). This is a picture of the heart of the church at Sardis. More and more of their focus was on other seeds, other plants, other issues and elements of the surrounding culture, until the original gospel seed was ineffective.

The fourth kind of heart is "a noble and good heart." This is a heart that hears the word of the Lord, understands it, guards it faithfully, and perseveres in living out the implications of it. This heart bears a consistent harvest, "yielding a hundred, sixty or thirty times what was sown" (Matthew 13:23). It is possible to remain spiritually awake and alert, but not without keeping a soft heart.

The Challenge of Revival

Fortunately for Sardis there was a faithful remnant. However, the pervasive effectives of death in the congregation were having an influence even on these few. Their faith distinctives were beginning to die. They were in need of a Holy Spirit revival, and if they could receive one, they could be the instruments of revival in the entire congregation. The call to "wake up . . . strengthen what remains . . . remember . . . obey . . . and repent" was a call to revival.

The prophet Hosea issued such a call to his generation. "Come, let us return to the Lord" (6:1). Heartfelt repentance would result in God healing them and binding up their wounds. "He will revive us . . . he will restore us, that we may live in us presence" (6:2). If we shake ourselves and arise from our slumber, if we press on to acknowledge the Lord, "he will appear . . . he will come to us" (6:3). Later Hosea prophesied, "Sow for yourselves righteousness, reap the fruit of unfailing love, and break up your unplowed ground" (10:12). The hearts of the people had become hard and unresponsive. They needed to turn to the Lord and cry out for a new heart, "for it is time to seek the Lord, until he comes and showers righteousness on you."

"If my people, who are called by my name, will humble themselves and pray and seek my face and turn from their wicked ways, then I will hear from heaven and will forgive their sin and will heal their land" (2 Chronicles 7:14). Revival comes when people turn to the Lord in repentance and intercession, crying out for mercy. "Will you not revive us again, that your people may rejoice in you?" (Psalm 85:6). That prayer will always be heard and answered by our merciful, faithful Father. We can know revival, and we can be sparks of spiritual life, spreading new fires wherever we go.

The Story of The City Church

Wendell and Gini Smith had served as youth pastors in Portland, Oregon, for twenty years when they were sent to plant a local church in Seattle, Washington, in 1992. They went out with twenty-one members of their church plant team, including their daughter Wendy and son Judah, and began conducting public gatherings in August. They rented a facility in a hotel in Bellevue and forty people were in attendance at their first service.

From the beginning, The City Church had a vision of being "a city within a city." They saw themselves as a community of believers gathered in the city for the city. They sought to be a place of refuge for people of all races, ages and economic levels, "preaching a message of good news and building a church for the 21st century." Pastor Wendell stated his vision this way: "Our vision is to see a New Testament local church proclaiming the good news about Jesus Christ to young and old, rich and poor, red and yellow, black and white. Extending the kingdom of God by building people, families, and leaders—first in our city and then in the ends of the earth."

They defined themselves as "a multi-denominational congregation," an "evangelical charismatic church," identified by Dr. C. Peter Wagner as a "new apostolic church." They have maintained an apostolic relationship with ministries outside of the congregation and are governed internally by a body of elders. Their historical roots are in the holiness movement, the Pentecostal heritage and the evangelical tradition.

Their openness to every community in Seattle resulted in rapid growth. One month after their first public service they had to move to larger facilities, renting space in an office complex. By their first anniversary, their number had grown to 300 people from every background. By 1997 they were serving 1200 believers in their weekend services and purchased the campus of Overlake Church in Kirkland.

One of the works of the Holy Spirit among them was a powerful youth revival in 1996. Having been youth pastors for many years, Wendell and Gini had a clear vision for reaching young people. Their son and daughter along with other anointed youth ministers saw a significant harvest among the youth of Seattle and the birth of Generation Church. But that was just the beginning of their "city within a city vision." Ultimately they wanted to serve and impact their community in a variety of ways, including youth and children's outreaches, food and clothing distribution, ministry to the needy, facilities for compassionate care, training, education, recreation, and a daily ministry to people in need from all walks of life.

As a result of their "multi-denominational" identity, The

City Church and Pastor Wendell have been able to actively engage in fellowship with a variety of churches in the Seattle area, including pastors from the Church of the Nazarene, the Assemblies of God, the Foursquare Church, Baptist churches, Open Bible churches, Presbyterian, Church of God in Christ, and many others. Their functional ecumenism has enabled them to effectively network throughout the city in the process of serving the city.

This overarching vision for the city resulted in the birth of City Ministries. At a certain time a couple in the congregation began distributing food to the needy in their area. Their goal was very simple: to provide immediate help to those in need, and to form relationships based around Christ-centered values. At first they distributed food from the back of a pick-up truck. Before long they were serving literally hundreds of people. It soon became apparent that they had identified a clear need that required the expanded involvement of more people in the congregation—and City Ministries was born.

As it developed, City Ministries was committed to supporting people in need from every social and ethnic background. They began distributing food and clothing to low-income apartment complexes, retirement homes, homeless shelters and missions. Eventually their distribution included day care centers, grade schools and other local churches. Partnerships were formed with companies such as Associated Grocers, Safeway, Rite Aid, Top Foods, QFC, Starbucks, Cannon Fish, Toys for Tots, and others. Every day volunteers collected and distributed bread, pastries, produce, dairy products, and non-perishable food items from over thirty-five vendors. Within a fairly short time they were operating three refrigerated trucks, employing five staff members coordinating eighty volunteers, distributing 2.2 million pounds of food per year out of a 10,000 square foot warehouse located in Redmond. Over 20,000 people in the Seattle area were being fed every week.

According to Director of Operations, Joel Pike, City Ministries has developed a three-fold strategy: 1) distributing to individuals and families, personally touching lives; 2) networking and partnering with area churches with a common mission to help the community; and 3) training other organizations to establish practical community outreach. "This threefold strategy . . . serves as a platform for the power of God to transform lives, communities, cities and nations."

The stated mission of City Ministries includes:

- Encouraging growth in unprecedented and previously unexplored ways as God directs, reinventing themselves and adapting quickly to change.

- Recognizing that God's enablement is expressed through partnerships with other people, resulting in a high priority being placed on relationships.

- Showing spiritual and practical support for people in need characterized by dignity and respect.

- Facilitating ongoing discipleship and training of volunteers in the various areas of ministry.

- Working to build trust and unity with other local churches and ministries.

Pastor Gini Smith sees serving the community as salt and light to be essential kingdom ministry. "Reform in the American welfare system, threats of natural disasters, and social and political upheaval give the church an unprecedented opportunity go serve the natural needs of people through the demonstration of the power of God and good works." Demonstrating the love of God in the midst of a sick world is the only thing that can bring healing and transformation. As Gini testifies, "The ministry endeavors of the local church are a means of demonstrating the love of God to individual lives for the purpose of redemption." However, the essential task of preaching the gospel is never far from view. "In the pursuit of good works, we must never lose sight of the goal that people know Christ, the real answer to all their needs. As Spirit-filled believers we not only embrace the means to meet people's immediate need for food, clothing, and shelter, but also know the power of God which is able to bring deliverance to their lives."

Perhaps one of the most significant ramifications of the

work of City Ministries has been the need to network with area churches. The work grew so quickly it was impossible for any one congregation to provide enough resources and volunteers to meet the need. The City Church quickly realized the need to facilitate cooperation among other congregations. As a result, a network of 150 churches in the greater Puget Sound area came together to extend the work of City Ministries. Forty of the churches received direct distributions from the Redmond warehouse. Eighteen of these churches served as ministry hubs in their city. Three clothing and home furnishing distribution centers have also been opened. It seems as though the shared vision of serving their communities has served to unite the local congregations in visible and effective ways.

In fact, the growing unity of the churches has become central to the vision of The City Church and City Ministries. The vision to serve their "ministry partners" has grown to a clear commitment:

- They are committed to supporting their partners with prayer, encouragement and practical training.

- They are committed to working to empower their partners to take active responsibility for the welfare of their communities.

- They are committed to encouraging their partners to further extend the network by forming working partnerships with other congregations and ministries.

The vision for an effective network of local congregations serving their communities has become their passion. Pastor Gini explains it this way: "Reaching a city requires a comprehensive biblical strategy and the cooperation of networking churches. A single church with limited resources cannot meet all the needs of a city. As a local church we are only one expression of the Body of Christ, with a limited ability to serve a community. In unity, networked together with other churches, we multiply our capacity to attain the common goal—people reconciled to Jesus Christ and established in a local church. Unity enables us to truly be effectual in reaching our city." In this way, the work of transformation not only touches a city but also a region, a nation, and beyond.

CHAPTER EIGHT:

THE PROMISE OF BEING A PILLAR CHURCH IN A PRECARIOUS CITY

THE LETTER TO PHILADELPHIA

"What's our assignment, Paul?"

"I and the elders are sending you on a mission to a town that has been destroyed by an earthquake, one so severe most of the population died in the disaster and the rest now live outside of the city walls for fear of aftershocks."

"Who will we be ministering to?"

"To the citizens of a town that used to be a missionary center for Greek culture and is now just trying to survive."

"And what will our objective be?"

"To be a steadfast, stable, secure community, a missionary community, in the midst of a devastated, desperate city."

If that had been a conversation you participated in, chances are you were headed to Philadelphia.

The Story of Philadelphia

King Attalus II (159–138 BC) of Pergamum was known by the nickname "Philadelphus" because of his love for his older brother, King Eumenes II (197–159 BC). When Attalus II came to the throne he wanted to build a city at the place where the ancient regions of Lydia, Mysia and Phrygia came together. It would need to be built on the main north-south trade route connecting to Smyrna and Troas on the coast as well as the chief cities of Sardis and Pergamum. The purpose of the city would be to spread Greek culture into the surrounding regions and ultimately into the interior of Asia Minor.

Attalus II built his city and called it Philadelphia. It was located on the southeast side of Mount Tmolus in the Cogamis River valley, a tributary of the Hermus. This valley was known for its rich volcanic soil that would be able to support a prosperous vine growing enterprise. The city was in an ideal location for trade and became the center of Hellenistic culture in central Asia Minor. Sir William Ramsay summarized the mission of the city of Philadelphia:

> Philadelphia was founded more for consolidating and regulating and educating the central regions subject to the Pergamene kings. The intention of its founder was to make it a center of Greco-Asiatic civilization and a means of spreading the Greek language and manners in the eastern part of Lydia and Phrygia. It was a missionary city from the beginning, founded to promote a certain unity of spirit, customs, and loyalty within the realm, the apostle of Hellenism in the Oriental land.[153]

The city succeeded in its mission to such an extent that by AD 19 Greek was the only language spoken in the areas surrounding Philadelphia.

Philadelphia was the newest of the seven cities of Asia. Like Thyatira it was organized around trade guilds. Like Sardis and Smyrna it had a strong, influential Jewish community. Like Ephesus it was a center of the worship of Artemis. Like Pergamum Dionysus was the patron of the city. During the Roman period Philadelphia found itself on the main Roman postal route in the province of Asia, further extending its influence. It was known as "the Gateway to the East."

All that changed in AD 17. The earthquake that devastated the acropolis of Sardis seriously damaged a total of twelve cities in the province of Asia. The city closest to the epicenter was Philadelphia. Most of the population was killed in the earthquake. Because it was so close to the epi-

Transformers

center of the earthquake, serious aftershocks continued for many years afterward. When the Roman historian Strabo visited the area in AD 20 he reported that most of the city's population lived in huts outside of the city walls. His report indicated, "Philadelphia . . . has not even its walls secure, but they are daily shaken and split in some degree. That is why the actual town has few inhabitants, but the majority live as farmers in the countryside, as they have fertile land."[154] The emperor Tiberius came to the aid of Philadelphia as he had of Sardis, remitting their taxes for five years. To show their gratitude the city changed its name to "Neocaesarea," built a monument to Rome and a temple to Germanicus, the adopted son of the emperor. However, the city continued to exist in a state of ruin, the people living in fear and poverty.

The city reacquired the name "Philadelphia" in AD 42. However, when Vespasian became the Roman emperor the city of Philadelphia, to gain the support of the new dynasty, it changed its name to "Flavia." The city had lost all sense of itself, all sense of stability, security or identity. It tried to make up for this lack by closely identifying itself with Rome and the emperors.

In AD 92 Domitian passed a law requiring all the vine growers in Asia to destroy half of their crops and to not plant new ones. Rumor was that the emperor was protecting and promoting the wine industry in Italy at the expense of the other provinces. There is also some reason to believe that the province of Asia was experiencing a famine at the time. Since it takes a long time for vines to grow back, this single imperial decree further devastated the economy of Philadelphia. "Hopes in the Flavian dynasty had finally been dashed by the action of the imperial patron himself."[155]

In the midst of this situation a serious conflict developed between the synagogue and the church. It's probable that many of the early converts were from the synagogue, always a source of tension. In addition, the laws of Domitian affecting the "Jewish tax" may have also been an element of this conflict. The inhabitants of the city lived in insecurity and poverty as it was. The chance of escaping the Roman tax by joining the synagogue must have been very appealing to some of the Christians. Eventually the synagogue officials forced the issue by excommunicating those who did not confess that Jesus was a false Messiah. "The difficulties of this Church arose from Jewish rather than pagan antagonists, and [there is] no reference to direct persecution from without or heresy within the brotherhood."[156]

In AD 117 Ignatius of Antioch wrote a letter to the church of Philadelphia addressing an ongoing problem with the synagogue. Evidently some of the Christians had in fact reconverted to Judaism and were putting pressure on the other Christ-followers to do the same. Ignatius reported that the validity of the gospel was being actively questioned. "For I heard certain persons saying, If I find it not in the charters, I believe it not in the Gospel.[157] And when I said to them, It is written, they answered me, That is the question. But as for me, my charter is Jesus Christ."[158] This points to continuing opposition from the synagogue, led by former members of the church.

According to Ramsay, "The Jews boasted themselves to be the national and patriotic party, the true Jews, the chosen people, beloved and favored of God, who were hereafter to be the victors and masters of the world when the Messiah should come in his kingdom. They upbraided and despised the Jewish Christians as traitors, unworthy of the name of Jews, the enemies of God."[159] However, the church as a whole remained faithful.

When John wrote the letter to the believers in Philadelphia, the city and surrounding area was disillusioned with Rome and ready for an alternative. It was time for the church to begin a new phase of their mission to that part of Asia and beyond.

The church in Philadelphia continued to be influential for centuries to come. The story of the martyrdom of Polycarp, bishop of Smyrna, indicates that when he died, certain believers from Philadelphia died with him. When the Turks invaded Asia Minor the city of Philadelphia was the last to fall, surrendering to the Turkish army in 1391. To this day the church is alive and well in the city.

The Letter to Philadelphia

To the angel of the church in Philadelphia write: These are the words of him who is holy and true (Revelation 3:7).

As with the other letters, Jesus addressed the church in Philadelphia in terms that would draw attention to the fact that he was all they needed. His address did not draw from the language of the vision of chapter 1 but came instead from the Old Testament.[160] In this case he was "the holy." "The Holy One" is a frequent title for God in the Old Testament, at times with Messianic indications. Psalm 16:10 praises the Lord, for "you will not abandon me to the grave, / nor will you let your Holy One see decay." Isaiah's favorite title for God was "the Holy One of Israel" (see 1:4; 37:23; etc.). Jesus here identifies with God as the Holy One, and even as the Holy One of the "Israel of God" (see Galatians 6:16).

Jesus also identifies himself as "the true." The Greek word *alethinos* can mean "genuine." Some of the believers were under pressure to confess that Jesus was a false Messiah. Here Jesus himself confesses that he is instead the true. This word can also mean "faithful." Jesus was the faithful Lord of the church and the Lord of the city of Philadelphia. He was the true Lord of the province of Asia, the interior of Asia Minor, in fact of the whole Roman Empire. While the emperor Domitian had proven himself to be an unfaithful lord as it pertained to Philadelphia, Jesus was and would always be faithful and true.

> *. . . who holds the key of David. What he opens no one can shut, and what he shuts no one can open* (Revelation 3:7).

The idea of the "key of the house of David" is only found twice in the Bible. The original reference is Isaiah 22:22. In that passage Eliakim is receiving a prophetic word concerning his future role in the royal palace. He would have a place of authority: he would hold the key that would give him access to the king and his palace. He would be second only to the king himself. In this way, "Eliakim with his key of office slung over his shoulder, is the antitype of the exalted Christ, set over the House of God and exercising all authority in heaven and on earth."[161] While Eliakim is said to have "the key," Jesus is said to "hold the keys." He has all the keys and they are his unique possession. He has all authority in heaven and on earth.

Both Revelation 3:7 and Isaiah 22:22 describe authority as opening doors in a way that forbids others to close them, and closing doors with equal persuasion. The use of the present tense in the letters draws attention to the present activity of Christ in the church. Jesus had told his disciples that he was going to give them the keys of the kingdom so that "whatever you bind on earth will be bound in heaven, and whatever you loose on earth on earth will be loosed in heaven" (Matthew 16:19; 18:18). Jesus is the one who possesses all the keys of authority in the kingdom of God. It is his prerogative to give his church, including the church in Philadelphia, access to those keys to accomplish his kingdom purpose.

> *I know your deeds. See, I have placed before you an open door that no one can shut* (Revelation 3:8).

As with four of the other churches Jesus begins his comment on the church by reminding them that he is personally aware of their deeds. However, as with Smyrna Jesus does not offer any words of correction. In fact, no specific deeds are listed, giving a sense of unconditional approval of the church in Philadelphia. Instead the emphasis is on their future deeds, not the past. Jesus had arranged an open door for them. No one has the ability to close that door. All they now need is the courage to go through it.

The apostle Paul often spoke of an open door. He referred to a "door for effective work," even in the face of those who opposed him (1 Corinthians 16:9; see also 2 Corinthians 2:12; Acts 14:27). He requested prayer that "God may open a door for our message" (Colossians 4:3). In this sense, an open door is a God-sent opportunity to preach the Gospel with power and persuasion. Revelation 4:1 also refers to an open door in heaven. In this sense an open door may picture entrance into the kingdom of God. This would be meaningful to the Christians who had been conflicting with the Jewish community. "While the church has been excommunicated from the synagogue, Christ has the 'keys' to the kingdom. He has opened the 'door,' and 'no one could shut it.'"[162]

> *I know that you have little strength, yet you have kept my word and have not denied my name* (Revelation 3:8).

Jesus acknowledges the fact that the church has "little power." They were considered to be a small church with little influence located in a precarious city. They were looked down upon by the city and the synagogue, and perhaps even by other churches in the area. But Jesus had placed before them an open door and given them authority to go through it.

Jesus was not just commiserating with the Philadelphians because of their powerlessness. The text literally says, "because you have little power." Jesus was demonstrating his power and authority through a Christian community that had very little of their own. Why? Because they had kept his word and not denied his name. They had proven faithful to the Lord during very difficult and frustrating times and now he was coming to them with a significant reward: increased authority and enlarged influence and fruitfulness.

In the face of pressure from the synagogue, they had not denied their Lord. Unlike the majority in Sardis, they had been faithful to the word of the Lord. "The church lacked size and stature in the community and was looked down upon and persecuted. They had 'little authority' or influence. 'But' they were faithful, and that has always been the test of divine blessing rather than success."[163] As with Smyrna, the church in Philadelphia is being favored by the Lord because of their faithfulness, even though they seemed to be a small, weak church.

Because of their loyalty to Jesus the Philadelphian church is being given the opportunity to move into increased areas of influence. Their location on the border of Mysia, Lydia and Phrygia gave the church a unique opportunity to spread the gospel into new areas. The road passing through Philadelphia continued on to the central plateau of Asia Minor. "Along this route the new influence was steadily moving eastward from Philadelphia in the strong current of communication that set from Rome across Phrygia towards the distant East."[164] If they take advantage of their opportunity, although small and weak, they can become the premier missionary church in the province of Asia.

> *I will make those who are of the synagogue of Satan, who claim to be Jews though they are not, but are liars—I will make them come and fall down at your feet and acknowledge that I have loved you* (Revelation 3:9).

Now the conflict with the synagogue is specifically addressed. The nature of the conflict is not described, but instead Jesus draws attention to his intention to vindicate his faithful followers. There was evidently a connection with the situation in Smyrna. In 2:9 there is a reference to "those who say they are Jews and are not, but are a synagogue of Satan." This letter to Philadelphia repeats the reference to "those who are of the synagogue of Satan, who claim to be Jews though they are not." This reference adds the phrase, "but are liars."

Jesus is going to give the church a gift of personal vindication by making those in the synagogue who have been opposing Christ and the Christians come and bow down before them. He will make the "synagogue of Satan" give way before the believers and humble themselves before them.[165] He will make the "false synagogue" acknowledge that Jesus has consistently demonstrated his love for the church that had been loyal to him. And now, he is going to reward them for their faithfulness by giving them expanded influence.

The idea of "falling down at the feet" of the people of God can be found in the prophets (see Isaiah 49:23; 60:14). The idea of demonstrations of the love for God for his people was also a common prophetic theme (see Isaiah 43:4). However, the

Old Testament prophecies pertain to the Gentile nations bowing before Israel and acknowledging God's love for them. Here in Philadelphia those who claim to be "Jews" because of their ethnicity and history but are not spiritually, will acknowledge that those whom they claim to be false Jews but are the faithful followers of Jesus are in fact the people of God. "When the 'false Jews' submit in the day of fulfillment, the roles will be reversed."[166] "Once you were not a people, but now you are the people of God" (1 Peter 2:10).

> *Since you have kept my command to endure patiently, I will also keep you from the hour of trial that is going to come upon the whole world to test those who live on the earth* (Revelation 3:10).

An authoritative open door is not the only gift the Lord is giving Philadelphia. They have consistently obeyed "my word of perseverance." Jesus had opportunity to exhort the believers to persevere during difficult times, and they had responded steadfastly. Now he makes a promise to them. When the hour of testing comes upon the whole world, he will personally keep, guard and protect them.

A universal "hour of trial" seems to have eschatological significance. The church had already experienced a significant trial in the past, and there would no doubt be additional trials in the future. But in the end, the whole world would be tested. Daniel 12:1 refers to "a time of distress" that would exceed anything previously known. Jesus also refers to a time of "great distress" (Matthew 24:21). But that final test will not be intended for the people of God but rather for "the inhabitants of the earth." This phrase is also used in Revelation 6:10; 8:13; 11:10; 13:8, 14; 17:2, 8, and always refers to "the earthly ones," to the enemies of God and the people of God. The final trial of the enemies of God is the wrath of God. Jesus promises to "keep" his loyal, obedient servants "out of" the trial of God's wrath. The preposition implies "protection from within" the trial and not the elimination of the trial. Jesus does not promise to spare his people from trials. Rather he promises to preserve them from the wrath of God in the midst of trials.

Throughout the NT, persecution is seen as the believers' lot, indeed their great privilege. In Revelation martyrdom is seen as a victory over Satan, not a defeat. Therefore, the point is that the Philadelphia church will be protected from the wrath of God against the unbelievers but not from the wrath of Satan, and that this protection is within and not a removal from that wrath.[167]

"He who stands firm to the end will be saved. And this gospel of the kingdom will be preached in the whole world as a testimony to all nations, and then the end will come" (Matthew 24:13, 14).

> *I am coming soon. Hold on to what you have, so that no one will take your crown* (Revelation 3:11).

Jesus now promises a sudden coming to them. The promise of Jesus' coming in 2:5, 16 and 3:3 was more of a threat than a comfort. However, in this verse Jesus promises to come to them in comfort and protection. He promises to come to vindicate them and increase their measure of power and influence.

However, in the meantime they are exhorted to "hold on to what you have." They are to maintain a firm grip on what the Lord has given them, including the open door he has placed before them. They are to continue to persevere in the midst of very challenging circumstances. If they don't, there still is the possibility of losing their crown. The church at Smyrna had been promised the victor's crown (2:10). The promise of a crown for the faithful in Philadelphia is clearly implied, but the possibility of someone taking their crown continues to be a possibility.

Paul had remarked on the fact that everyone runs the race but not everyone wins the prize. Therefore, "Run in such a way as to get the prize" (1 Corinthians 9:24). And the prize? "A crown that will last forever" (verse 25). No one, either in the synagogue or in the city, has the power to take their crown from them. They only way they can lose it is to drop out of the race. If they do not persevere to the end, they will forfeit the race.

Transformers

Historians have noted that "the use of the athletic metaphor was appropriate in Philadelphia, on whose inscriptions games and festivals are specially prominent."[168] "If anyone competes as an athlete, he does not receive the victor's crown unless he competes according to the rules" (2 Timothy 2:5). Their enemies would surely attempt to put obstacles in their way, to discourage them and distract them. But if they kept their vision clear and persevered, they would win the crown.

Him who overcomes I will make a pillar in the temple of my God. Never again will he leave it (Revelation 3:12).

Now promises are given to those who win the victory. But what is it that they need to overcome? What are the enemies the faithful in Philadelphia need to conquer? In a weak, devastated city they are known as a church with "little strength," but with a powerful open door in front of them. Surely there will be times when they will need to overcome the tendency to doubt the word of the Lord to them, to doubt the vision, because of their sense of weakness. They may even have times of discouragement and wonder whether or not their stubborn perseverance is worth the effort. The battle to be fought and won will be in their own souls. They will need to win a faith-victory every day.

The overcomers will receive a special blessing. Jesus will make them a pillar in God's house. This was a promise of a new security and a new identity. This must have been a very meaningful promise to a people living in an unstable, earthquake-prone city. To a people so filled with fear and insecurity they lived in huts outside the city walls Jesus said, "I will make you a pillar." The leaders in the church at Jerusalem had been known as "pillars" (Galatians 2:9). The church itself is also referred to as a "pillar" (1 Timothy 3:15). A pillar is both stable and permanent. A pillar was also known for the amount of weight it could support and the size of structure that could be built upon it.

Part of their new stability and strength was the promise that they would never again have to go out of God's temple.

They had been forced to abandon the city in years past, but they will never leave God's house. They will have permanent security in the presence of the Lord.

> *I will write on him the name of my God and of the city of my God, the new Jerusalem, which is coming down out of heaven from my God; and I will also write on him my new name* (Revelation 3:12).

As wonderful as it will be to be known as a "pillar" church—strong, steady, stable—they will be a very special pillar indeed. They will be a pillar with three names written on them. The idea of an inscribed pillar would have been a familiar one to the Philadelphians. In the Old Testament the temple of Solomon had two inscribed pillars. The first one was named "Jachin," which means "He establishes." The second pillar was inscribed with the name "Boaz," meaning "In him is strength" (see 1 Kings 7:21; 2 Chronicles 3:15–17). Both of these pillars in God's temple made reference to great strength. In addition, it was the custom in Greek temples to write the names of prominent citizens on the pillars.

The first name inscribed on this pillar church was "the name of my God." Bearing the name indicated membership in his family as a son or daughter. Bearing the divine family name indicated character and destiny. In the Old Testament the name of God was placed on every Israelite to identify them as being his authentic people (see Numbers 6:27; Deuteronomy 28:10; Isaiah 43:7; 62:2). The high priest wore a plate of gold with the words "Holy to the Lord" engraved on it (Exodus 28:36). Later John sees a vision of the people of God sealed with the "Father's name written on their foreheads" (Revelation 14:1; see also 7:3; 22:4). Bearing God's name indicates that his people in Philadelphia belong to him and share in his nature and authority.

Second, the Philadelphians will have "the name of the city of my God" written on them. The city of Philadelphia couldn't make up its mind what it name ought to finally be. It vacillated between Philadelphia and Neocaesarea, back to Philadelphia then on to Flavia and then back to Philadelphia again. But the church will always be known by one name: New Jerusalem. Paul had referred to "the Jerusalem that is above" in contrast to "the present city of Jerusalem" (Galatians 4:24–26). For Paul, the present Jerusalem was the result of the covenant made at Sinai, while the new Jerusalem was the result of the coming of Christ and the new covenant (see also Hebrews 12:22; 13:14). Bearing the name of the city was an indication of full citizenship in that city.

When John wrote the letter to Philadelphia the old Jerusalem had been destroyed and was no longer a covenantal factor. What mattered was their citizenship in the city "which is coming down out of heaven." "But our citizenship is in heaven" (Philippians 3:20). This was not only a reference to the new covenant community in Philadelphia but to the full expression of that covenant and that community at the end of the age. When Ezekiel saw a vision of the new temple and the new city he was told its name: The Lord Is There (48:35). At the end of his vision John also sees the city of God coming down from heaven—Paradise restored (21:2ff). For the church at Philadelphia, their identity was connected to that city in a way that gave them a sense of security as well as hope.

They also received a third name—"my new name." We know and love the name of Jesus. It tells us that he is our Savior and Lord. Yet we have not yet begun to grasp the full glory of his name. Paul sings about this new name: "Therefore God exalted him to the highest place / and gave him the name that is above every name" (Philippians 2:9). When John sees the return of Christ at the end of the age he says that "he has a name written on him that no one knows" (Revelation 19:12). Surely we see the willingness of Jesus to identify himself with his people, to allow them to share in his victory, his authority and his glory. "Both the victorious Christian and the victorious Christ will receive a new name, i.e., sustain a new character and appear in a new light."[169] Jesus shares his glory with his victors now and in all the ages to come. "When Christ, who is your life, appears, then you also will appear with him in glory" (Colossians 3:4). Sharing in the glory of Christ ultimately involves knowing him and being like him. "He will share with him all His honours and rewards. There is to be a most perfect oneness between the overcomer and the King."[170] "We know that when he appears, we shall be like him, for we shall see him as he is" (1 John 3:2).

> Here, on the one side, were the ruined temple and the obsolete worship of the imperial god and the disused new name which for a time the city had been proud to bear. None of all these things had been permanent, and there remained from them nothing of which the city could now feel proud. On the other hand, the letter gives the pledge of safety from the hour of trial, of steadiness like the pillar of a temple, of everlasting guarantee against disaster and eviction, of exaltation above the enemies who now contemn, and insult. In token of this eternal security it promises that the name of God and of the city of God and of the divine author shall be written upon the victor.[171]

He who has an ear, let him hear what the Spirit says to the churches (Revelation 3:13).

Those individual members of the church of Philadelphia, or of any of the churches, are called to listen carefully to the message of the Holy Spirit, and to demonstrate the fact that they have heard by the way they live. For the Philadelphian believers their true listening will be the fact of their refusal to lose their crown, to hold on tight to all the Lord has given them. When the Lord comes to them with a seemingly impossible mission, they won't hesitate because they are small. They will remind themselves of their new identity in Christ and go forth in faithful perseverance. All that's called for is simple obedience.

The Key of Obedience

John's special word for obedience (Greek *tereo*) is used three times in the letter to Philadelphia. Although they had little strength, they have "kept" his word (verse 8). Since they had "kept" the word to persevere, Jesus will "keep" them from the hour of trial (verse 10). This word refers to more than simple obedience. It means steadfast obedience during difficult and trying circumstances. It is usually used in the context of keeping God's Word.

This idea of obedience is an important theme throughout the book of Revelation. A blessing is pronounced on those who "take to heart" what they hear (1:3). The overcomers in Thyatira who "do his will" to the end will be blessed (2:26). The remnant in Sardis are exhorted to "obey" what they had received and heard (3:3). Later the dragon is seen waging war against those who have "obeyed" God's commands (12:17). The saints who "obey" God's commands are exhorted to patiently endure (14:12). A final blessing is pronounced on those who "keep" the words of the prophecy (22:7). "In Revelation, repentance and obedience are highlighted over belief and faith. The verb 'believe' does not occur in Revelation; the noun 'faith' always means faithfulness; the adjective 'faithful' means loyalty or endurance, not belief."[172] The commitment to obey the word of the Lord is an important key to being overcomers in any generation.

In other places the word translated "obey" is the Greek verb *hupakouo*. It is a compound verb made up of the preposition *hupo*, "under," and the verb *akouo*, "hear," and literally means "to hear under." It gives a picture of those who have placed themselves under someone or something else and as a result have made a commitment to do anything they might hear. Obedience implies a determination that the subject is worthy; that is, we decide to obey someone because it is an appropriate aspect of our relationship with them. Our obedience shows our respect for that person or thing. While obedience is unconditional, the subject of our obedience is selective. We must always ask, "Whom or what must we obey?"

We must obey God. One of the most basic truths of our faith is that God is God and we are not. By definition God is worthy of our obedience. The apostles went so far as to say, "We must obey God rather than men" (Acts 5:29). If we are forced to choose between the two, God always has priority.

Love for God implies obedience. Because he is God, love for God will always be loving obedience. If we love him, we will obey him (John 14:15; 15:10; 1 John 5:3). Entering into a love relationship with Father, Son and Holy Spirit will include obeying his commands (John 14:21, 23). On the other hand, those who do not love God will not obey him (John 14:24). A personal knowledge of God is confirmed by the fact that we obey his commands (1 John 2:3–5). Those who obey his commands have made their home in him (1 John 3:24).

We must obey God's Word. Faith sometimes involves making every thought obey Christ (2 Corinthians 10:5). We are not to replace our obedience of God's word with obedience to our own traditions (Mark 7:9). Faithfully keeping God's word is a foundational commitment to every follower of Christ.

Preaching the gospel involves teaching people to obey the commands of the Lord. The Great Commission instructs us to teach them "to obey everything I have commanded you" (Matthew 28:20). We are not just calling people to believe; we are calling them to obey, to enter into a life of obedience to Christ.

The Christian life is a lifestyle of obedience. Our confession is "Jesus is Lord." If he is Lord, we will obey him at every point. "We must obey. We must make every effort to embrace the righteous way of life that the New Testament commands and promises are possible. Obedience means unconditional submission to Jesus as Lord as well as Savior."[173] Jesus knew that his followers would live so differently from the surrounding society that the world would hate them (John 15:19, 20). "Today, unfortunately, many people despise Christians, not for the unswerving obedience to Christ, but because of the hypocritical disconnect between Jesus' teaching and our actions."[174]

Faith leads to obedience. Faith is not a passive mental assent. Faith is active and always leads to certain steps of faith. Obedience comes from faith (Romans 1:5). Faith is the choice to obey God's Word (Romans 15:18; 16:19, 26). A "good confession" of faith will result in obedience to the commands of Christ (1 Timothy 6:12–14) The Christian "faith" can be described as "the obedience to Jesus Christ" (Acts 6:7; 1 Peter 1:2). Abraham not only believed the Lord, he obeyed his word (Hebrews 11:8). If that is true of the "father of those who believe," it is certainly true for his spiritual children.

214   *Transformers*

We become the "slaves" of whatever we obey. If we obey sin, we become slaves of sin (Romans 6:12, 16). On the other hand, if we obey God, we become slaves of God (Romans 6:17). That kind of slavery is the only true freedom (John 8:31, 32). Those who obey the truth purify themselves (1 Peter 1:22). Obedience is more than a choice; it is a life-long commitment that will affect every area of our lives.

Obedience leads to acts of compassion. The obedience that accompanies our confession of faith will overflow in generosity (2 Corinthians 9:13). Although we cannot earn our salvation through works, faith without works is "dead" (James 2:17). "Good works and righteousness are evidence of repentance . . . . Salvation, while not achieved by works, is demonstrated and maintained in what is done."[175]

An attitude of obedience will also empower us to receive the servants of the Lord with honor and respect. Whoever has a relationship of obedience to Jesus will also obey the servants of the Lord (John 15:20). The Corinthians were commended for their obedience of Titus (2 Corinthians 7:15). Children are commanded to obey their parents (Ephesians 6:1; Colossians 3:20). Servants are to obey their masters (Ephesians 6:5; Colossians 3:22). We are to obey our leaders in the local church (Hebrews 13:17). An attitude of obedience toward our spiritual leaders can contribute to the working out of our salvation (Philippians 2:12). Obedience is a heart condition. Either obedience is in our hearts or it is not. If it is, it will be demonstrated in all our relationships.

God rewards those who obey him. Whoever obeys the word of the Lord will never see death (John 8:51). God has given the Holy Spirit to those who obey him (Acts 5:32). Jesus is the source of salvation to those who obey him (Hebrews 5:9). Answers to prayer are sometimes contingent upon our obedience to the word of the Lord (1 John 3:22). God loves us unconditionally, but he cannot reward disobedience.

Disobedience has consequences. Those who reject the truth of God and choose to follow evil will suffer appropriate consequences (Romans 2:8). Therefore, we must learn to obey God rather than our own sinful inclinations (Romans 6:12). Those who do not obey the gospel will be punished (2

Thessalonians 1:8). Those who refuse to obey the instructions of the Lord are to be led to repentance (2 Thessalonians 3:14). In the end judgment will come to those who refuse to obey the truth (1 Peter 4:17).

The Message of the Letter to Philadelphia

I love preaching from the letters to the seven churches of Asia. It seems like I have preached most often from the letter to Philadelphia. Its application to some situations seems obvious, especially to churches that are small but considering greater involvement in missions or evangelistic outreaches. But everyone is blessed if they heed the word of Jesus to the church at Philadelphia. Most people face similar challenges at one time or another in their lives. What is the message to us today in this letter?

The Challenge of Insecurity

If Jesus openly acknowledged that the church in Philadelphia had "little power," I'm sure everyone else was well aware of that fact. Surely the Philadelphians knew they were relatively powerless. If they compared themselves to Sardis or Laodicea they would be convinced of their own failure to be a successful, influential congregation. They would have tended to have a small identity to go along with their small power.

And they wouldn't have been the first people of God to have a poor identity. When the Lord appeared to Moses on Mount Sinai he had spent 40 years herding sheep. He had long since given up any aspirations of being a deliverer. When the Lord called him to go to Pharaoh and lead the Israelites out of Egypt, Moses understandably replied, "Who am I?" (Exodus 3:11). Moses couldn't connect the idea of his life circumstance with delivering a couple of million slaves from the great Egyptian empire. To help him make the connection the Lord responded, "I will be with you" (3:12). Moses' personal sense of self had to be connected to God and to the presence of the Lord in his life, not to his own sense of whether or not he was capable of delivering the people. Because Moses took cautious steps with the Lord, he eventually had the privilege of seeing a great exodus.

However, when the nation of Israel was given the opportunity to enter into the promised land, they sent explorers ahead who brought back a report that frightened them. Their conclusion: "We can't attack these people" (Numbers 13:31). They were convinced they were unable to take the land the Lord had given them. Why? "We seemed like grasshoppers in our own eyes" (verse 33). Joshua and Caleb had a different perspective. "We should go up and take possession of the land, for we can certainly do it" (verse 30). But the insecurity of the people led to their disobedience, which ultimately led to their death in the wilderness.

When the Lord appeared to Jeremiah, the future prophet was only sixteen years of age. In an oriental culture that meant little power, and yet the Lord called him to be a prophet to the nations. Jeremiah was simply being honest when he said, "I am only a child" (1:6). However, his youth was not a limitation to God. As with Moses the Lord responded, "I am with you" (1:19). All Jeremiah had to do to be successful was to be faithful and obedient.

The Lord was placing a powerful open door before the church at Philadelphia. Although we don't know exactly what that door entailed, it's easy to imagine the church responding, "We have little power; we can't do it." But if their insecurity led to disobedience, they would in fact have lost their victor's crown. It was essential that they connect their identity as a church to the presence of God in their midst and to the power of God enabling them to do whatever he might purpose for them.

The same is true for us. Our limitations do not define us. Our limitations are no limitations to God. All we need to successfully do God's will, no matter how stupendous, is to be faithful and obedient. The Lord is with us.

That requires faith. A life of faithfulness begins with a life of faith in God. Yet faith can be an elusive thing, especially in a crisis.

"Without faith it is impossible to please God" (Hebrews 11:6). Faith has everything to do with our personal relationship with God. It is chiefly our ability to trust him; it is "faith in God" (Hebrews 6:1). We can trust him to the extent that we know him. And that trust leads to hope and certainty (Hebrews 11:1).

Our growing relationship with God will lead to an increased ability to hear his voice, which will ultimately lead to greater faith, because "faith comes from hearing" (Romans 10:17). Faith is the dynamic of our heart connection to the Father, one that grows as our intimacy with him grows.

It took faith for the believers to go to Philadelphia to begin with. They had to trust that the Lord was calling them and would always be with them as they attempted to be faithful to his call. It took even greater faith when he sent word through John that he was preparing to open a new door of authority and opportunity to them. They had to believe the Lord could use them in a powerful way, even though they were known for their powerlessness. They had to trust the Lord in the small things and the big things.

It was Hudson Taylor who faced many harsh trials in the process of establishing the gospel in China. There were moments of hardship and discouragement, moments when he felt his faith wane. But it was in those moments he realized the truth—that God is not so much looking for great faith as he is people who will trust his great faithfulness. That was true for the church in Philadelphia. It was true for Hudson Taylor in China. It is true for us today. No matter what our circumstance, we can trust God's faithfulness. To do so is great faith.

The Challenge of Costly Discipleship

Although the church in Philadelphia had little power, they had proven their faithfulness and loyalty at certain times in their past. The church planting team knew what they were getting into when they went to Philadelphia. They knew they were going to a devastated, precarious city, a city where the survivors lived in huts outside of the walls in fear of further earthquakes. The city had little power. How much influence could a congregation in that situation have? How successful could any local church appear, ministering to "squatters" living in fear and poverty?

It cost the believers to go to Philadelphia. They gave up alternative ministry opportunities to be faithful to their call.

When Jesus sent the twelve out on a mission he sent them with very little. "Take nothing for the journey—no staff, no bag, no bread, no money, no extra tunic" (Luke 9:3). They were not sent with much support. The cities where they went were not going to put them up in the best hotels and wine and dine them. They had to take whatever hospitality was offered them. "Whatever house you enter, stay there until you leave that town" (verse 4). They couldn't go with the thought of personal success in mind.

When they returned Jesus clarified the call to costly discipleship. "If anyone would come after me, he must deny himself and take up his cross daily and follow me" (verse 23). The Lord does not necessarily design our ministry assignments to contribute to our self-esteem. He commissions us in a way that will contribute the most to the extension of the kingdom of God. "For whoever wants to save his life will lose it, but whoever loses his life for me will save it" (verse 24). Since true life comes out of death, true spiritual productivity requires us to set ourselves aside for the sake of the will of God. If we insist on asking, "What's in it for me?" the answer might be, "Death." But a death that will lead to multiplied life.

My experience of adult life paints a picture of the pursuit of "success" during the early decades. The focus is on achievement and proving one's worth. At some point, that transitions to a pursuit of "significance." Just achieving is no longer enough; we must know our life is making a difference. But even significance is mostly about me. Both success and significance are a result of reflecting on our own value in life. There is perhaps one thing greater than significance: self-forgetfulness. Giving ourselves for the sake of others, whether or not it seems successful or significant, is surely the greatest contribution anyone could make.

Going to Philadelphia would have necessitated costly discipleship. The believers had been faithful for decades by the time John wrote his letter. They had given themselves to serving the city and the people there. Now Jesus was coming to them with enlargement.

The Challenge of Being Faithful in the Little Things

The believers in Philadelphia started with very little. Their assignment was to serve a frightened, insecure people with the love of Christ. They had a small mission in a small community with little to work with. But their requirement was the same as that of the congregation in Ephesus: faithfulness.

Jesus taught his disciples (and whoever was willing to listen) about the need for faithfulness. He taught them that their faithfulness would be tested with small things first. To some extent faithfulness is faithfulness. Faithfulness with small things would have the same value as faithfulness with great things. "Whoever can be trusted with very little can also be trusted with much, and whoever is dishonest with very little will also be dishonest with much" (Luke 16:10). All that matters is whether or not we can be trusted. If we can be trusted with little, it will be an easy step to trust us with much.

Paul made a similar statement concerning the faithfulness of deacons. "Those who have served well gain an excellent standing and great assurance in their faith in Christ Jesus" (1 Timothy 3:13). One who serves faithfully is in a position to receive whatever the Lord may have in mind for them. The Philadelphian church had been faithful with little. Now a great door was opening before them. As David Ravenhill has written:

Because of their faithfulness in "little things" they were to be rewarded with greater opportunities, namely, that of having greater influence. The promise of "spiritual enlargement" remains today for all those who have stepped out in faith, investing the little that they have been entrusted with, watching as God breaks it and feeds the multitudes through them. The Christian life is always progressive; we go from faith to faith and move from victory to victory. How we invest that will determine whether we receive more or not. Jesus says to the church: "If you sow the little you have, I will see to it personally that you are rewarded with great gain in the Spirit. And yours will be the increase.[176]

The Story of Salem Christian Center

Oradea is a beautiful city in northwest Romania, close to the Hungarian border. In ancient times it was part of the Roman province of Dacia. Later the areas around Romania were devastated by the Mongols and eventually became a part of the Turkish empire. It was part of the Austro-Hungarian empire until 1919 when modern-day Romania was formed. Oradea is considered the main gate from western Europe into Romania. It has a population of 230,000, and is the marketing and industrial center for the region. There are also popular health resorts in the area. Almost half the city's population is Hungarian.

Teodor Ciuciui grew up in communist Romania. He was born into a Christian family, his father spending time in prison for his faith. Ted had a personal conversion experience at an early age and began to preach the gospel as a twelve-year old. As a member of a Pentecostal church he was baptized in water and in the Spirit. He had another life-changing encounter with God at the age of fourteen, when he made a commitment to ministry. As he said, "I was so touched at that time. My cousin and I were in a forest where we encountered a heavenly atmosphere, including angelic visitations." That same year the Ciuciui family moved to Oradea.

The Christian community in Oradea was about 60%

Orthodox, 12% Reformed, 8% Roman Catholic, 6% Pentecostal, and 4% Baptist. Under the communist regime even the Evangelical and Pentecostal churches became very traditional, struggling simply to survive. After communism, many of the older churches seemed somewhat irrelevant to a new generation. To reach the children and young people a new way of doing church would be necessary.

In 1990 Teodor, his wife Zamfira, and their four children decided to move to Portland, Oregon to prepare for a new chapter of ministry. Ted completed the Church Leadership Program at Portland Bible College and then went on to complete a Masters of Art at Multnomah Biblical Seminary. While in the U.S. they began to network with churches and leaders who would be a source of relationships and resources in the years to come.

When the Ciuciui family returned to Oradea they had a passion in their hearts to see a new generation of believers formed into a company of overcomers in Romania. They had a vision to see a local church that was Spirit-filled, culturally relevant, and effective as salt and light, both in Romanian society, in the city of Oradea, and among the other Christian congregations.

From the beginning, Salem Christian Center (*Centrul Crestin Salem*) sought to attract the hurt and the rejected, non-Christian seekers, and young people. The name "Salem" means peace, and communicates a vision to provide a place where people can experience the peace of God in the presence of God. Their first meeting place was the Cultural Hall of the city. This unusual location sent an immediate message to the community: S.C.C. was not going to be a traditional congregation. In fact, during their first few months as a church they were fairly controversial:

- They chose to be an unaligned, nondenominational church. For that reason, the other congregations didn't know how to "label" them.

- They broke out of traditional worship forms and encouraged "free" worship, including things like clapping their hands, raising their hands, etc.

- To be sensitive to the real lifestyles of the people they were trying to reach, they chose non-traditional times for corporate services and other events.

- They emphasized church "membership" as a relational process in building community rather than the traditional forms of official membership.

- They targeted unchurched people in the community.

They were not content to stay inside of any one building and sought ministry opportunities in community parks and neighborhoods. They used drama, pantomime, and music to communicate the gospel. These practices made them so controversial some of the evangelical churches in town did not even consider them to be Christian.

Salem Christian Center had clear spiritual goals from the outset. First of all, they wanted to see people in the community come to Christ. They also wanted to help facilitate relationships among the various local churches in Oradea, encouraging partnership and unity. In the end, S.C.C. hoped to build a strong local church that would be a model for other churches, including new church plants, in Romania.

Their founding vision also included certain social goals. They wanted to build bridges between the church and the local community. Romanians tended to view the church as isolated and irrelevant. S.C.C. sought to engage the community, including the local government, with social projects, and to take on some of the social problems facing the community. This would include the problem of the many orphans in Romania, seeking to help care for them and see them successfully integrated into Romanian society. Their work with children would include children's clubs and a Christian school. They also sought to reach out to young people with things like an internet café. Ultimately, the S.C.C. congregation planned to facilitate foster care for seniors and to provide medical services to the poor.

The families of Oradea also have significant needs. The Ciuciui's are committed to serving the families in a variety of ways. They seek to provide relationship training, counseling and mentoring to young people. They work to provide training classes in parenting skills. They do all they can to foster better communication between husbands and wives.

After serving the community for a time, Ted approached the local government for permission to buy property and build on it. The officials were surprised at the scope of S.C.C.'s vision—pleasantly surprised. Usually the city only allows a local church enough land to build an auditorium on. However, in this case they made an exception and gave the church five acres on which to build an auditorium, a school, a clinic, and an orphanage. The Lord had given the church great favor in their city.

As a result, the church has a growing impact on the city. People in the community look at S.C.C. as an open place for all, a place where everyone is welcome, a place of refuge from the pressures of life in Romania. They are also beginning to see the church as a place where God is, a place of miracles. Not only are the corporate gatherings filled with visitors, so are the prayer meetings.

The congregation of S.C.C. has gained an entrance into the local public schools, serving them with a variety of children's programs. They hold public Christmas and Easter plays that are well attended by the community. The congregation is also actively engaged in providing clothing, medical services and counseling to the poor in the community.

Now Salem Christian Center is conducting a Friday night event for young people, attended by teens from non-Christian families. Some of the youth have begun Bible clubs in their high schools. Every Saturday a children's program is offered for the kids in the community. About 80% of those coming are from non-Christian families. In these ways the congregation is having a profound impact on a new generation of Romanians.

Even though other churches in Oradea questioned the "orthodoxy" of Salem Christian Center in the beginning, they are now responding to the new vision with increasing openness. This can be seen in the worship patterns of the local churches, singing many of the same songs with the same freedom. An atmosphere of unity and fellowship is growing between all the churches in the city.

In the future, S.C.C. would like to influence the business community. They want to build a Business Center that will offer help with start-up businesses and will provide jobs for people in the community. They have plans to build an auditorium that will seat 3,000, and a Christian school that will serve 300 students. They also plan to launch a Bible college to train a new generation of pastors and church planters. Future plans also include a sports center for the young people in the area and a retreat center.

A truly healthy congregation ultimately reproduces itself. S.C.C. has plans to plant ethnic churches in Oradea for the Hungarian community and the Gypsy community. They also have plans to plant five local congregations in the region.

What would it be like to have an overcoming congregation in Romania that serves as salt and light and leaven in all aspects of society? The Salem Christian Center is impacting Romanian children and youth, education, local government and business. The light of the gospel is shining through them, bringing transformation to a new generation, bringing hope to a land so often devastated. They are redeemed transformers in the midst of the world.

CHAPTER NINE:

THE PROMISE OF BEING A SELF-GIVING CHURCH IN A SELF-SATISFIED CITY

THE LETTER TO LAODICEA

All too often people who love the book of Revelation tend to also be people who love "doom and gloom prophecies," who are attracted to bad news. Those same people also have a special fondness for the letter to the church in Laodicea, especially when they can view it as a summary picture of "the end-times church," or even the American church.

Unfortunately, that approach runs the risk of missing the point. Like the other six, this letter must be seen in its original context. And then we must have ears to hear what the Spirit is saying to the church then, to the church today, and to our own individual lives. If we would be overcomers in our generation we will listen to this final letter.

The Story of Laodicea

The city of Laodicea was built sometime between 260 and 253 BC by the Seleucid king Antiochus II (260–242) in honor of his wife, Laodice. His ultimate motivation was to establish Seleucid control in the area. Like Philadelphia, Laodicea was established to spread Greek culture into the area of Phrygia. Unlike Philadelphia, Laodicea failed in its "missionary task." Instead it developed mostly as a commercial center.

The city was built in the Lycus River valley at the spot where the main postal and trade routes crisscrossed—the north-south route connecting Troas, Pergamum and Sardis in the north with the Mediterranean Sea in the south, and the east-west route connecting Ephesus and Miletus on the Aegean coast to the west and Syria to the east. It was located 100 miles east of Ephesus and 45 miles SE of Philadelphia. Those entering the city passed through the "Ephesian Gate" on the western wall and exited through the "Syrian Gate" on the eastern wall. The citizens of Laodicea levied taxes on all trade traveling through their city. Both the Attalids in Pergamum and the Romans paid special attention to the building and upkeep of these principle highways, resulting in rapid growth and prosperity in the new city of Laodicea.

Laodicea was built on a plateau about a half-mile square with the fertile plain of the Lycus Valley below. This valley was the crossroads of Lydia, Phrygia and Caria. There were three cities built together in the valley: Laodicea, Colossae, 10 miles to the east, and Hierapolis, 6 miles to the north. At first Colossae was the principle city, located at the foot of a snow-covered mountain that was a source of clear, cold water year round. In fact, it was the only drinkable water in the area. Hierapolis was known for its hot mineral springs and became a popular health spa. The hot water flowed over cliffs to the south of the city, leaving behind white sediment visible from Laodicea. The city of Laodicea had no springs, no sources of water, and the water of the Lycus River was not drinkable. Instead Laodicea built an aqueduct piping water from Denizli six miles to the south. Unfortunately this water was also hot mineral water that became lukewarm mineral water by the time it reached Laodicea. "So the hot waters of Hierapolis were medicinal, the cold waters of Colossae pure and life-giving . . . . The affluent society [of Laodicea] was far from the sources of its life-giving water, and when by its own resources it had sought to remedy the deficiency, the resulting supply was bad, both tepid and emetic."[177]

The original settlers were mostly Syrian, including a large Jewish colony. Several Jewish families became prominent in

Transformers

the city and adopted Greek names and Greek culture. The Jewish colony organized itself into trade guilds and became very prosperous. The Talmud refers to the Jews of Laodicea as the epitome of the ease and laxity of the Diaspora. In 62 BC the Roman proconsul confiscated the gold traveling to Jerusalem. The amount of gold indicated a Jewish population around 7,500. "The Jews of Laodicea may have become so integrated with their affluent society that they were indistinguishable within it, perhaps even leaders in its commercial expansion and its most vigorous and united class."[178] There was no hint of ethnic tension in Laodicea.

The oldest Asian god of the city was Men Karou. "Men" was an ancient moon god associated with agricultural fertility, the underworld, and the protector of tombs. The local population called on Men for healing, safety and prosperity. "Karou" indicated the location of his shrine between Laodicea and Carura, thirteen miles east of Laodicea. There was a famous medical school associated with the Men temple. Followers of the teaching of the ancient physician Herophilos (330–250 BC) believed in the use of compound medicines made from local herbs. They developed a compound for curing eye diseases known as "Phrygian Powder." The famous physician Galen wrote of this unique "collyrium," making the city even more famous and prosperous.

Under Greek influence the god Zeus Laodicenus became the patron of the city. The city also paid homage to the god Apollo. Ancient inscriptions refer to the prophets of Apollo from Laodicea. The worship of Asklepios was no doubt connected to the temple of Men. In fact, as the commercial prosperity of the city grew so did their religious syncretism, eventually including shrines to Dionysus, Helios, Nemesis, Hades and Mithra.

After the defeat of Antiochus III the Romans signed a treaty with the Seleucids in 188 BC giving Laodicea to Pergamum. In 133 BC the city became a part of the Roman province of Asia. However, the city maintained a stubborn independence from Rome. During the rebellion of Mithridates IV, king of Pontus (88–63 BC), Laodicea sided with Pontus, surrendering the Roman commander to

Mithridates. When the rebellion was eventually crushed, Rome exacted crippling taxes on the area. Among other things, Rome enforced the power to requisition lodging when passing through town. They exploited the wealthiest citizens, forcing entry into their homes and demanding hospitality for as long as they wished. "The exploitation of local wealth by corrupt Roman officials and the enforced hospitality for their staff fell heavily and persistently on Laodicea as an affluent *conventus* capital."[179]

Relations with Rome improved somewhat under the proconsulship of Cicero (51–50 BC). Laodicea became the administrative and judicial center for the region under Cicero. It was also established as a banking center, bringing even more wealth to the city. The local farmers developed flocks of sheep known for their soft, raven-black wool, resulting in the establishment of the manufacture of black garments and carpets. The coins minted at the time depicted cornucopias, a symbol of material wealth.

From the time of Cicero on the wealthiest families in Laodicea became famous throughout the region. One of the most famous was the orator known as Zeno (90–38 BC). The Zenonid family was considered the greatest in all Asia. In 40 BC Labienus Parthicus invaded Asia, and only Laodicea, led by Zeno and his son Polemo, was able to resist him. Polemo was named the first ruler of Cilicia and ultimately king of Pontus by the Romans. Several of his sons became kings in turn, a heritage the Laodiceans were justly proud of.

Like Philadelphia, Laodicea was located in a volcanic area subject to frequent earthquakes. The earthquake of AD 17 resulted in severe damage to the city. As was true of other cities in Asia, Laodicea received much-needed aid from the emperor Tiberius. According to the *Annals* of Tacitus, when a second earthquake damaged the city in AD 60, the citizens of Laodicea rejected Roman aid. Several very wealthy citizens donated large sums of money and personally rebuilt the city. Citizens such as Nicostratus and Q. Pomponius Faccus were remembered by name. A man named Hiero donated 2,000 talents, several million dollars in today's currency. They built a large gymnasium, a sports stadium with a track 900 feet long, a triple gate and towers, and several buildings. If anything the city was more beautiful and prosperous after the earthquake.

Under the Romans Laodicea became famous for its gladiatorial games. They also hosted musical contests. The city prospered greatly under the Flavian dynasty. A temple to the emperor was built to Vespasian in AD 79, making Laodicea a center of the imperial cult.

It's quite possible that Epaphras of Colossae, sent out by Paul, planted the church in Laodicea (Colossians 1:7; 4:12-15). It appears that the two churches were closely related (Colossians 2:1). Evidently Paul wrote an epistle to Laodicea (Colossians 4:16) that is no longer extant. John's letter to Laodicea was sent about thirty-five years later. Church history records a local bishop up until c. 1450. The plateau on which Laodicea was built is without inhabitant today.

The Letter to Laodicea

To the angel of the church in Laodicea write: These are the words of the Amen, the faithful and true witness, the ruler of God's creation (Revelation 3:14).

Jesus begins his address to the Laodiceans by identifying himself as "the Amen," a Hebrew word which means, "to verify something as true, to confirm." It implies strong agreement with a desire to bring something to a conclusion or fulfillment. It indicates that something is reliable or trustworthy. This word is used in both Testaments to authenticate a statement as being particularly important. It indicates the truthfulness, authoritativeness, and the divine origin of a saying— or in this case, of a person. In Isaiah 65:16 the Lord is identified as *Elohim Amen*, usually translated the "God of Truth." As G. Campbell Morgan noted, "He is the Certainty, the Finality, the Ratification, the ultimate Authority, the Amen."[180] Whenever John records an especially important saying of Jesus, he introduces it with a double "amen amen," translated as "I tell you the truth" in the NIV (see John 13:28; 16:23). Paul tells us that the promises of God are "Yes" in

Christ, eliciting an "Amen" from us (2 Corinthians 1:20). When Jesus identified himself as "the Amen" he was guaranteeing the trustworthiness of his person, deeds and words.

The faithful and true witness. In order to elaborate on Jesus as the Amen, he is further described as the "faithful and true witness." Jesus is referred to as the "faithful witness" in 1:5. These are the only two places in the book of Revelation where Jesus is said to be the "witness" (Greek *martus*). This designation refers to human "witnesses" in 2:13; 11:3; 17:6, and usually in the context of suffering and/or martyrdom. In his passion Jesus was the ultimate faithful witness. Jesus is also called "the true" in 3:7; 19:11. "The true witness" is one who fulfills his word, whose testimony never falls short of the truth. Jesus in the only completely reliable representation of the Father and of the Father's kingdom purpose. His witness does not change from circumstance to circumstance. "Jesus Christ is the same yesterday and today and forever" (Hebrews 13:8).

The ruler of God's creation. The ultimate demonstration of the authority and reliability of Christ can be seen in his role in creation. He is the "head" (Greek *arche*) of God's creation. The word *arche* means "the beginning" or "the preeminent one." It may also mean "source" or "origin." In the prologue to his gospel John sings, "In the beginning (*arche*) was the Word" (John 1:1). Paul's epistle to the Colossians declared that Christ is "the firstborn over all creation" (1:15). He went on to say that all things, visible and invisible, were created "by him and for him" (1:16). In fact, all things in creation literally hold together "in him" (1:17). Paul then described Jesus as "the beginning (*arche*) . . . so that in everything he might have the supremacy" (1:18).

Jesus is "the uncreated principle of creation, from which it took its origin . . . the head of the family as well as the first in point in time. The Creation is subjected to the Eternal Word with Whom it began."[181] Jesus is the source and sum of all things (see Ephesians 1:10). If Jesus is the source of creation, he alone is the source of everything the Laodiceans have and of everything they might ever need. He is their all-sufficiency. If he is in control of creation, he can be trusted to be the Lord in Laodicea.

Transformers

I know your deeds, that you are neither cold nor hot. I wish you were either one or the other (Revelation 3:15).

As with the other assemblies Jesus acknowledges he is aware of the fruit of the lives of the Laodiceans. Instead of saying what that is, he simply remarks that the Laodiceans and their deeds are "neither cold nor hot." Both words refer to temperature extremes, icy cold or boiling hot.[182] It's probable that the two sources of water in the area were in view. Colossae was known for its refreshing, life-giving, icy cold water. Hierapolis was known for its hot, healing mineral water. Laodicea had no sources of water. "The Laodiceans should have been known for their spiritual healing (like Hierapolis) or their refreshing life-giving ministry (like Colossae)."[183] Instead, they are not known for any particularly impacting ministry.

Jesus would have preferred that the believers in Laodicea had been either cold or hot. Instead, the best they could hope for was lukewarm. Because they had no springs in or around Laodicea, with neither cold nor hot water, all they could do was build man-made aqueducts to pipe in water. If they had attempted to pipe cold water in, it would have been lukewarm by the time it arrived. Their strategy was to pipe hot mineral water in from the south, but of course, by the time it arrived, it was lukewarm mineral water.

When the prophet Jeremiah summarized the Lord's complaint against Israel he lamented, "My people have committed two sins: They have forsaken me, the spring of living water, and have dug their own cisterns, broken cisterns that cannot hold water" (2:13). Instead of relying wholly on the Lord as an always-flowing artesian well, the Israelites of Jeremiah's day had opted for a more controllable faith in a more predictable God. They wanted to be in control of their relationship with God, so they built their own religious cisterns. The problem was, they ended up with something other than faith in a god other than Yahweh. The same could now be said for Laodicea.

So, because you are lukewarm—neither hot nor cold—I am about to spit you out of my mouth (Revelation 3:16).

The problem with lukewarm mineral water is that it is good for nothing except as an emetic. When Romans participated in their pagan feasts they were able to continue eating long after they were satiated by drinking lukewarm mineral water, resulting in regurgitation, making room for more food. Jesus is telling the Laodicean believers that they are lukewarm mineral water and good for only one thing. As a result, he is about to vomit them out of his mouth.

The inner spiritual condition of the church at Laodicea was lukewarm. They looked good on the outside but appearances were deceiving. The white cliffs of Hierapolis, formed by overflowing tepid mineral water, were strikingly beautiful, but their impressive appearance belied the fact that the cause was useless lukewarm water. The resulting "deeds" of the Laodiceans were also lukewarm, neither healing nor refreshing. Their apparent success covered the reality of their inner barrenness.

As a result, Jesus is coming to them in a decisive act of "vomiting." He is about to bring judgment to them, but a judgment that will have redemptive potential, if embraced by them.

> You say, "I am rich; I have acquired wealth and do not need a thing" (Revelation 3:17).

What brought about such a desperate state of useless lukewarmness? Their claim, their self-definition, was, "I am rich." They thought of themselves in terms of material wealth, extreme wealth. In fact, they went even further, claiming, "I have acquired wealth," literally "I have made myself rich and will continue to do so." Their boast was of their business acumen, their ability to be successful in the only way the city of Laodicea would recognize. There's clearly nothing wrong with wealth per se. What is fatally wrong is the attitude the success of these Christians led to the idea that "I do not need a thing," or literally, "I have no need." The immense wealth of the believers led to an attitude of self-sufficiency and complacency.

When the Seleucid kings established the city of Laodicea

they gave it a mission to spread the Greek language and culture throughout the area of Phrygia. However, they became so involved with the commercial opportunities presented by their locale they never succeeded in their mission. They learned how to adapt themselves to whatever was necessary to gain wealth and in the process lost their enthusiasm for their assignment. It's now obvious that the same fate befell the church planted in that city.

When the Romans offered assistance after the devastation of the earthquake in AD 60, the citizens of Laodicea felt no need. They had so much wealth in the city they were confident they could rebuild on their own, and took pride in their independent ability to do so. The spirit of arrogant independence eventually found its way into the church, so much so that they lost their sense of neediness, even for the presence of Christ. Their claim, "I am . . . I have . . . I have," shouts their boastful pride and self-sufficiency.

But you do not realize that you are wretched, pitiful, poor, blind and naked (Revelation 3:17).

Although Jesus is aware of their true condition, the believers are completely unaware. The problem with the gradual development of lukewarmness is the blindness to its development. The more the church developed a confidence in their ability to succeed, the more they lost their sense of need. "The Laodiceans may have interpreted their material wealth as a blessing from God and thus have been self-deceived as to their true spiritual state."[184]

Jesus' understanding of their spiritual condition is the exact opposite of theirs. In the view of the Christians, they have no needs. In the view of Jesus, they are "wretched" and "pitiful." These two adjectives summarize the condition of the Laodiceans. The first word means "to be miserable or filled with distress, to be oppressed with a burden," and connotes extreme unhappiness. The second word paints a picture of someone deserving only pity (or mercy). Both adjectives are words of pity, words implying the availability of mercy, not words of anger.

The next three adjectives are reflections of the specific context of Laodicea. They saw themselves as extremely wealthy. *You are poor.* Jesus sees them as beggars living in abject poverty. *You are blind.* Instead of taking advantage of their famous "Phrygian Powder," they have become blind, but unaware of their blindness. *You are naked.* Although famous for their rich garments, they are "covered" with shame. They are poor, blind beggars, standing in their rags along the road needing help, but when the King passes by they only say, "I have no need."

When Jesus healed the man born blind in John 9 he taught the people concerning the true nature of blindness. "For judgment I have come into this world, so that the blind will see and those who see will become blind" (9:39). Jesus came to expose the fact that all people are born spiritually blind and that only he can heal them of their blindness. But to be healed, they must admit they are blind. Unfortunately, the Pharisees missed the point. "What? Are we blind too?" (9:40). In their spiritual pride they refused to "see" their true blindness. Jesus responded, "If you were blind, you would not be guilty of sin; but now that you claim you can see, your guilt remains" (9:41). The ultimate guilt of the Pharisees—the ultimate guilt of the Laodiceans—is to claim they could see when in fact they were blind. Because of their pride and self-sufficiency they were blind to their blindness, stumbling into judgment.

In the same way every person is wretched, pitiful, poor, blind and naked—apart from Christ. The only difference is some "see" it and some don't. Those who are aware of their desperate need and willing to come to Christ to have that need met will see true riches.

> *I counsel you to buy from me gold refined in the fire, so you can become rich* (Revelation 3:18).

Jesus now attempts to reason with the blind Laodiceans. To a city given over entirely to commerce he advises that they make a financial decision. They were to enter into the marketplace of the kingdom of God and make the purchases that would reverse their lukewarm condition. And there was only one possible source for those purchases. "Buy from me" makes it clear that Jesus alone has all the essential items needed by the believers in Laodicea.

The first decision Jesus advises the Laodiceans to make is to purchase "gold refined in the fire." Laodicea was a prosperous banking center known for its deposits of gold. But this was not the kind of gold being referred to by Christ. The church possessed an abundance of material wealth, but they were living in abject poverty. The gold Jesus is providing them has been purified by fire. It is a purity that is attained by removing dross. Gold purified by fire is also referred to in 1 Peter 1:7 where it refers to the trying of one's faith (see also Zechariah 13:9). The image refers to a fiery trial that purifies the faith of the one being tried.

And the purpose of this trial? In order that "you can become rich." Jesus seeks abundance for his people, but a different kind of wealth than they had been seeking. If they embrace the trials coming their way, they will obtain true riches that will benefit them and others for eternity.

> . . . and white clothes to wear, so you can cover your shameful nakedness (Revelation 3:18).

Laodicea was famous for its manufacture of sleek, black clothing. No doubt the members of the church had their share of those garments, but from Jesus's point of view, they were naked. Instead of black garments, Jesus advises them to buy from him the white garments that only he can provide. As with the righteous remnant in Sardis (3:4, 5) white garments represent the robes of righteousness washed in the blood of the Lamb. They are the garments of the overcomer (see Revelation 6:11; 7:9; 19:14).

The purpose of this purchase was to keep their shame from being revealed. The Jewish view of nakedness always involved shame. Nakedness involved disgrace brought by divine judgment. Every human being is born in sin and shame. The Laodicean believers have lost sight of their disgrace. Jesus came to cover their shame. The only way the

Laodiceans can avoid a revelation of their disgrace is if they buy white garments from Jesus. Jesus alone can remove their shame.

> . . . *and salve to put on your eyes, so you can see* (Revelation 3:18).

The local medical school was famous for their success in treating diseases of the eye. They were no doubt confident in their ability to treat eyes and keep them healthy. In the midst of that situation the Christian believers were blind, and worse yet, blind to their blindness. Jesus now advises them to buy an eye-salve that only he can provide.

Jesus reveals a special treatment for their blindness. They must not only make the decision to buy it from Jesus, they must apply or "anoint" their eyes with the salve. Indeed, it is a Holy Spirit eye-salve. It is an anointing that will bring them a "Spirit of wisdom and revelation" (Ephesians 1:17). It will give them insight into the things that only the Spirit can show them (see 1 Corinthians 2:9, 10).

Jesus has revealed to the Laodiceans their unique need: they are poor, naked and blind. He has also revealed to the church the only solution to their need. "There is only one way open to it. It must cease to trust to itself. It must be recognized that it is poor, and seek riches where the true riches can be found."[185] He alone possesses those things that will bring them back to a place of true riches, righteousness and revelation.

Their Need	The Prescription	The Result
You are poor	Buy from me gold refined in the fire	You will be rich
You are naked	Buy from me white garments to cover yourself with	Your shameful nakedness will not be exposed
You are blind	Buy from me salve to anoint your eyes with	You will see

Ultimately, Jesus Christ himself is all they need. If they see Jesus, they will have true vision. If they have a relationship with Christ, they will be truly wealthy. If they are clothed with his righteousness, they will never know shame again. "The Lord would teach the church that the true wealth, the true raiment, the true wisdom, the true vision is Himself possessed in all the aspects of His perfection."[186] The ultimate revelation of the mystery of God is—Christ, and Christ alone (see Colossians 1:27; 2:2; 4:3).

Those whom I love I rebuke and discipline (Revelation 3:19).

Even though Laodicea has become useless, if not nauseating, Jesus declares his love for them. He not only loves them, he likes them.[187] He does not threaten judgment; he calls them to repentance. And he promises to "rebuke" them and "discipline" them. The word translated "rebuke" means "to convict, or refute; to point out a problem and convince the person to do something about it." It's the same word that refers to the "conviction" of the Holy Spirit in John 16:8. Indeed, the conviction of the Spirit is the first step toward repentance and restoration. The word translated "discipline" means "correction that has as its goal the training and guiding of the individual." It is used to describe the training of children or of education in general. This is the same word used in Hebrews 12:6, "The Lord disciplines those he loves, and he punishes everyone he accepts as a son."

Because the Lord loves the believers in Laodicea, he is committed to their correction and training. Because he is a Father to his beloved children, he will do what is necessary to see them flourish, and that means discipline (see Proverbs 3:11–12). Some have speculated that the church at Laodicea had experienced little in the way of discipline since there is no mention of any trials, persecution or opposition, from within or without. Because Jesus loves them, that is about to change. And if they will embrace his discipline, it will lead them to repentance and back to the truth (see 2 Timothy 2:25).

So be earnest, and repent (Revelation 3:19).

Therefore, what is the conclusion to the matter? What is the solution to the dilemma in Laodicea? First of all, they must "be earnest," that is, be zealous, be passionate, show a warm interest in Christ and his concern for the city of Laodicea. The believers must first move from their luke-warmness and return to a condition of spiritual heat and zeal. They had been passionate about their own success. Now they need to return to a new enthusiasm for Jesus.

If they do, it will lead them to a sincere decision to repent, to turn back to Christ and his purpose for their mission in Laodicea. As with Ephesus, Pergamum, Thyatira and Sardis, the cure to their backsliding is sincere, heart-felt repentance. "The way back to blessing will be that the church should get down into the dust, into the place of humbling, into the place of heart-break,"[188] into the place of repentance. This is the only true cure to anyone's backsliding. We must take the time to repent, to acknowledge our backsliding, and turn back to God with all our being.

Here I am! I stand at the door and knock (Revelation 3:20).

Jesus now draws the attention of the Laodiceans to himself. "Behold!" Jesus is about to offer the believers himself, his presence, and he wants them to be fully aware of that offer.

"I have been standing at the door." Jesus has been with them from the beginning, and he is still with them. But the tragedy is the picture of Jesus standing on the outside of the door. At some point in time Jesus moved from the inside to the outside, the real cause of their lukewarmness. "I am knocking." Unlike the Roman officials who demanded the right of hospitality, Jesus patiently waits on the outside. He is not waiting passively; he is actively knocking, inviting a response.

This picture is similar to the one described in the Song of Solomon. The Shulamite admits, "I slept" (5:2), but while asleep she hears her beloved. "Listen! My lover is knocking."

And the Lover sings an invitation: "Open to me, my sister, my darling, / my dove, my flawless one." In the same way, Jesus calls to his bride to not leave him out in the cold, to open to him.

> *If anyone hears my voice and opens the door, I will come in and eat with him, and he with me* (Revelation 3:20).

Jesus has been knocking all along, but the Laodicean believers have not heard his knock. They aren't even aware that they have moved Jesus to the fringes of their lives. A heart of repentance will restore sufficient spiritual hearing to make them aware of his patient, incessant knocking.

They must make a new commitment to hear. They must push the envelope of their sensitivity to Jesus. He's not shouting to them. He's not attempting to beat the door down. He's just patiently knocking. They have to move beyond listening for his voice to listening to any movement he might be making. They must draw near with all their hearts.

And they must make a decision to respond to his knock. This is a unique door. "The door has no latch on the outside. It can only be opened from the inside."[189] They must take the step of opening the door. It's not enough to take the time to listen. There must be an active response. They must give Jesus access to their lives in a new and personal way. They must turn from their self-satisfaction to the place where only Jesus can satisfy.

If they do, Jesus will take it from there. He will come in to them. Indeed, he is not the one who has been resistant to ongoing intimacy. He has been there all along. All he needs is an opening and he will come to them with arms opened wide.

More than that, Jesus will include them in a special time of "table fellowship."[190] This is a reference to the main meal of the day and the daily time of family fellowship. (This is also the same word as that used in Luke 22:20 and 1 Corinthians 11:25 to refer to the "Lord's supper.") "Table fellowship" was a very important part of eastern culture. It was a meal of covenant relationship. It was a meal of reconciliation. The "supper" communicated acceptance, sharing and blessing, a time of deep, intimate fellowship. Jesus here offers the luke-warm Laodiceans a return to intimate fellowship with him, perhaps even greater intimacy than they've ever known. "What was missing was the passion—the passion to press on into greater intimacy and knowledge of God."[191]

In fact, this is the only solution to their lukewarmness. It seems unlikely that one could simply decide to be red hot with spiritual passion. That passion would have to be restored in the presence of the Lord. Jesus offers his presence at all times. We are the ones who moved him outside and shut the door. Even then he didn't go away. He continued to stand there, knocking, loving, hoping we would hear and open and return to a life shared with him.

> *To him who overcomes, I will give the right to sit with me on my throne* (Revelation 3:21).

Every member of the church in Laodicea has the possi-bility of overcoming. The enemy to conquer seems obvious. They need to triumph over lukewarmness and all that led to that nauseating state. They must triumph over their self-suf-ficiency and self-satisfaction. They were sent to Laodicea with the prospect of being a community of intimate relation-ships in a city filled with independent people who felt no need for intimacy. They could have been examples of self-giving and self-sacrifice in a city of proud people. But they had squandered their opportunity, absorbed the "strong-holds" of the city, lost their saltiness, and pushed Jesus out in the process.

Now they are being called to repent and overcome. If they do, Jesus promises a gift. He will give them a place with him on his throne. They will sit with him. They will sit in a place of intimate fellowship with him. At the original Lord's supper, John himself had reclined next to Jesus at the table (John 13:23). In a similar way Jesus is offering a permanent place of fellowship to everyone who overcomes their luke-warmness.

More than that, Jesus offers the overcomers a place of

authority. They will not just be sitting next to Jesus at the banquet table, they will be sitting in a place of intimacy with him on his throne. Jesus had promised the Twelve that they would sit on twelve thrones (Matthew 19:28). This promise is greater than that. The overcomers will sit with Jesus on his throne. This is a throne of dignity and judicial authority (see 1 Corinthians 6:2f). They will reign in life through Jesus Christ (cf. Romans 5:17), and they will share in his triumphant glory in his eternal kingdom.

> *. . . just as I overcame and sat down with my Father on his throne* (Revelation 3:21).

Jesus as the ultimate Overcomer, the final Victor—the Christus Victor—is the great theme of the book of Revelation. Jesus has already overcome, winning the victory in his death on the cross (see Colossians 2:15). Jesus told his disciples at the last supper, "I have overcome the world" (John 16:33).

When Jesus was raised from the dead and ascended into heaven he sat down at the right hand of the Father (see Ephesians 1:20; Hebrews 1:3; 8:1; 12:2). Jesus shares the throne of the Father. He alone has all authority, in heaven and on earth (see Matthew 28:18).

The great enthronement Psalm 110 is no doubt in view. "The LORD says to my Lord, / sit at my right hand / until I make your enemies / a footstool for your feet" (verse 1). The Father had sent his Son into the world to save the world, but he had also sent his Son to be its King. "The LORD will extend your mighty scepter from Zion; / you will rule in the midst of your enemies" (verse 2). Even as the Lamb of God, Jesus ruled as the Lion of Judah.

"Therefore God exalted him to the highest place / and gave him the name that is above every name, / that at the name of Jesus every knee should bow, / in heaven and on earth and under the earth, / and every tongue confess that Jesus Christ is Lord" (Philippians 2:9, 10). Jesus is enthroned in the very glory of God. But his ascent to that place involved making "himself nothing" (verse 7), humbling himself and becoming obedient to the point of "death on a cross" (verse 8).

Because Jesus is ruling now, we too can and will rule. But we will rule from a position of intimacy, out of a relational flow of life and love, not from self-made wealth and power.

He who has an ear, let him hear what the Spirit says to the churches (Revelation 3:22).

In some ways the promise to the overcomers at the end of this letter can be applied to every one of the seven churches—and to all of our churches today. There is a vital need to hear what the Spirit is saying to us today. If we would rule with Christ, we must find a place of intimate dependence in his presence. Finding our own place of power and success instead will just make us lukewarm mineral water.

The Key of Brokenness

Understanding the extent of their neediness was the key to overcoming in Laodicea. Like every human being they were all essentially blind, poor and disgraced. Being willing to admit that required more humility than they could muster. As a very wealthy, successful congregation they didn't feel the need they still had—in fact, they were genuinely unaware of it—and therefore were not able to confess it. And without a deep understanding of their need, intimacy with Christ would not be possible.

What would it take for them to return to a place of humble responsiveness to the Lord? The prophet Hosea exhorted the people to "break up your unplowed ground" (10:12). What is brokenness, why is it important, and how can we see the power of it working in our lives?

Brokenness can lead us back to a love relationship with God. In a time of trial the Psalmist confessed, "I have become like broken pottery" (31:12). His life was like a clay jar smashed on the ground. But instead of bitterness his response was, "But I trust in you, O LORD; / I say, 'You are my God. / My times are in your hands'" (31:14, 15). His experience of brokenness led him to a deeper faith and trust in the Lord. David sang that his confession of sin and humble repentance was like breaking his bones. Yet, "Let me hear joy and gladness; / let the bones you have crushed rejoice" (Psalm 51:8). Rejoicing would follow brokenness when combined with true repentance. He went on to declare, "The sacrifices of God are a broken spirit; / a broken and contrite heart, / O God, you will not despise" (51:17). A deep relationship with God is unlikely apart from brokenness.

When Simon the Pharisee invited Jesus to his house for the evening meal he failed to show him the common courtesies due a guest (Luke 7:36ff). Into that situation came a woman, a known "sinner" in the community, who was weeping so hard her tears fell on the feet of Jesus. She responded by wiping Jesus's feet with her hair and kissing his feet. She then broke a very expensive jar of perfume, pouring the contents over Jesus's feet. When the Pharisees grumbled about Jesus allowing a sinner to touch him, he responded with a parable. One man owed a moneylender five hundred denarii (a silver coin worth a day's wage) and another fifty. The moneylender cancelled the debt of both men. Which one loved him more?

Jesus was explaining the love response of the sinful woman. However, he was also speaking ironically. Every person has sinned against the Lord equally. For that reason, every person is guilty of an infinite degree of sin. Everyone is forgiven equally. Everyone is in a position to love the Lord with a deep, passionate love. Simon was just as much a sinner as the woman. He just didn't know it—or was not willing to "see" it. As a result, only the woman heard the words, "Your sins are forgiven."

None of us are any more or less a sinner than anyone else. Grace comes to those who see their need, are willing to acknowledge it and then respond from the heart.

Brokenness is poverty of spirit. When Jesus began his Sermon on the Mount, he started by pronouncing important blessings, the first one being, "Blessed are the poor in spirit, for theirs is the kingdom of heaven" (Matthew 5:3). What a wonderful blessing, to be promised an inheritance in the kingdom of God! But what does it mean to be "poor in spirit"? Most commentators would agree that this kind of poverty is a profound, deep sense of one's neediness apart from Christ. To the extent we are convinced deep in our hearts that we are utterly undone apart from Christ, we are poor in spirit. If we really understand that without Christ we can do nothing (see John 15:5), have nothing and are nothing, we are poor in spirit.

Luke's version of this beatitude is, "Blessed are you who are poor, for yours is the kingdom of God" (6:20). The phrase "in spirit" does not modify poverty for Luke. It's true that those who, in every way, have nothing, are more conscious of their neediness. It's easier for them to have a humble response to the Lord and to acknowledge their need for him at every point in their lives. That response results in potential intimacy. However, pride and the tendency toward self-sufficiency are universal human weaknesses. It's possible to be poor and still be proud, to resist turning to Christ. For that matter, it's possible to be genuinely humble and not pursue intimacy.

By his grace God may allow us to experience things that will focus attention on our need for him and give us an opportunity to lean more heavily on him. But is it possible to be wealthy and successful and still be profoundly aware of our neediness? Obviously Abraham and David, or even Noah and Job, would answer in the affirmative. But it might be a less automatic response. It would be necessary to meditate regularly on the pre-eminence of Jesus Christ in all areas of life. It would require a regular examination of values to discern the difference between those that are transitory and those that are transcendent. Poverty of spirit—brokenness— can be consciously cultivated by anyone. And the benefit? The possibility of growing relational intimacy with Christ.

Brokenness is a complete dependence on God's grace. Paul testified to an experience he called "a thorn" in his flesh (2 Corinthians 12:7). He said God sent it to him "to keep me from becoming conceited." No one agrees on what that thorn was, but it was clearly uncomfortable. Paul prayed three times that God would remove it. I'm sure there was nothing wrong with Paul's faith. If anyone could walk with Christ in a place of brokenness and intimacy it would have been Paul. Yet the Father saw a necessary benefit in the thorn. His response to Paul's request? "My grace is sufficient for you" (12:9).

Transformers

Grace is God's unmerited initiative in our lives. Grace is the favor of God, the resources of God, offered freely to his children. Grace is available to everyone equally, but not everyone avails themselves of grace to an equal extent. There is still something in our nature that wants to earn at least a part of our salvation. To admit that everything we need, everything we must have, and everything we could ever want, can be found in God alone and is available by grace, requires a basic humility, a fundamental brokenness.

The Lord went on to tell Paul, "for my power is made perfect in weakness." This literally means, "power is brought to completion in weakness." The power of God has freest reign in the context of human weakness. God has the greatest access to the life of someone who knows they are weak. As a result, Paul proclaimed, "I will boast all the more gladly about my weaknesses, so that Christ's power may rest on me" (12:9). Paul sought God's glory, not his own. He understood the need for him to decrease in order that God might increase (see John 3:30). "For when I am weak, then I am strong" (12:10). Paul was prepared to exchange even his strength for God's strength in order to see Christ alone exalted in and through his life.

If we are honest, we can admit that all of us have broken areas in our lives. "Ruthless honesty about what is happening inside of us will lead to brokenness."[192] Healing comes, not by covering up, but by opening up and receiving God's grace and love.

Brokenness can be learned in the desert. The Lord gave Jeremiah a very strange revelation of the wilderness journey of Israel. When I read the book of Numbers it sounds like the years spent in the desert were all bad news. But the Lord's perspective was very different. "I remember the devotion of your youth, / how as a bride you loved me / and followed me through the desert, / through a land not sown. / Israel was holy to the LORD, / the firstfruits of his harvest" (Jeremiah 2:2, 3). The Lord viewed Israel's wilderness experience as a period of engagement. Israel was betrothed to the Lord in the desert. To me it looked like a time of murmuring and judgment, but that represents the narrow viewpoint of the rebels in the nation. God had a different perspective.

For God the wilderness was an idyllic time. It was difficult and uncomfortable. But it was a circumstance that created the possibility of growing intimacy. Why? Because the people were forced to be dependent on the Lord alone for everything. They depended on him for "angels' food" and water out of the rock. They even relied on the Lord to keep their clothing from wearing out. And the reality of dependence created the possibility of intimacy.

All of us go through wilderness experiences. At times we might just experience a sense of "dryness." When we do we usually focus our faith on asking God to get us out as quickly as possible. Maybe we should allow that time of dependence to push us into the arms of the Father. We might be well advised to allow our dryness, our experience of "thirst," to motivate us to come to the Lord for a fresh drink of living water. The end of the Revelation gives an invitation to those who have heard and acted on the word. "Whoever is thirsty, let him come; and whoever wishes, let him take the free gift of the water of life" (22:17). "Brokenness is realizing He is all we have. Hope is realizing He is all we need. Joy is realizing He is all we want."[193]

Brokenness can be facilitated with "spiritual disciplines." The power of brokenness is that it leads us to greater grace. "But he gives us more grace. God . . . gives grace to the humble" (James 4:6). Anything that has the possibility of producing a humble response in us creates the potential for more grace. A right approach to spiritual disciplines as "means of grace" can enable a life filled with grace.

A classic example is fasting. The Psalmist testified, "I humbled my soul with fasting" (35:13 NAS). It's possible to dedicate time to prayer and fasting as an expression of our neediness. It can be a way of reminding us that we need the Lord alone, to let hunger focus our attention on our dependence on God. Unfortunately, it's possible to approach fasting as a "hunger strike," an attempt to manipulate God into doing what we want him to do, or just to impress the Lord with our spirituality. In that case, we have completely missed the point. (Other spiritual disciplines can function in much the same way.)

Brokenness can be thwarted. In Jeremiah's day it was the ministry of false prophets to circumvent brokenness. "They have healed the brokenness of My people superficially, / Saying, 'Peace, peace,' / But there is no peace" (Jeremiah 6:14 NAS; see also 8:11). The true prophet was using the circumstance of the discipline of the Lord to call the people to repentance. But they needed to feel their need to turn to the Lord. To deflect them from that felt need the false prophets preached the blessings of the Lord—"Peace, peace"—even though the Lord was attempting to discipline them. The false prophets maintained their influence by preaching peace, but the avoidance of brokenness would waylay true repentance. As a result, discipline would become judgment.

Brokenness is necessary in order to be made new. At one point the Lord told Jeremiah to go to the potter's house and observe him at work (18:1ff). As he worked, the vessel became marred and therefore useless. In order to make it into another vessel, the potter had to break it and then form it into another pot. The prophet was then moved upon to announce the coming of judgment because of the corruption that had filled the nation. However, after prophesying judgment on the nation, Jeremiah called them to repentance. "If that nation I warned repents of its evil, then I will relent and not inflict on it the disaster I had planned" (18:8).

There are no throw-away vessels. It is always the purpose of God to remake marred vessels into new ones, but that requires a certain response on the part of the vessel. The Lord always responds to genuine, heart-felt repentance, but that kind of repentance rarely occurs apart from brokenness. Without it judgment is inevitable. "He who falls in this stone will be broken to pieces, but he on whom it falls will be crushed" (Matthew 21:44). The one who falls on Christ who is the Rock will be broken. The one who resists will be scattered by the wind like chaff.

The last generation will be a broken generation. At the end of Daniel's visions he saw the final salvation of the people of God (12:1), the resurrection of the dead (12:2), and the eternal glory of the saints (12:3). It's one of the most beautiful pictures of God's eternal plan anywhere in Scripture. Daniel must have been overwhelmed at the thought of it. Then he heard two angels discussing the implications of this end-time revelation. One asked the other, "How long will it be before these astonishing things are fulfilled?" (12:6). The answer is one of the most mysterious messages given in Daniel's book. "When the power of the holy people has been finally broken, all these things will be completed" (12:7). I would have thought the answer might have been, "When the power of the enemies of God has been broken, these things will find their completion." Instead, what is in view is the power of God's people.

The word translated "power" is the Hebrew word "yad," or literally, the "hand" of the holy people. It is a reference to the natural power or strength of the people. God's perfect plan of redemption will be brought to its successful conclusion when the people of God have come to a place of brokenness, when they have learned to no longer trust in their own strength but rather in the strength of God alone. Then and only then will God have free reign to bring his plan and purpose to an end.

A similar picture is painted in Revelation 11. There we see "two witnesses" or "prophets" successfully preaching the gospel with signs following (verses 3f). They are supernaturally protected with fire from heaven. Like Elijah, they are able to keep rain from falling while they prophesy. Like Moses, they can strike the earth with plagues of blood (verse 6). But one very important observation is made of these end-time prophets. While they preach the gospel with power, they do so "clothed in sackcloth" (verse 3). In other words, their posture is one of humility, repentance and mourning. They are a powerful, overcoming generation. But they are first and foremost a broken generation. They understand their desperate need for God and for grace and preach from a position of self-forgetfulness. They succeed in bringing the work of the gospel to a victorious end, and then they give their lives as the ultimate witness (verse 7).

We want to be a powerful generation. But are we willing to pay the price?

Even now, in our normal daily lives, we need to hear this message. We need the Lord! Every moment of every day! He is our hope. He is our strength. "Those who wait for the Lord / Will gain new strength [change and renew their strength and power, Amp.]; / They will mount up with wings like eagles, / They will run and not get tired, / They will walk and not become weary" (Isaiah 40:31 NAS). He who has ears to hear, let him hear.

The Message of the Letter to Laodicea

I'm not comfortable with the view that the "modern church" or the "American church" is the Laodicean church, or that we find ourselves trapped in some kind of "Laodicean Age." At the same time, the message of the letter to the Laodiceans has clear relevance to a prosperous congregation in an affluent society. We would do well to heed its warning and apply the principles involved to our own specific context.

The Challenge of Material Wealth

If there's one thing that stands out about Laodicea it is its wealth. They were materially rich, very aware of it, and proud of it. According to G. Campbell Morgan, "The one great peril threatening the church at Laodicea was its wealth."[194] They obviously attached more value to material wealth than God does, and that error led them to self-satisfaction and spiritual lukewarmness.

First of all, Scripture is clear that God is our faithful provider. One of the covenant names for God is "The LORD Will Provide" (Genesis 22:14). The Lord promised to bless his people with abundant provision (Psalm 132:15). Paul was clear that "my God will supply all your needs according to His riches in glory in Christ Jesus" (Philippians 4:19 NAS).

At the same time, God's material provision has only temporary value. It is morally neutral and is either good or evil depending on how it is used. To place a higher value on wealth than God does is idolatry. "You cannot serve God and wealth" (Matthew 6:24).

Some people have more than enough provision. They are the "wealthy" among us. Some people don't have enough provision. These are the "poor" among us. After giving many just laws to Israel, Moses told them, "There will always be poor people in the land" (Deuteronomy 15:11). Both poverty and riches come from the Lord (1 Samuel 2:7).

One of the reasons why God would give some more than enough is so they could share with those who don't have enough. The way the people treat the poor is very important to God. "Do not be hardhearted or tightfisted toward your poor brother" (Deuteronomy 15:7). The Law called for great care and sensitivity toward the poor. They were to be paid at the end of the day and nothing done to threaten their livelihood (Deuteronomy 24:12–15). No interest was to be charged for money loaned to the poor (Exodus 22:25; Leviticus 25:35–38). Redemption is provided for those who fall onto hard times (Leviticus 25:25–27).

The Lord himself looks out for the interest of the poor (Psalm 68:10; 72:13; 112:9; 113:7; 140:12). The prophets declared the judgment of God against those who did not care for the poor (Isaiah 1:17; 3:14, 15; 10:1–3; 11:4; 58:7, 8). Generosity toward the poor was a distinctive of the New Testament church (Acts 4:37; Romans 15:26; 2 Corinthians 8:2–4; Galatians 2:10; James 2:2–6).

Human nature makes it difficult for the rich to be truly humble before the Lord. When the man with great wealth asked about getting eternal life, Jesus discerned his undue attachment to his riches, and advised him, "If you want to be perfect, go, sell your possessions and give to the poor, and you will have treasure in heaven. Then come, follow me" (Matthew 19:21). When he could not, Jesus concluded, "It is easier for a camel to go through the eye of a needle than for a rich man to enter the kingdom of God" (19:24). At one point Jesus went so far as to say, "Woe to you who are rich, for you have already received your comfort" (Luke 6:24). In a parable Jesus described the fruitless, self-centered life and death of a rich man and concluded, "This is how it will be with anyone who stores up things for himself but is not rich toward God" (Luke 12:21).

The apostles understood the challenge of material wealth. One of the qualifications of local church elders was that they not be "a lover of money" (1 Timothy 3:3). Paul prophesied that in the last days, "people will be lovers of themselves, lovers of money" (2 Timothy 3:2). The writer to the Hebrews exhorted them, "Keep your lives free from the love of money and be content with what you have" (13:5). James advised the rich man to not take pride in his riches, "because he will pass away like a wild flower" (1:10, 11). He also warned the rich to not misuse their wealth or place too high a value on it (5:1–5).

Paul's advice was "contentment" in every situation. "I know what it is to be in need, and I know what it is to have plenty. I have learned the secret of being content in any and every situation, whether well fed or hungry, whether living in plenty or in want" (Philippians 4:12). To Timothy he advised, "Godliness with contentment is great gain. For we brought nothing into the world, and we can take nothing out. But if we have food and clothing, we will be content with that" (1 Timothy 6:6–8).

The Laodiceans not only attached an inordinate value to material wealth, they took their error one step further: they promoted "the fallacy that material success is synonymous with blessing."[195] It wasn't that they were wealthy; it was that they drew a false conclusion from their wealth. To the Laodiceans, the fact that they were wealthy indicated that the blessing of the Lord was upon them. And if the Lord was blessing them, they must be spiritually healthy.

Evidently there were those in Ephesus in Paul's day who had made the same mistake. As a result, Paul concluded, "the love of money is a root of all kinds of evil. Some people, eager for money, have wandered from the faith and pierced themselves with many griefs" (1 Timothy 6:10). He didn't respond by commanding the rich to sell all their goods and give the money to the poor, but he did have important counsel for them:

> Command those who are rich in this present world not to
> be arrogant nor to put their hope in wealth, which is so
> uncertain, but to put their hope in God, who richly pro-
> vides us with everything for our enjoyment. Command

them to do good, to be rich in good deeds, and to be gen-
erous and willing to share. In this way they will lay up
treasure for themselves as a firm foundation for the com-
ing age, so that they may take hold of the life that is truly
life (1 Timothy 6:17–19).

George Barna uncovered the fact that in 1968 American evangelical Christians gave an average of 6.15% of their income to the church. By the year 2001, those evangelicals had greatly increased their average household income, but their giving had fallen to an average of 4.27%. By the year 2002, 6% of born-again American Christians tithed, a 50% decrease from 2000. "As we got richer and richer, evangelicals chose to spend more and more on themselves and give a smaller and smaller percentage to the church."[196] If there was ever a time the message of the letter to Laodicea needs to be heard, it is now.

The Challenge of Consumer Christianity

Placing a false value on material wealth and the misuse of wealth results in what Jack Hayford calls "me-ism." "We need to come to terms with the fact that material success is not synonymous with blessing. Let that sink in deep. And let us recognize the 'me-ism' that occupies the Church."[197] "Me-ism" is viewing the church and the Christian faith with me at the center. It's all about getting my needs met.

How many times have I heard the question, "Are you going to the service tomorrow? Who's preaching? Who's leading in worship?" We're not assembling together because we have important covenant relationships with brothers and sisters; we're "going to church" because of the possibility it might be somewhat entertaining. We don't come together "in his name" because it is an important spiritual discipline and a command of Scripture, but because we might run into some of our friends.

Why do so many people leave the church—excommunicate themselves—in today's church? In my experience it's often, "Because I'm not being fed"—as if being fed, having my needs met, is the only reason why I would participate in the Body of Christ.

Modern commentators have often noted the American "mall" approach to doing church. When an American Christian goes "shopping" for a local church, it's about what programs are being offered, how user friendly the worship service is, the availability of parking, or the condition of the carpet. We have to lure people in by offering the best deal in town. Consumerism is not only the driving force in our society as a whole, it's become the driving force in the church as well.

If there had been multiple congregations in Laodicea I can easily imagine that this mindset would have been at work. Instead, a church filled with needy, poor-in-spirit believers would have been excited about any opportunity to worship God together, any context in which they could serve in and with a faith community.

The Challenge of Compassionate Christianity

The alternative to commercial Christianity would be compassionate Christianity. Compassionate Christians would be looking for opportunities to serve and not be driven by whether or not their personal needs were being met. A Jesus church will be passionate about representing him at every opportunity.

Toward the end of his ministry Jesus taught a parable about the final judgment. At one point he is seen pronouncing, "Depart from me, you who are cursed, into the eternal fire prepared for the devil and his angels" (Matthew 25:41). Who was he talking about? Why were they being judged? What was his complaint against them? "I was hungry and you gave me nothing to eat, I was thirsty and you gave me nothing to drink, I was a stranger and you did not invite me in, I needed clothes and you did not clothe me, I was sick and in prison and you did not look after me" (25:42, 43). If we heard those words I'm sure we would be shocked. We love Jesus, but we've never seen him. How is it possible to not have met his needs? If we had seen him we would have gladly done anything he might have asked of us.

"I tell you the truth, whatever you did not do for one of the least of these, you did not do for me" (25:45). The infinite, selfless love Jesus has for all people is to be seen among his covenant people. If we love him, if we have a real give-and-take love relationship with the one who is "Love," that love will be seen in us. And it will be seen most specifically toward the least and the lost among us.

Because the Laodiceans were supremely self-satisfied, because they felt no need, they saw no need. I'm sure they were as insensitive to the needs of others as they were to their own needs. On the other hand, a broken people are a compassionate people, freely giving of themselves to others.

The Challenge of Authentic Community

According to David Ravenhill, the core issue in Laodicea was relational. Much like Ephesus, while they were "successful" in every way, the passion of God's love was missing. "The 'life' of most churches revolves around the numerous activities, not to mention their facilities. What was missing in Laodicea was what is missing in many congregations—relationship."[198] That missing ingredient was seen first in their relationship with Christ. Jesus is seen standing outside of the door, knocking, seeking admittance. And they didn't seem to really miss his presence. "Today, more than ever, we have learned how to 'excel' without the abiding presence of God in our midst. With our slick marketing techniques, professional staff, and motivational speaking, we are able to operate successfully without God."[199]

In fact, their self-satisfaction made intimacy impossible. When you think about it, true intimacy requires a significant level of vulnerability. Being vulnerable requires us to be open and transparent, ready to give and receive love in the midst of our brokenness. What the world is seeking more than anything else is authentic community. Just being a Christian church does not guarantee that we are a real community. Authentic community requires vulnerability, commitment, and the presence of God.

In *The Safest Place on Earth,* Dr. Larry Crabb defines community this way:

> A spiritual community consists of people who have the integrity to come clean. We must admit to our community . . . who we are at our worst. We must tell our stories to someone without consciously leaving out a chapter. The response of community comes next. If the response is anything less than unconditional love, our brokenness becomes fragmentation.
>
> A spiritual community, a church, is full of broken people who turn their chairs toward each other because they know they cannot make it alone. These broken people journey together with their wounds and worries and washouts visible, but are able to see beyond the brokenness to something alive and good, something whole.[200]

For that level of authentic community to be possible, the members of the community must each be convinced of their neediness—their need for God and their need for each other. The atmosphere of such a community will be one of unconditional love and acceptance. It will be a safe place for anyone and everyone to find healing and wholeness. "A central task of community is to create a place safe enough for the walls to be torn down, safe enough for each of us to own and reveal our brokenness. Only then can community be used of God to restore our souls."[201] Only the atmosphere of unconditional love can liberate us and empower us to be transformed.

As a Christian counselor Crabb has become convinced that vulnerable, committed relationships in an authentic community is the only environment in which true healing and transformation can take place. He wrote, "[It] is my growing conviction that all substantial change depends on people experiencing a certain kind of relationship."[202] The apostle Paul wrote that we are all built up and grow "by every supporting ligament," that is, by our relational connections, "as each part does its work" (Ephesians 4:16). "We yearn for intimacy. We were made for community . . . and to the degree we experience it, we change, we grow, we heal."[203]

The Laodicean believers could have never known authentic community. They were too self-sufficient. Perhaps answering the call to enter into intimacy with Christ would have set the stage for their own transformation into a safe place of healing. May it be true for all of us.

The Story of Life Center

(As told by Pastor Derrill Corbin.) During my years at Portland Bible College, a number of things were placed in my heart—one thing in particular was a love for the local church. Having grown up in the church, I always loved being involved in its ministry efforts, but I never really understood the church as the final instrument of God to fulfill His purpose in the earth as I do today. As my understanding of God's intent (see Ephesians 3) deepened, my love for the body of Christ increased. As my love for the church increased, my passion to plant and pastor a local congregation became stronger and stronger.

During a prophetic gathering in Portland, Oregon, at City Bible Church in May, 1996, God spoke specifically to me that I could have what I wanted. I knew in my heart that God was speaking of a city to pioneer a dynamic work in. I went to a map and began to circle communities in southwest Washington that I knew needed a good church. As I circled various towns and cities, one thing became apparent to me—we needed to plant a community-oriented church with a regional focus, not just a little inward focused group of believers.

With over twenty towns and cities circled on my map, I noticed that "Centralia" was right in the middle of all my little dots. As I began researching the city more, I realized it was called "Hub City" in its early days, and is known for its central location. As far as I was concerned, the course was set and the vision was clear—we would plant a church that would reach an entire region, not just one town.

Many circumstances ensued, including graduation from college, marriage, full-time employment at CBC, and gaining eldership approval for this new venture. On August 17, 1997, we launched what is now a thriving church in Centralia, WA. With just over twenty-five people from the community present on that first Sunday, we began to worship, celebrate and proclaim the breadth of our vision for Southwest Washington. I had a strong burden from the Lord that I was not only to pastor Life Center, but I was also to pastor our city.

Centralia was known for its low economic status and high divorce rate. The attitude we encountered regularly was, "Why Centralia?" It quickly became our passion to change that attitude. We received a word from the Lord that "money would never be a problem, and we would be used to raise the economic standard of the city." We also believed that in time, we would turn the tide of marriages in our region. It was a large vision, but we knew we had a word, so our faith was strong.

The little group began to grow in numbers and in understanding of God's purpose and vision for the local church and its part in this region. We preached about God's plan for the body of Christ, His future return for a spotless bride, and the work of the five-fold ministry today. We established ourselves as an equipping house with a passion to REACH the hurting and the lost, RESTORE them by the washing of God's Word, and RELEASE them to fulfill their God-given destiny.

In the first year, we purposed to make ourselves known to the area with name recognition. We advertised in the newspaper, prayer-walked every major neighborhood, and hung over 3,000 door hangers, offering prayer for any need that anyone had. We prayed regularly over the city and region in both our corporate services, and special early-morning prayer meetings, which were attended by nearly 1/2 of the church family.

Purpose-filled outreach was one thing we did and continue to do. Our first free oil change day for single mothers turned out to be a huge success. Over forty moms were served lunch, kids enjoyed clowns and fire trucks, and cars were serviced by the people in the church. All supplies were donated from local businesses, and the church was able to experience hands-on community ministry for its first time collectively. This first major outreach took place within the first twelve months of the church's birth. After that, these oil change days took place at least yearly.

One Sunday, while preaching through Ephesians and looking at the house of the Lord in Paul's great epistle, we took a check for $2,000 (which for us was like $1,000,000) to another local church and presented it to them at the end of their service. The church clapped and shouted, and the leaders responded very well, believing God was truly up to something big in our area. The statement we were attempting to make was, "We want to work together as a team, and we will put our money where our mouth is."

Our strategic outreach efforts have included neighborhood clean-up days, work on people's homes, various community service projects, grocery drop-offs at holiday times, giving a significant contribution of finances to every local church building project that we're aware of, leading community worship events that have drawn hundreds, and focusing on prayer for other churches during our corporate worship and prayer time every week.

Our philosophy of outreach is based in the parable of the sower. Scripture declares plainly that seed must be sown—that is the job of the one who has seed. We believe that in due season we will reap, so we must "sow now" what we hope to reap in the future. We have built a mindset in our church that every door-hanger is a seed, every dollar is a seed, every kind act is a seed, and every prayer is a seed. We are truly convinced that the church in the community will have significant impact in time, and we are daily seeing the fruit of this effort.

Over the years, our strategy has also been to meet different needs at different times. More recently, we've begun ministering to a different sub-culture within our city through Friday concert nights. We have seen hundreds come to hear various types of music in a concert venue we call "theRift." This place is a safe place for teens to go one Friday a month and hear local Christian bands and ultimately find a message of hope and life. The concert year culminates with one large event called "Mountain Dew Float Fest" which draws hundreds from the Northwest to a day of music, gospel presentation, and free Mountain Dew Floats.

We have sought to address the problem of dysfunctional marriages and families in a variety of ways. We have formed marriage groups in the Life Center congregation we call "Couples Relationship & Accountability" groups. These groups meet weekly to discuss communication, conflict management, family values, and so on, and are meeting an important need. We are also offering a variety of parenting classes for the community. One couple in particular is very gifted in this area. These classes are having a significant influence in our city, forming a new community standard for parenting and relationships.

Recently we networked with fifteen area churches to host the "Celebrate the Family Rally." An organization called Families Northwest partnered with us to conduct an outdoor worship and prayer rally focused on the sanctity of marriage. There were over 1,200 people from the area in attendance. An older man from the congregation and I are also teaching a class for fathers in our local college. The director of the Family and Parenting department of the community college visited our church and observed the relationships between parents and children and asked us to teach a parenting class for fathers. There has been a very positive response to our class.

Our future outreach plans include free music lessons for kids, after school tutoring programs, and a transitional shelter for the abused, battered, and drug addicted. Our vision is to meet the REAL needs of today's families by "Building a family-friendly community relevant to the 21st century."

The equipping ministry of the church continues to expand regionally as well. We have seen people coming from several surrounding communities. Many drive more than a half hour to be here multiple times each week.

Our strategy as a regional church is to develop satellite campuses in 6 surrounding communities. These locations will be focused on leading recovery groups, pastoral care ministry, and outreach ministry into various neighborhoods and communities. Sunday morning, we will continue to have a large hub of dynamic worship and word which meets together in one location, but all mid-week activity will take place in various locations around the region.

We've currently laid the groundwork for this by splitting up the region into six districts and appointing a prayer captain over each region. This person is equipped and responsible for praying for the people in that region, taking care of any prayer needs, and alerting others in that region to pray for any pertinent needs.

In phase two of our development, we will train care leaders who will serve the ministry and pastoral needs of each of those regions. Those leaders will begin to draw that region together for fellowship and prayer and outreach ministry. As that group grows, we will purchase buildings in those communities to house the ministries which focus on that community. These community centers will be called "The City of Refuge."

After just seven short years, we can say we have seen dramatic change in the atmosphere of our community. The churches are more unified than ever before. The passion to reach the lost is very evident in many local churches. We are continually seeing economic growth with additional industry coming to the area every year. The Word of the Lord has been true to us—we have never lacked financially, and the economic standard of the city is changing.

CHAPTER TEN:

LISTENING TO THE CHURCH'S CALL:

HAVING EARS TO HEAR

The only phrase that appears in all seven letters to the churches of Asia is, "He who has an ear, let him hear what the Spirit says to the churches" (Revelation 2:7, 11, 17, 29; 3:6, 13, 22). This appears to be the key exhortation of the letters, addressed to the person (singular) who "has an ear." Obviously this is referring to more than the appendage most people have on the sides of their heads. It refers to a spiritual capacity, an attentiveness of heart, to the Holy Spirit. The Spirit is communicating a distinct message to each of the churches, but it is the individual who really hears the message that will gain the long-term benefit of it.

The idea of "hearing" in Scripture means more than our common use of the word. When the Lord wanted to capture the attention of his people he began by saying, "Hear, O Israel" (see Deuteronomy 5:1; 6:4; 20:3; etc.). The Hebrew word being used is *shema*, which refers to more than hearing the sound of a voice but also to hearing the meaning of the message. It implies a certain active quality of listening, not passive or selective listening. It involves listening with a prior commitment to obey whatever is heard.

The same idea is found in the New Testament. Jesus told parables to test the hearing of his listeners (see Mark 4:33). He pronounced a blessing on the Twelve because of the quality of their hearing. "But blessed are . . . your ears, because they hear" (Matthew 13:16). The Greek word *akouo* has the same sense as the Hebrew parallel. This is made clear by combining the preposition *hupo* ("under") with *akouo*, resulting in the verb *hupakouo*, the word for "obedience." An active response of "hearing under" will naturally result in obedience.

The hardness of heart that resulted in spiritual hearing loss was long a concern of biblical authors. Moses acknowledged that the Lord had not given Israel "a heart to know . . . nor ears to hear" (Deuteronomy 29:4). When he was commissioned Isaiah was told that the people would be unable to "hear with their ears" (Isaiah 6:10; see also Matthew 13:15; Mark 8:18; Acts 28:27; Romans 11:8). Jeremiah prophesied to a "senseless people . . . who have ears but do not hear" (Jeremiah 5:21), to a people whose "ears are closed and they cannot listen" (6:10). Ezekiel was also sent to "a rebellious house" who have "ears to hear but do not hear" (Ezekiel 12:2). "And though the Lord has sent all his servants the prophets to you again and again, you have not listened or paid any attention" (Jeremiah 25:4).

On the other hand, there is the promise of accurately perceiving the voice of the Lord. The wise are exhorted to "incline your ear and hear" (Proverbs 22:17). The Lord is willing to heal his people, so that "the ears of those who hear will listen" (Isaiah 32:3). The prophets' ability to communicate the word of the Lord depended on their ability to listen, as the Lord told them, to "hear with your ears, and give attention to all that I am going to show you" (Ezekiel 40:4; 44:5). Jesus continually exhorted his hearers, "He who has ears to hear, let him hear" (Matthew 11:15; 13:43; Mark 4:9, 23; 7:16; Luke 8:8; 14:35).

Jesus was concerned about the quality of hearing on all levels. First, they were to be careful about what they heard. "Consider carefully *what* you hear" (Mark 4:24). Not all knowledge or information is created equal. Some constitutes truth and some error. Discerning the content is vital to the practice of spiritual hearing. They were also to be careful *how* they listened. "Consider carefully how you listen" (Luke 8:18). Not all perception is created equal. Everyone has their own frame of reference. The condition of the heart determines the extent to which real hearing will take place. In the

Parable of the Sower, the seed sown along the path is a picture of hearing the message but not understanding it (Matthew 13:18), resulting in the word being snatched away by the evil one. The seed that fell along rocky soil is a picture of hearing and receiving the word superficially (Matthew 13:20), resulting in a falling away in the face of trouble or persecution. The seed falling among thorns pictures hearing the word but being distracted by the worries of this life (Matthew 13:22), making the word unfruitful. The seed falling on good soil shows us a person hearing and understanding the word and bearing good fruit (Matthew 13:23). All these are descriptions of various ways to hear, different conditions of the human heart. Embracing God's Word in a way that will bear good fruit depends on both what we hear and how we hear it.

All of us share a sincere desire to hear and obey God's voice. We want to understand and embrace every word "that proceeds out of his mouth." His word is our daily food, nourishing our lives and the lives of others. So how can we develop our spiritual hearing? Our fruitfulness in God's kingdom depends on our ability to hear and obey. Exploring the potential of our ability to hear God's voice is one of the most important and beneficial things we can do. Here are some ideas—a place to start (in no particular order).

Garbage In—Garbage Out. Whether we like it or not our brains are very sophisticated computers with a vast capacity to store information. We literally "remember" in 3D, including not only the content but also the sights and sounds and feelings associated with that content. To some extent we are in control of what gets stored in our brains. We can control the quantity and quality of the information (and the effects of that information) in our heads. If we fill our heads with "garbage," our thoughts will tend to revolve around that garbage. To the extent that our minds are being filled with thoughts that are "against the knowledge of God" (see 2 Corinthians 10:3–5) it will be more difficult to "screen" new knowledge in a godly way. It will be more difficult to accurately discern the voice of God. On the other hand, filling our minds with God's thoughts will make the practice of listening to his voice that much easier. If we fill our minds with "whatever is true, whatever is noble, whatever is right, whatever is pure, whatever is lovely, whatever is admirable" (Philippians 4:8), it will be that much easier to discern the pure voice of God.

Take Time to Listen. The prayer practices of the average American Christian (including American pastors) are not that great. Even those who do "pray" regularly tend do more talking than anything else. For many of us prayer is a matter of reminding God of our needs and advising him on what to do about it. It's simply difficult to hear if we don't spend much time listening. One of the best petitions we could present to the Lord is, "Speak, for your servant is listening" (see 1 Samuel 3:10), and then actually take time to listen. If you are like me and have a "Type A" personality, slowing down enough to really listen can be a challenge, to say the least. Cultivating a listening heart must therefore be a high priority. Books on "centering prayer" are very helpful in learning how to deal with a wandering mind and keeping the heart centered on the Lord.

Listening with a Heart of Love. Communication is the heart of any relationship. Ultimately our desire to listen to God is a relational issue. It's all about growing intimacy. A heart filled with genuine love for the Lord will automatically result in greater attentiveness to him. If we love him we will want to hear anything he might have to say to us. As our love grows for him, a life of hearing and obeying will be our passion. A loving heart, a grateful heart, a heart of trust and confidence in God and his love, will greatly facilitate our growing ability to hear and respond to God's voice.

Establish a Listening Atmosphere. Timing is important to truly hearing someone you love. It's not possible to jump into a topic without being prepared for it. If you're too tired or too upset, a better time to talk needs to be found. The same is true in our relationship with the Lord. We need to take the time to establish an atmosphere of listening, and the very best way to do that is worship. When we praise the Lord we build a throne for his presence (see Psalm 22:3). We "tune up" our spirits, our spiritual ears, by fixing our hearts on the

Transformers

Lord in adoration. It's so much easier to stop and listen if we have spent time bowing and worshiping first.

God Has Already Spoken Clearly to You. Being nourished by "every word that comes from the mouth of God" (see Matthew 4:4) must be seen in an overarching, objective context. It's vitally important to "hear" in the context of the revelation already given us by God. God has already spoken to us in a written word and a living word—in Scripture and in the person of Jesus Christ (see Hebrews 1:2–3). This prior, authoritative revelation of God forms the larger context for our hearing. Since the Holy Spirit inspired Scripture, his word to you today will not contradict what he has already revealed. In fact, learning to listen to the voice of the Holy Spirit in Scripture is a lost art. Meditating on Scripture, praying Scripture, responding to Scripture as it truly is, the word of the Lord to us, is our starting place in a life of hearing and obeying.

God's Voice Disguised in Human Voices. God can also speak to us through other people in a variety of ways (see Hebrews 1:1). The Lord has always provided his people with certain "prophets" to communicate a message from him. However, God can speak to you through almost anyone—proven prophet or new believer, young or old, educated or uneducated, male or female, rich or poor, or even (dare I say it) Christian or non-Christian. If God can speak through a donkey, he can speak through any human being he wishes. Knowing that, we are well advised to not reject communication from anyone, no matter how they might say it. If we have ears to hear, we just might discern the voice of God in that human voice.

Non-verbal Communication. Those who study communication in marriage have pointed out that up to 93% of all such communication is non-verbal. The verbal content of a message is just 7% of the actual communication taking place. It's not just the words themselves but the dynamics of the relational context, facial expression, tone of voice, body language, and so on, that determines what is actually being communicated. Since we are made in the image of God, it should be easy to conclude that much of our communication with God is also non-verbal. God speaks to us in many creative ways, not just in words. We have to "listen" to the message God is communicating to us in the depths of our hearts, in our emotional responses (or those of others), in our circumstances, in creation, in the world around us (see Psalm 19:1–4). I believe God is speaking to us all of the time; we just aren't listening. Learning to listen to God's non-verbal communication is an important part of our growing listening skills.

Communication Styles. Not only do we all communicate in a variety of ways, we also have different listening "styles." Gary Chapman has served us well by pointing out our various "love languages." These are simply ways we uniquely and effectively receive communications of love. Our personal temperament and personality type will affect the way we perceive communication. Since the Lord created us, we can assume he understands that about us. Some of us receive communication in pictures, some in concepts, some in intuitive bursts of insight. Some "hear" best in a musical context, some a visual context, some in complete silence. You need to find out how you uniquely hear and then learn to develop that unique sense of hearing.

Wait for Confirmation. No matter how spiritual you are, you don't have a hotline to heaven. Everyone sees "but a poor reflection" (see 1 Corinthians 13:12). Knowing that, God always speaks to us in more than one way. In fact, he has taught us to test all communication "by the testimony of two or three witnesses" (see Deuteronomy 19:15; 1 Corinthians 14:29; 2 Corinthians 13:1; 1 Timothy 5:19; Hebrews 10:28). Especially when making a decision based on your discernment of the voice of the Lord, look for multiple words to come to you in a variety of ways. The Lord is faithful and will make sure he has confirmed his word to you so you can move forward with faith and confidence.

Discern the Fruit of the Word. Part of our discernment must be an evaluation of the fruit of whatever we are "hearing." Is the word producing clarity or confusion? Is it bearing the fruit of peace or anxiety? Is the word encouraging or condemning? The wisdom of heaven is "pure . . . peace-loving, considerate, submissive, full of mercy . . . impartial and sincere" (James 3:17). In other words, it is full of "good fruit," fruit that can be discerned and evaluated.

Be Filled with the Spirit. Your relationship and responsiveness to the Holy Spirit is central to your ability to hear and obey the word of the Lord. We are called to a life-style of being filled with the Spirit (see Ephesians 5:18). All expressions of that relationship—praying in the Spirit, singing in the Spirit, and so on—help to empower our life of listening (see 1 Corinthians 14:15). It's possible to have an experience of being carried along by the Spirit, as in a river (see 2 Peter 1:21). The Holy Spirit can be like "streams of living water" flowing from within (see John 7:37–39). Participating in that "flow" makes it so much easier to hear and obey.

Soften Your Heart. Unfortunately, the human heart, if left to itself, tends to get hard. A hard, unresponsive heart has great difficulty listening to the voice of the Spirit. If a heart gets hard enough, even the desire to hear God's voice fades away. If we really want to cultivate a hearing ear and an obedient heart, we must regularly do whatever is needed to keep our hearts soft (see Hosea 10:12). Being quick to confess and repent, to turn our hearts back to the Father, will keep our hearts soft. Keeping our hearts soft through forgiveness, by refusing to accumulate offenses against others, is vital. The practice of spiritual disciplines—fasting, serving, assembling together, among others—can also keep the ground of our hearts duly plowed.

Renew Your Mind. One of the most important aspects of our growth in grace is the renewing of our minds (see Ephesians 4:22–24; Romans 12:2). The "strongholds" in our minds are patterns of thought that keep our minds imprisoned and alienated from God's thoughts. Systematically tearing down anti-God strongholds and replacing them with pro-God strongholds is not just an educational issue, it is necessary to our ability to accurately hear and respond to God's voice. Every time we discern and apply a word from the Lord, we contribute to a whole new mental structure, a new perspective and attitude. Eventually we will find ourselves thinking God's thoughts after him (without even being consciously aware of it).

Cultivate Obedience. The ability to hear depends significantly on our willingness to obey (see John 7:17). If God were to speak to you, knowing that you would not obey the word, it would be a curse to you. His word is a blessing only if you obey it. In the mercy of God he will only speak to you if he knows you will obey his word. So cultivate obedience. Make a clear determination to do whatever he tells you to do—no matter what.

Step Out of the Boat. Sometimes your commitment to obedience will result in radical moves. In reality, we don't always know what we are hearing, what it means, or what we should do about it. Is Jesus really saying, "Come"? Surely not! Doesn't he know that the circumstances are unfavorable and the timing horrible? But just in case, because we are committed to a life-style of listening, it's best to just step out of the boat (see Matthew 14:29–31). Some kind of "step of faith" is always necessary to our life of hearing. Every act of obedience increases the accuracy of our spiritual hearing. Every act of disobedience dulls our hearing. It would be far better to think we are hearing "Come," step out of the boat and sink, than to hear "Come" and refuse to step out of the boat and be "safe."

Celebrate a Lifetime of Listening. The success of any relationship requires a lifetime commitment. Our communication skills, including listening skills, grow and improve throughout our lives. As we grow, sometimes we will hear accurately and sometimes we won't. It's not a contest. Our egos aren't attached to our spiritual hearing. We're on a journey with Jesus, learning to stay close, listening for his voice. We're committed to a lifetime of growing intimacy with him and are ready to celebrate every lesson learned along the way.

APPENDIX A

Interpreting the Book of Revelation:
Learning How to Wear Apocalyptic Glasses

One of the most important aspects of biblical studies is hermeneutics—the art and science of Bible interpretation. If we were reading a contemporary work in our own language in the context of our own culture, we would have little difficulty interpreting it. In addition, we would need to be reading something in a literary genre we are personally familiar with. Some of us are better than others at interpreting poetry or history or journalism, simply because we have more of a background in those kinds of writing.

The same is true of interpreting Scripture. The Bible was written by at least forty authors, in three languages, spanning sixteen centuries, in a variety of historical and cultural contexts. In addition, the Bible has a great variety of styles of writing, from legal writing to wisdom literature, from Hebrew poetry to historical narrative, from prophetic literature to gospel or epistle. Each of these requires a different interpretive grid. I like to think of it as having a variety of tinted glasses available to put on when needed in order to see more clearly what I'm reading. I have a different set of glasses (mindset, interpretive perspective) on when I'm reading a Psalm than I do when I'm reading one of Paul's epistles.

Perhaps the most interesting and challenging case involves apocalyptic literature. There isn't a lot of apocalyptic writing in the Bible. The latter chapters in Ezekiel and Daniel are good examples in the Old Testament. Obviously the "Apocalypse" or Revelation of John is a full expression of apocalyptic writing in the New Testament. Interpreting these portions of Scripture requires a unique set of glasses. However, I'm convinced that all of the Bible, as God's objective written revelation, is intended to be understood. All we have to do is place ourselves in the original context and the original audience and read and hear God's word in the way it was originally intended to be read.

With that in mind, let me describe our apocalyptic glasses.

First of all, apocalyptic literature took a written form from the beginning. This contrasts with prophetic literature that was spoken first and only later took a written form. For this reason, apocalyptic writing shows a clear written structure. This can actually make apocalyptic writing more "predictable" as a form of literature.

Apocalyptic writing was presented in the form of visions and dreams. Its language was very symbolic and its presentation highly figurative and stylized. The visions usually included an angelic guide communicating information. The images are often very "fantastic," combining elements in an unearthly way. How many times have you actually seen a beast with seven heads and ten horns?

The formalized style of apocalyptic writing makes frequent use of symbolic numbers. The number "7" can be found throughout the vision in a variety of ways. Visions are often arranged in numbered sets (usually in sets of seven). John's "seven seals," "seven trumpets" and "seven bowls" are obvious examples.

The arrangement of visions usually follows a pattern known as "progressive parallelism." There is a repetition of parallel images and visions used to reinforce the message. The key is to discern where the vision ends and then starts over again. Every time a vision repeats there is some form of intensification in the new presentation. In addition, each time a vision is repeated it tends to give us even more details concerning the end, the culmination, of the message. This use of the repetition of parallel images is intended to progressively increase the effect of the message on the reader.

The effect of the message on the hearers / readers is the ultimate function of apocalyptic writing. Apocalypse functions much like poetry, only using graphic images and language. It is designed to capture the mind and imagination of the reader. It intends to move the emotions of the reader, leading to action. Often that action is simply to persevere in the midst of difficulties.

Apocalyptic writing vividly portrays the unseen world that lies behind the actions in the material world. In this way, the sovereign intervention of God in the affairs of humans on behalf of his people is clearly portrayed in a variety of ways. The message is often quite simple: If God is this much in control of big events, how much more can he be in control of our lives now. We can trust him!

Apocalyptic writing always presents the big picture, the cosmic context, of human events. Kingdoms clash, and not just human kingdoms. The kingdom of the world clashes with the Kingdom of God. "Chaos" and "cosmos" conflict from time to time. There are times when it looks as though chaos is winning, Satan is triumphing. In reality, God is always in control. Indeed, just when we are convinced Satan has won the day, God's greatest victory is revealed.

For that reason, apocalypse is always a call to action. It presents the sure means by which God's people overcome, leading to final victory.

So, what are the special principles of interpretation that must be kept in mind as we read books like Revelation? What are the elements that go into our apocalyptic glasses?

Seek the author's original intent.[205] The basic mantra of hermeneutics is, "It cannot mean what it could not have meant—to the original author and his original audience." There is no hope of discovering the meaning (and the application) of any passage without being able to place ourselves in the original context. With effort we can do this so effectively we are free to simply hear to the word of the Lord as it was originally intended to be heard.

Don't push the analogy of Scripture too far. The "analogy of Scripture" is a basic principle of hermeneutics that teaches, "Scripture interprets Scripture." It's not enough to identify an Old Testament allusion used, for instance, in John's Revelation, and then bring forward the meaning of that Old Testament passage. John's writing is unique, in a unique context. However, the many passages from the prophetic literature form an overall frame of reference for the Apocalypse.

The symbolic imagery must be interpreted. Apocalyptic symbols are not intended to be representations of reality. They are symbols that need to be interpreted in their context. Remember: some symbols are constant in their meaning while others are more fluid. Some have a specific interpretation, while others have a more general reference. Some key apocalyptic symbols have more than one historical fulfillment. The details of the symbol are not to be allegorized—the apocalyptic symbols usually communicate one simple theme. Fortunately, the author usually interprets the symbol in the context, so that the author's interpretation must be considered the authoritative one.

The eschatological scenes must also be interpreted. Pictures of the future must not be confused with pictures of reality—they are symbols of reality designed to communicate an important spiritual theme. The specific details of a picture do not necessarily have a separate meaning—the picture must be viewed as a whole. Pictures of "the end" are designed to communicate a "not-yet" dimension in the present. Because of the fluid nature of the future scenes, it's best to be cautious and undogmatic about their interpretation.

A detailed chronology is not the intent of an apocalyptic presentation. While God's sovereign control over history is always the point, setting forth a specific timetable is not. In fact, "certainty" is often communicated in terms of "soonness."

Now, having calibrated your apocalyptic glasses, try them on and read the book of Revelation in a new light.

APPENDIX B

The Problem of Gnosticism:

Overcoming Nicolaitans in the First Century (and Every Century)

J esus commended the Ephesian believers for hating the deeds of the Nicolaitans, "which I also hate" (Revelation 2:6). On the other hand he rebuked the believers in Pergamum for having some among them who "hold the teaching of the Nicolaitans" and called them to repent (Revelation 2:15). Jesus hated both their deeds and their teaching. References to "the teaching of Balaam" (Revelation 2:14) and to the prophetic ministry of "Jezebel" (Revelation 2:20) also appear to be references to the deeds and the teaching of the Nicolaitans. Who were these people, and what did they believe?

The church fathers referred to the Nicolaitans as an early group of Christian "Gnostics," established first in Ephesus by a man named Cerinthus. Some claimed they named themselves after the Nicolas of Acts 6:5. It's more likely they simply used the meaning of the name—"to conquer the people"—to indicate their true agenda.

Cerinthus and the Nicolaitans did not invent Gnosticism. Gnostic philosophy and spirituality had been around for hundreds of years. Historians see Gnostic thought in ancient Babylon and Persia. A well-known school of Jewish Gnosticism operated in Alexandria, Egypt. Gnostic ideas could be attached to almost any religion. It was perhaps only a matter of time before someone thought of attaching them to the new Christian faith. Once it began in Ephesus, various forms of Gnostic Christianity have been proposed in various places throughout the history of the church. In fact, Gnosticism in a variety of forms experienced a resurgence at the end of the twentieth century.

Thus, it's more important than ever that we be clear about Gnostic thinking. In many ways the twenty-first century parallels the first century, the church facing similar challenges.

The way they addressed the challenge of the Nicolaitans in the seven churches of Asia can be very instructive to us today. And so, here is a simple outline of Gnostic thought:

"God." Gnostics believe in a true, ultimate, transcendent, unknowable God, who is beyond all creation and who, in fact, has never created anything. However, the true God, the "Unknown Father/Parent," brought forth or "emanated" from within himself the substance of everything else. These emanations or "Aeons" are, in a way, divine beings. The sum total of these Aeons constitutes the "Fullness" or "Pleroma." The emanations furthest from the Unknown Father underwent unwholesome changes, becoming corrupt expressions of the divine essence.

This brings us to the Old Testament. One of the furthest emanations was "Sophia" or Divine Wisdom. In the course of her journeyings she emanated a flawed consciousness who, in his state of corruption, blindness, and pride, erred by bringing into being the world of "mind" and even of "matter." This Aeon is unaware of his own origin and so imagines himself to be the ultimate, absolute God. Although he exists as divine essence, he has emanated mind and matter, resulting in a "dualism" throughout his creation.

This "Demiurgos" ("half-maker") is the God of the Old Testament and the originator of ethical monotheistic religion. The Demiurge also created seven cosmic minions, the "Archons" ("rulers") to help him rule the psychic/physical creation. Ultimately he created human beings who reflect his dual nature. Although they are soul and body, they have an essential divine spark they are unaware of. They are trapped in a world of mind and body, are ignorant of their true nature, and therefore unable to escape.

"Anti-Cosmic Dualism." This cosmology results in a certain kind of dualism. For the Gnostic, the world of mind/matter is essentially evil. Only the realm of pure spirit is good. The visible universe is essentially corrupt and temporary. It is flawed and created in a flawed manner. Life is filled with suffering because the world is twisted. And it's twisted, not because of human sin, but because a flawed deity emanated a flawed realm of existence.

276   *Transformers*

"*Christ.*" From time to time the True God has sent his Messengers of the Light to assist humans in their quest for True Knowledge ("Gnosis"). For Christian Gnostics, Christ came from the Unknown Father to give the purest revelation of Gnosis. He is the principal "Savior" ("Soter"). However, the early Christian Gnostics varied on how they defined Jesus as the Christ. Some, known as "Docetists," claimed Jesus only had an apparent physical body. Because matter is evil he could not have had a real material body and been a Messenger of Light. Another school taught that Jesus of Nazareth was inhabited by the "Christ-Spirit" or the "Christ-Consciousness" when he was baptized in the Jordan River. That Christ-Spirit left Jesus in the Garden of Gethsemane. Thus, what the man Jesus taught between his baptism and betrayal reflected true Gnosis. However, the circumstances of his birth and death were irrelevant.

Humanity. Human beings exist both as a part of the Light of the True God and as a creation of the false Demiurge. Every human being has a divine spark within him/her. However, existing in the material universe reinforces a condition of ignorance. In addition, the Demiurge and his Archons continually work to reinforce human ignorance of Gnosis, the true knowledge of human nature. If an individual human becomes enlightened, the process of liberation from the bonds of physicality back to the Pleroma will begin. Death releases the divine spark from its physical prison. However, if a human being is "unenlightened," if they have not been initiated into the true Gnosis, that divine spark will fall back into the physical order to be re-embodied.

Gnostics taught that the Serpent in Genesis 3 was not a seducer into sin but rather a liberator, leading human beings in their rebellion against the evil Demiurge and into the true "Knowledge of Good and Evil."

The Gnostics taught there are three kinds of human beings:

1. "Spiritual ones" who are ready for full initiation into Gnosis and the resulting liberation. They can also be used to initiate others to a state of enlightenment.

2. "Soulish ones" who have some knowledge but not true enlightenment. They are religious ones who mistake the Demiurge of the Old Testament for the Unknown Father. They follow a way of religion and morality but do not see the way to true spiritual freedom.

3. "Fleshly / Earthly ones" who are completely ignorant and unable to see Gnosis. They can only see physical reality and are not candidates for enlightenment.

"Salvation." True liberation is the release of the divine spark from the bonds of matter. The true knowledge of the divine origin of the human spirit is required. Gnostics are not looking for salvation from sin but salvation from ignorance. The potential for such salvation exists in every human being, but it must be brought into consciousness by initiation into the "mysteries," mediated by enlightened Gnostic teachers and prophets/prophetesses. The indwelling spark must be awakened by the true saving Gnosis.

Christian Gnostics had a variety of rites. All practiced baptism, some baptizing "in the name of the Unknown Father, of Sophia, the Mother of all, and the Christ-spirit who came down on Jesus." They also practiced a rite of Anointing, intended to keep the evil Archons away. They also anointed the sick and even the dead. Gnostics also celebrated various forms of the Eucharist. There were also pagan rituals, including a secret mystery known as the "Nymphon," that involved a mystical marriage to the pure Aeons in the Pleroma. Magic spells also played an important role in the Gnostic mysteries, often involving the repetition of the seven Greek vowels (corresponding to the seven planets and the seven Archons). These magic spells would be necessary after death, in the struggle of the enlightened human spirit against the Archons to reach the Pleroma.

Because Gnostics are not seeking salvation from sin, their view of right conduct is non-moral. The Nicolaitans were "libertines." They believed that the spirits of enlightened humans were perfect. Thus what they did with their bodies was irrelevant. Indeed, they taught that ethics or systems of morality originated with the Demiurge and are ultimately designed to serve his evil purposes. Only "soulish disciplinarians" were concerned about ethical rules. "Spiritual" persons were concerned about higher matters, namely the exploration of the true Gnosis.

Later Gnostics were "ascetics," believing that, because the physical body is essentially evil, it must be renounced if not punished. All Gnostics encouraged a passive detachment from the world. It's easy to see how the Nicolaitans in the province of Asia could advocate compromise with emperor worship, paganism and immorality.

In his first epistle the apostle John worked to specifically counter the teachings of the Nicolaitans in the province of Asia. He used language that would have been easily understood by Gnostics when he taught, "God is light, in him there is no darkness at all" (1:5). He then clarified what he meant by saying, "If we claim to have fellowship with him [as the Gnostics did] yet walk in the darkness, we lie and do not live by the truth" (1:6). Furthermore, it was not the darkness of ignorance but of sin John was referring to. "If we claim to be without sin, we deceive ourselves and the truth is not in us" (1:8); and again, "If we claim we have not sinned, we make him out to be a liar and his word has no place in our lives" (1:10). The Gnostics in Asia erred in a false understanding of God and Jesus, of sin and salvation. Ultimately they erred in their lives by modeling arrogant exclusivism rather than humble love for their brothers and sisters.

"Restoration." The spirit of an enlightened human being has the potential of escaping the world of mind and matter and gaining entrance back to the Pleroma. Christian Gnostics taught that Christ awaited the spiritual person at the entrance of the Pleroma to guide him back to the Unknown Father. In the end, every being will receive Gnosis and will be reunited with its higher self. Ultimately, every corrupted, "fallen" emenation from God, including the Demiurge and his Archons, will be restored. All the stray divine sparks will return to a state of rest and the natural order will cease to exist.

The early church fathers spent much of the second and third centuries battling Gnosticism. Yet, in the process many Gnostic ideas were absorbed into Christian thought.

Whenever there was a strong emphasis on the Spirit, Gnostic ideas tended to surface. False expressions of Christianity such as Christian Science are a modern version of Gnosticism. Even "New Thought," "New Age" teachings, and the more recent Scientology, reflect those ancient ideas.

They are in fact very ancient Indo-European concepts, found in the teachings of both Socrates and Plato in Greece and Gautama Buddha in Aryan India. They are a mixture of philosophy, paganism, and the occult. And they are contrary in every way to the revelation of God in Scripture. They were a problem in the churches of Asia and they are a problem today. Only a clear understanding of Scripture will bring into focus their error.

BIBLIOGRAPHY

Conner, Kevin J. *The Book of Revelation: An Exposition.* Victoria, Australia: KJC Publications, 2001.

Crabb, Larry. *The Safest Place on Earth: Where People Connect and Are Forever Changed.* Nashville, TN: W Publishing Group, 1999.

Friesen, Steven. "Ephesus: Key to a Vision in Revelation." *Biblical Archaeology Review* (May/June 1993): 25–37.

Hayford, Jack. E Quake: *A New Approach to Understanding the End Time Mysteries in the Book of Revelation.* Nashville, TN: Thomas Nelson Publishers, 1999.

Hemer, Colin J. *The Letters to the Seven Churches of Asia in Their Local Setting.* Grand Rapids, MI: William B. Eerdmans Publishing Company, 1986.

Humble, Bill, and Ian Fair. *The Seven Churches of Asia.* Nashville, TN: Gospel Advocate Company, 1995.

Ignatius of Antioch. "To the Philadelphians," trans. J. B. Lightfoot, in *The Apostolic Fathers* (1891). Grand Rapids, MI: Baker Book House, 79–82.

Lovelace, Richard F. *Dynamics of Spiritual Life: An Evangelical Theology of Renewal.* Downers Grove, IL: InterVarsity Press, 1979.

McClendon, James Wm., Jr. *Ethics: Systematic Theology, Vol. 1.* Nashville, TN: Abingdon Press, 1986.

Morgan, G. Campbell. *A First Century Message to Twentieth Century Christians: Addresses Based upon the Letters to the Seven Churches of Asia.* London, UK: Fleming H. Revell Company, 1902.

Osborne, Grant R. *Revelation: Baker Exegetical Commentary on the New Testament.* ed. Moises Silva. Grand Rapids, MI: Baker Academic, 2002.

Ramsay, William M. *The Letters to the Seven Churches.* Peabody, MA: Hendrickson Publishers, 1904.

Ravenhill, David. *The Jesus Letters: Seven Secrets That Can Change You and Your Church.* Shippensburg, PA: Destiny Image, 2003.

Sider, Ronald J. "The Scandal of the Evangelical Conscience." *Books & Culture* (Jan/Feb 2005): 8–9, 39–42.

_____. *The Scandal of the Evangelical Conscience: Why Are Christians Living Just Like the Rest of the World?* Grand Rapids, MI: Baker Books, 2005.

Smith, Christian. "What American Teenagers Believe." *Books & Culture* (Jan/Feb 2005): 10–11.

Swete, Henry Barclay. *The Apocalypse of St. John.* London, UK: Macmillan, 1911.

Tenney, Merrill C. *Interpreting Revelation: A Reasonable Guide to Understanding the Last Book in the Bible.* Grand Rapids, MI: Eerdmans Publishing Company, 1957.

Yeatts, John R. *Revelation.* Scottdale, PA: Herald Press, 2003.

NOTES

[1] Henry Barclay Swete, *The Apocalypse of St. John* (Macmillan: London, UK, 1911), cliv.

[2] William M. Ramsay, *The Letters To the Seven Churches* (Peabody, MA: Hendrickson Publishers, 1904), 18.

[3] John R. Yeatts, *Revelation* (Scottdale, PA: Herald Press, 2003), 31.

[4] The question is whether or not we are reading an "objective" or "subjective genitive," i.e., is Jesus Christ the object or the subject of the revelation. Although a stronger case can be made for the subjective usage, it's quite possible John was seeing both. Compare Swete, 1.

[5] The Greek word *dei* refers to something that is necessary or required, something that arises from Divine appointment.

[6] The phrase *en tachei* simply means "without delay." Swete says this phrase indicates "the sure fulfillment of the purpose of God revealed by the prophets" (2).

[7] The Greek term *semaino* was often used as a technical term in ancient literature. It simply means "to give a sign," but was also used to convey truth by means of images rather than definitions. This verb is once again in the aorist tense, confirming that the communication of the revelation took place at a certain time.

[8] Yeatts, *Revelation*, 32.

[9] There are six other blessings pronounced in the book of Revelation: 14:13; 16:15; 19:9; 20:6; 22:7, 14.

[10] The Greek present participle, *ho on*, is used in the LXX to translate "I am who I am" in Exodus 3:14.

[11] Swete, *The Apocalypse of St. John*, 5.

[12] The present participle of *agape* is used here.

[13] Swete, *The Apocalypse of St. John*, 8.

[14] Ibid., 10.

[15] Swete noted that the Rabbinic symbol of the first and last letters of the Hebrew alphabet. "Aleph Tau" "was regarded as including the intermediate letters, and stood for totality; and thus it fitly represented the Shekinah" (10).

[16] In fact, *pantokrator* is somewhat unique to the book of Revelation. The only other place it is used in the NT is 2 Corinthians 6:18. In the LXX it is used either for *shaddai* or *tsabaoth*.

[17] The use of *pantokrator* contrasts with the claims of the Roman empire. The emperor was commonly called the *autocrator*, i.e. the "self-ruler," but God is the "ruler of all."

[18] Ramsay, *The Letters to the Seven Churches*, 75, 76.

[19] Ibid., 132.

[20] Ibid., 141.

[21] In fact, the Pergamene kings, as well as some of the Seleucid kings, had long considered themselves to be incarnations of certain Greek gods.

[22] Steven Friesen, "Ephesus: Key To A Vision In Revelation," *Biblical Archaeology Review* May/June 1993: 34.

[23] Yeatts, *Revelation*, 20.

[24] Ramsay, *The Letters to the Seven Churches*, 70.

[25] Yeatts, *Revelation*, 460.

[26] Colin J. Hemer, *The Letters to the Seven Churches of Asia in Their Local Setting* (Grand Rapids, MI: William B. Eerdmans Publishing Company, 1986), 8.

[27] Ibid., 10.

[28] Swete, *The Apocalypse of St. John*, xcvi.

[29] Ramsay, *The Letters to the Seven Churches*, 33.

[30] Hemer, *The Letters to the Seven Churches of Asia*, 21.

[31] Ramsay, *The Letters to the Seven Churches*, 48.

[32] Richard F. Lovelace, *Dynamics of Spiritual Life: An Evangelical Theology of Renewal* (Downers Grove, IL: InterVarsity Press, 1979), 184.

[33] Ibid., 190.

[34] Ronald J. Sider, "The Scandal of the Evangelical Conscience," *Books & Culture* (Carol Stream, IL), January/February 2005, 9.

[35] Ibid., 8.

[36] Ibid.

[37] Yeatts, *Revelation*, 24.

[38] Ramsay, *The Letters to the Seven Churches*, 61.

[39] This phrase occurs at the beginning of each of John's visionary experiences. See also 4:2; 17:3; 21:10.

[40] Swete, *The Apocalypse of St. John*, 14.

[41] Kevin J. Conner, *The Book of Revelation: An Exposition* (Victoria, Australia: KJC Publications, 2001), 31.

[42] David Ravenhill, *The Jesus Letters: Seven Secrets That Can Change You and Your Church* (Shippensburg, PA: Destiny Image, 2003), 34, 34.

[43] Jack Hayford, *E Quake: A New Approach to Understanding the End Time Mysteries in the Book of Revelation* (Nashville, TN: Thomas Nelson Publishers, 1999), 15.

[44] The Greek word translated "bronze" (*chalkolibanos*) is only used here and in 2:18 and is apparently unique to the situation in Thyatira.

[45] John R. Yeatts, *Revelation* (Scottdale, PA: Herald Press, 2003), 42, 43.

[46] Ibid.

[47] The statement that Jesus is the *eschatos* creates the possibility of developing a Christocentric eschatology, i.e., a doctrine of last things that centers around the revelation of the person and work of Jesus Christ.

[48] John here uses the present participle *ho zon*, from the verb *zoe*. John prefers to use this word for "life" when describing the divine quality of life or eternal life.

[49] Merrill C. Tenney, *Interpreting Revelation* (Grand Rapids, MI: Eerdmans Publishing Company, 1957), 198.

[50] Bill Humble and Ian Fair, *The Seven Churches of Asia* (Nashville, TN: Gospel Advocate Company, 1995), 36.

[51] Apocalyptic literature usually contains the interpretation of the key symbols within the text itself. It is not necessary for us to invent our own interpretation. Scripture interprets scripture.

[52] There are various views of who the angels of the seven churches are: (a) They could simply be human messengers, perhaps delegates from the seven churches. The use of *angeloi* in Luke 7:24; 9:52 and James 2:25 would allow for this possibility. However, *angelos / angeloi* does not refer to human messengers anywhere else in the NT. (b) A variation on this view is that these are the elders of the local churches in Asia. The argument is that no individual messenger could be held personally responsible for the state of the churches. However, the elders

might be. (c) St. Augustine was the first to suggest that the *angelos* was the bishop of the church. However, there was no evidence that the office of the bishop was functioning in Asia when these letters were delivered. (d) A variation on this theme is that the *angelos* represents the "senior pastor" of the local churches. However, this is reading a modern church structure into a first century context. (e) Others have suggested that, because the book of Revelation is highly symbolic, the "angel" of the church simply represents the "prevailing spirit" of the church, i.e., the local church itself. (f) Then there is the view that the *angeloi* are simply angels. It has been noted that a distinctive of apocalyptic literature is the presence of angels as a picture of the connection between heaven and earth and God's sovereign control over both. Outside of chapters 1–3, "angels" are referred to sixty times in the book of Revelation. In no case are they human messengers.

[53] Yeatts, *Revelation*, 45.

[54] Christian Smith, "What American Teenagers Believe," *Books & Culture* (Carol Stream, IL), January/February 2005, 10.

[55] Ibid., 10.

[56] Ibid., 11.

[57] Smith, "What American Teenagers Believe," 11.

[58] This is a classical symbolic number found in apocalyptic literature. It is made up of 12X12X1000, the fullest symbol of God's covenant community.

[59] Yeatts, *Revelation*, 38, 39.

[60] Hayford, *E Quake*, 17.

[61] Although it looks a bit confusing, the various Greek kings after Alexander were all descendants of Alexander's generals, known as the *Diadochoi*. There was continual warfare between them for dominance of their various territories. The Romans were finally able to bring stability to the area.

[62] Hemer, *The Letters to the Seven Churches of Asia in Their Local Setting*, 38.

[63] Swete, *The Apocalypse of St. John*, 23.

[64] Ibid., lxxv.

[65] Ibid., 25.

[66] John is using the aorist imperative of *metanoeo*, which refers to

a change of heart, involving the repudiation of the past as well as the embracing of a new lifestyle.

[67] Swete, *The Apocalypse of St. John*, 26.

[68] Humble and Fair, *The Seven Churches of Asia*, 38.

[69] In the next generation, the epistle of Ignatius of Antioch to the Ephesians (prologue.1) indicated that the church had taken this warning to heart and had indeed returned to their first love.

[70] This is the present participle of the verb *nikao*, meaning "to conquer, to overcome; to come away victorious." This is an athletic or military metaphor that connotes superiority and victory over a vanquished foe. The participle is singular, pointing to the promise that any individual could hear the word of the Lord and overcome.

[71] Swete, *The Apocalypse of St. John*, 30.

[72] Ramsay, *The Letters to the Seven Churches*, 179.

[73] Yeatts, *Revelation*, 80.

[74] Ronald J. Sider, "The Scandal of the Evangelical Conscience," *Books & Culture* (Carol Stream, IL), January/February 2005, 40.

[75] Ibid.

[76] Hayford, *E Quake*, 48.

[77] G. Campbell Morgan, *A First Century Message to Twentieth Century Christians* (London, UK: Fleming H. Revell Company, 1902), 47.

[78] Ibid., 42.

[79] Ibid., 47.

[80] David Ravenhill, *The Jesus Letters: Seven Secrets That Can Change You and Your Church* (Shippensburg, PA: Destiny Image, 2003), 58.

[81] Ibid.

[82] Hayford, *E Quake*, 48.

[83] Yeatts, *Revelation*, 60.

[84] The Greek word for the laurel wreath or the "victor's crown" is *stephanos*. A different word, *diadema*, is the word for royal crown.

[85] Ramsay, *The Letters to the Seven Churches*, 197.

[86] Morgan, *A First Century Message to Twentieth Century Christians*, 63.

[87] The word for faith is *pistis* while the word for faithful is *pistos*. "Faithfulness" is the key characteristic of the saints in the book of Revelation (cf. 13:10; 14:12; 17:14).

[88] Osborne, *Revelation*, 134.

[89] In Revelation 12:11 John uses the word *psuche* for life, also translated "self" or "soul." In 2:11 John uses the word *zoe*, referring to a divine quality of life, abundant life.

[90] Humble and Fair, *The Seven Churches of Asia*, 51.

[91] Ibid. 52.

[92] Ravenhill, *The Jesus Letters: Seven Secrets That Can Change You and Your Church*, 84.

[93] Hemer, *The Letters to the Seven Churches of Asia*, 65.

[94] Ravenhill, *The Jesus Letters*, 81.

[95] Morgan, *A First Century Message to Twentieth Century Christians*, 73-75.

[96] Osborne, *Revelation*, 135.

[97] Ibid.,139.

[98] Ibid., 141.

[99] There are other views of why Pergamum is referred to as the "throne" of Satan. Some refer to the fact that the acropolis had the appearance of a throne. Others have pointed out the consistent symbol of the serpent, both on the altar of Zeus as well as in the worship of Asklepios.

[100] Osborne, *Revelation*, 142.

[101] The early church father Eusebius referred to others martyred at Pergamum, including Carpus, Papylus and Agathonike.

[102] Yeatts, *Revelation*, 64.

[103] Ramsay, *The Letters to the Seven Churches*, 219.

[104] Hemer, *The Letters to the Seven Churches of Asia in Their Local Setting*, 92.

[105] Swete, *The Apocalypse of St. John*, 38.

[106] Morgan, *A First Century Message to Twentieth Century Christians*, 102–04.

[107] Note that none of these traditions have any basis in Scripture or history.

[108] Some of the interpretations proposed for this stone by commentators include: (1) a jewel, either that fell with manna from heaven, or was worn on the vest of the high priest; (2) a judicial vote of acquittal; (3) a token of admission to a pagan banquet; (4) a token of membership in a mystery cult; (5) a token of discharge from gladiatorial service; (6) a magic charm with a divine name; (7) a testimonial of a cure from the cult of Asklepios; (8) a token given to one returning victoriously from battle; (9) a token of free citizenship in a Roman city; (10) a token between friends, divided with their names written it; (11) tickets given in exchange for food.

[109] Hayford, *E Quake*, 56, 57.

[110] Morgan, *A First Century Message to Twentieth Century Christians*, 95, 102.

[111] Hemer, *The Letters to the Seven Churches of Asia in Their Local Setting*, 117.

[112] Morgan, *A First Century Message to Twentieth Century Christians*, 114.

[113] Ibid., 199.

[114] Osborne, *Revelation*, 157.

[115] The noun *porneia* could refer to spiritual adultery, i.e., idolatry and covenant-breaking, or sexual immorality.

116 The phrase *thlipsin megalen* is used only here and in 7:14 in the book of Revelation.

[117] This phrase is also used in Ezekiel 33:27, referring to dying by a plague, and in Revelation 6:8, referring to the power of Death to kill by plague.

[118] Osborne, *Revelation*, 160.

[119] Ibid., 161.

[120] Morgan, *A First Century Message to Twentieth Century Christians*, 125.

[121] Osborne, *Revelation*, 164.

[122] Some commentators feel that the gnostic teachers actually advocated an initiation into the secret mysteries of Satan. For example,

Grant Osborne wrote, "Jezebel may have taught that Christians should experience 'the deep things of Satan' in order to triumph over them. In this sense, she would admit that the guild feasts and pagan environment are evil but claim that they have no power over the believer. She would even have taught that Christians should participate in those activities and experience the 'depths' of paganism in order to show their mastery over it. [Gnostic libertines] believed that their participation in sinful activities did not become sin because of their 'knowledge'" (*Revelation* 2002, 162, 163).

[123] Morgan, *A First Century Message to Twentieth Century Christians*, 121, 122.

[124] Ibid., 123.

[125] John may be using a play on words in this passage. The Greek word for "depth" is *bathos* while the word for "burden" is *baros*. John is also using the verb *ballo*, the same word he used when he referred to Jezebel being "cast" onto a sick bed.

[126] Ramsay, *The Letters to the Seven Churches*, 257, 258.

[127] Osborne, *Revelation*, 167.

[128] Other interpretations of the "morning star" symbol have been proposed: (1) an allusion to Daniel 12:3 where the righteous shine like stars in the resurrection; (2) a reference to Lucifer from Isaiah 14:12; or (3) a reference to Apollo, the patron god of Thyatira.

[129] Morgan, *A First Century Message to Twentieth Century Christians*, 116.

[130] Ibid., 132.

[131] Ravenhill, *The Jesus Letters: Seven Secrets That Can Change You and Your Church*, 111, 112.

[132] Ramsay, *The Letters to the Seven Churches*, 264.

[133] Hemer, *The Letters to the Seven Churches of Asia in Their Local Setting*, 132.

[134] Ibid., 133.

[135] Ibid., 134.

[136] Ramsay, *The Letters to the Seven Churches*, 266.

[137] Hemer, *The Letters to the Seven Churches of Asia*, 136.

[138] Ibid., 137.

[139] The video series entitled "Faith Lessons of the Early Church:

Conquering the Gates of Hell," Vol. 5, with Ray VanderLaan was especially helpful in picturing circumstances in Sardis (Focus On the Family Films, 1999).

[140] Morgan, *A First Century Message to Twentieth Century Christians*, 136, 137.

[141] Humble and Fair, *The Seven Churches of Asia*, 87.

[142] Grant R. Osborne, *Revelation, Baker Exegetical Commentary on the New Testament*, ed. Moises Silva (Grand Rapids, MI: Baker Academic, 2002), 175.

[143] Morgan, *A First Century Message to Twentieth Century Christians*, 141.

[144] Ibid., 138-40.

[145] Osborne, *Revelation*, 176.

[146] Swete, *The Apocalypse of St. John*, 51.

[147] Morgan, *A First Century Message to Twentieth Century Christians*, 150.

[148] Swete, *The Apocalypse of St. John*, 52.

[149] Ramsay, *The Letters to the Seven Churches*, 285.

[150] Ravenhill, *The Jesus Letters: Seven Secrets That Can Change You and Your Church*, 118.

[151] Ibid., 121.

[152] James Wm. McClendon, Jr., *Ethics: Systematic Theology, Vol. 1* (Nashville, TN: Abingdom Press, 1986), 18.

[153] Ramsay, *The Letters to the Seven Churches*, 286, 287.

[154] Hemer, *The Letters to the Seven Churches of Asia in Their Local Setting*, 156.

[155] Ibid., 159.

[156] Swete, *The Apocalypse of St. John*, 53.

[157] The "charters" were apparently the Hebrew scrolls.

[158] Ignatius of Antioch, "To the Philadelphians," trans. J.B. Lightfoot, in *The Apostolic Fathers* (Grand Rapids, MI: Baker Book House, 1891), 8.

[159] Ramsay, *The Letters To the Seven Churches*, 300.

[160] In fact, the letter to Philadelphia contains more Old Testament allusions than any of the other letters.

[161] Swete, *The Apocalypse of St. John*, 53, 54.

[162] Osborne, *Revelation, Baker Exegetical Commentary on the New Testament*, 188, 189.

[163] Ibid.

[164] Ramsay, *The Letters to the Seven Churches*, 297.

[165] John is using the future tense of *proskuneo*, ordinarily translated "worship." In this context it indicates rather the attitude of a beaten foe.

[166] Hemer, *The Letters to the Seven Churches of Asia*, 163.

[167] Osborne, *Revelation*, 194.

[168] Hemer, *The Letters to the Seven Churches of Asia*, 165.

[169] Swete, *The Apocalypse of St. John*, 58.

[170] G. Campbell Morgan, *A First Century Message to Twentieth Century Christians* (London, UK: Fleming H. Revell Company, 1902), 176.

[171] Ramsay, *The Letters To the Seven Churches*, 301, 302.

[172] John R. Yeatts, *Revelation* (Scottdale, PA: Herald Press, 2003), 85.

[173] Ronald J. Sider, "The Scandal of the Evangelical Conscience," *Books & Culture* (Carol Stream, IL), January/February 2005, 41.

[174] Ronald J. Sider, *The Scandal of the Evangelical Conscience* (Grand Rapids, MI: Baker Books, 2005), 33.

[175] Yeatts, *Revelation*, 85.

[176] Ravenhill, *The Jesus Letters: Seven Secrets That Can Change You and Your Church*, 129.

[177] Hemer, *The Letters to the Seven Churches of Asia in Their Local Setting*, 188, 191.

[178] Ibid., 184, 185.

[179] Ibid., 209.

[180] Morgan, *A First Century Message to Twentieth Century Christians*, 191.

[181] Swete, *The Apocalypse of St. John*, 59, 60.

[182] The Greek word *psuchros* means icy hot and *zestos* means boiling hot.

[183] Osborne, *Revelation, Baker Exegetical Commentary on the New Testament*, 206.

[184] Ibid., 207.

[185] Ramsay, *The Letters to the Seven Churches*, 316.

[186] Morgan, *A First Century Message to Twentieth Century Christians*, 206.

[187] Instead of *agapao* Jesus uses the more personal and emotional *phileo*.

[188] Morgan, *A First Century Message to Twentieth Century Christians*, 207.

[189] Humble and Fair, *The Seven Churches of Asia*, 101.

[190] John uses the aorist tense of the verb *deipneo*. The noun *deipnon* is a reference to the main meal of the day, the meal where significant "table fellowship" took place.

[191] Ravenhill, *The Jesus Letters: Seven Secrets That Can Change You and Your Church*, 143.

[192] Larry Crabb, *The Safest Place on Earth: Where People Connect and Are Forever Changed* (Nashville, TN: W Publishing Group, 1999), 32.

[193] Ibid., 39.

[194] Morgan, *A First Century Message to Twentieth Century Christians*, 188.

[195] Hayford, *E Quake*, 53.

[196] Sider, "The Scandal of the Evangelical Conscience," 9.

[197] Hayford, *E Quake*, 55.

[198] Ravenhill, *The Jesus Letters*, 139.

[199] Ibid., 137.

[200] Crabb, *The Safest Place on Earth*, 30–32.

[201] Ibid., 11.

[202] Ibid., 45.

[203] Ibid., 124.

[204] These hermeneutical principles are drawn from *How To Read the Bible For All It's Worth* by Gordon D. Fee and Douglas Stuart (Grand Rapids: Zondervan, 1982).

www.ingramcontent.com/pod-product-compliance
Lightning Source LLC
LaVergne TN
LVHW052015080426
835513LV00018B/2039